Pop Art Design

Pop Art Design

Vitra
Design
Museum

Roy Lichtenstein at work
in his studio, 1964
Photo: Ken Heyman

Charles and Ray Eames working
on the *Chaise* lounge chair, ca. 1968
Courtesy Eames Office

Tom Wesselmann (left) in his
studio with an assistant, 1964
Photo: Ken Heyman

Alexander Girard (left) and an assistant
preparing fabrics for the exhibition
Nehru: *His Life and His India*, 1965
Photo: Charles Eames

7

Walter Pichler (left) in his studio
working with an assistant on
TV-Helm (Tragbares Wohnzimmer), 1967
Photo: Georg Mladek

Andy Warhol (left) and an assistant at the
Factory on 47th Street, New York, 1964
Photo: Ken Heyman

Achille and Pier Giacomo Castiglioni with
plaster models of a cutlery set designed for
Reed & Barton, 1959

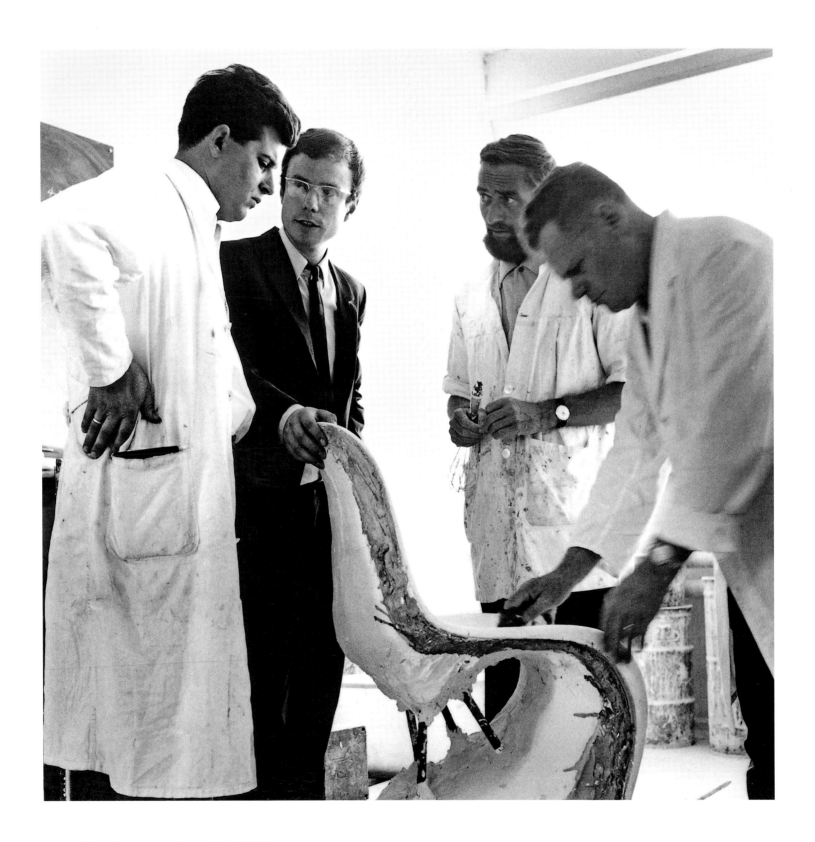

Verner Panton (second from right), Rolf Fehlbaum
(second from left), Manfred Diebold (left) and
another employee working on the *Panton Chair* in
the Herman Miller/Vitra development department
in Weil am Rhein, ca. 1966
Photo: Vitra

This catalogue is published on the occasion
of the exhibition „Pop Art Design".

„Pop Art Design" is an exhibition of the
Vitra Design Museum, Weil am Rhein, in
cooperation with the Louisiana Museum of
Modern Art, Humlebæk, and the Moderna
Museet, Stockholm.

Vitra Design Museum:
13 October 2012 – 3 February 2013
Louisiana Museum of Modern Art:
21 February 2013 – 9 June 2013
Moderna Museet:
27 June 2013 – 22 September 2013
Further venues are planned.

www.design-museum.de

Cooperation partners

LOUISIANA MUSEUM OF MODERN ART

MODERNA MUSEET

Supported by

vitra.

Catalogue

Editors: Mateo Kries,
Mathias Schwartz-Clauss
Editing: Mathias Schwartz-Clauss,
Bettina Korintenberg
Copy Editing: Ariel Krill (English),
Gudrun Altfeld (German)
Translations: Julia Thorson, Barbara Fisher,
Joel Agee
Image Rights: Bettina Korintenberg,
Johanna Thieme, Adrian Luncke
Art Work: Thorsten Romanus
Lithography: GZD, Ditzingen
Production Management: Jörn Strüker
Production Assistance: Johanna Thieme
Distribution: Irma Hager
Printing: E & B engelhardt und bauer,
Karlsruhe

© Vitra Design Museum and Authors, 2012

The Deutsche Nationalbibliothek lists this
publication in the Deutsche Nationalbiblio-
grafie; detailed bibliographic data are
available in the Internet at http://dnb.dnb.de.

ISBN 978-3-931936-96-9 (English Edition)
ISBN 978-3-931936-95-2 (German Edition)

Exhibition

Directors Vitra Design Museum:
Mateo Kries, Marc Zehntner
Curator: Mathias Schwartz-Clauss
Junior Curator: Bettina Korintenberg
Academic Advisors: Anders Kold,
Alexander von Vegesack
Exhibition Design: groenlandbasel, Basel
Technical Direction: Thomas Schmidhauser
Installations: Michael Simolka
Media Technology & Animation:
Ina Klaeden
Conservation: Susanne Graner
Registrar: Bogusław Ubik-Perski
Press & Publicity: Katharina Giese
and Gianoli PR
Exhibition Tour: Isabel Serbeto,
Reiner Packeiser
Supporting Activities: Kilian Jost
Visitor Services: Christina Scholten

Pop Art was arguably the most influential art movement of the postwar era. One of its fundamental elements was the dialogue between art and design that pervaded it. In order to investigate this very dialogue, the Vitra Design Museum has delved for the first time in its history into the field of fine art and with the exhibition *Pop Art Design* and its accompanying catalogue offers a comprehensive look at the exchange between art and design and its decisive impact on Pop Art.

The initial impetus for this project came from the many Pop-era pieces contained in the museum's collections. These include designs by Ettore Sottsass, Superstudio and Studio 65, as well as from the estates of Charles and Ray Eames,

Verner Panton, George Nelson and Alexander Girard. It had long been an interest of our curator Mathias Schwartz-Clauss to situate these pieces within the context of the Pop Art phenomenon, exploring their close links with the artistic tendencies of the period and thus contributing to a deeper understanding of the history of their design.

A further motivation stemmed from the still visible traces that Pop Art has left behind in both art and design. Works by such figures as Philippe Starck, Matali Crasset, Erwin Wurm or Tobias Rehberger, for instance, would be inconceivable without the playful approach to consumer aesthetics and commercial clichés that gained its credence and respectability through Pop Art. For this reason, too, we wanted to examine when and how the artistic strategies of Pop Art first emerged so as to facilitate such a dialogue between art and design – and how exactly this dialogue worked.

A final and decisive impulse for *Pop Art Design* was the fact that we were able to secure the Louisiana Museum of Modern Art in Humlebæk, Denmark, with its significant Pop Art collection, as a partner for the project. Soon thereafter, the Moderna Museet Stockholm came on board as a second major partner that not only owns an important collection of Pop Art but also enjoys close historical links with the history of the movement: Pontus Hultén, the legendary founder of the Moderna Museet, had shown works by Jasper Johns and Robert Rauschenberg as early as 1962 in the exhibition *4 amerikanare* (4 Americans) and in 1968 had organized the world's first Andy Warhol retrospective.

Thanks to the collaboration with these renowned partners, we were able to produce an exhibition and book that open up a whole new perspective on Pop Art – a perspective that finally recognizes design's central role in the history of the movement. Pop Art is not simply presented as a phenomenon of the times, as might have been the case a decade ago

Tobias Rehberger, *Was du liebst, bringt dich auch zum Weinen (Japanese franchise version)*, 2010
Installation view, Setouchi, Japan
Courtesy neugerriemschneider, Berlin
Photo: Osamu Nakamura, Takumatsu

during the height of the retro frenzy. Instead, the exhibition highlights the dialectic character of Pop Art, traces the migrations of images and motifs between the disciplines, sheds light on questions of media theory, and explores the boundaries between picture and appliance, between image and object. In short, it enables a more differentiated and complex assessment of the Pop phenomenon.

This perspective is particularly relevant today because it addresses the continued penetration of Pop Art – domesticated as pop culture – into all corners of daily life and thus opens up current issues for discussion. When artists like Elmgreen and Dragset transplant a Prada boutique into the middle of the Texan desert or Wim Delvoye tattoos a pig with a Louis Vuitton logo, they are doing something that would have been unthinkable without the artistic 'branding' and interdisciplinary incursions between art and design initiated by Pop Art. At the same time, global crises and anti-consumerist slogans such as 'No Logo!' show that critical questions of today's pop culture are growing louder. Can Pop also develop a critical attitude towards society? Does it supply sophisticated images of subversion – or is it merely a bag of tricks at the disposal of advertising strategists? For such questions, no clear-cut answers can be found. Yet one of the historic achievements of Pop Art lies in bringing these questions to the conscious attention of the viewer in ever-new ways.

Mateo Kries
Director
Vitra Design Museum

Jerszy Seymour, *Pipe Dreams*, 1998
Magis SpA, Torre di Mosto, VE, Italy
Watering cans
Courtesy of the artist

Pop Art Design is an exhibition that investigates the connections and cross-fertilizations, established during the 1950s and '60s, between art and design – or fine art and applied art, to use the distinctions that we today, thanks to Pop Art and to design, are hesitant to use. The attitude of Pop – the anti-highbrow interest in life as modern or contemporary people experience it, in life filtered through media – is still relevant today. This is a point worth stressing when considering the presentations of the exhibition at the Louisiana Museum of Modern Art and the Moderna Museet. For, in the case of Louisiana, it is exactly this point of view that, historically, has advocated its cross-disciplinarily and entirely non-departmental exhibition policy that spans art, architecture and design.

Louisiana and the Moderna Museet were both founded in 1958 and are, in a sense, children of the early Pop era—or perhaps one should say 'teenagers', another pop invention. This is evident in the collections of both museums. The present exhibition puts many of the works in these collections into a context that gives us a deeper understanding of the world they came from and helped shape.

Both museums have a long history with Pop. During the sixties, the Moderna Museet presented exhibitions such as *4 Americans* (1962), *American Pop Art* (1964), *James Rosenquist F-111* (1965), *Claes Oldenburg* (1966) and *Andy Warhol* (1968), to mention a few. These not only showed new art but also showed it in a new way. Louisiana, for its part, also exhibited *American Pop Art* (1964) and *James Rosenquist F-111* (1965), and throughout the late Pop era held such exhibitions as *American Art 1950–1970* (1971), *Robert Indiana* (1972), *David Hockney's Graphic Works* (1976), *Claes Oldenburg's Drawings* (1977) and *Andy Warhol* (1978).

From the very beginning, both museums have also shared a multidisciplinary notion of art. Over the years, a multitude of activities have been arranged for visitors to take part in: concerts and performances, film studios and happenings, readings and workshops. *Pop Art Design* celebrates this bridging of gaps – just as, historically, Pop Art and Pop design played a major role in bringing it about. We look forward to sharing this exhibition with our visitors.

Daniel Birnbaum und Ann-Sofi Noring
Director / Co-Director
Moderna Museet

Poul Erik Tøjner
Director
Louisiana Museum of Modern Art

The exhibition and catalogue *Pop Art Design* confronted the Vitra Design Museum with new and unfamiliar challenges. Never before had we dealt with so many and such significant works of fine art. Particularly in regard to the technical and logistical preparations, the presentation of these artworks had to satisfy much higher requirements than the objects of design typically featured in our exhibitions. At the same time, however, a central objective of the project consisted in the equal treatment of the two disciplines. In translating our ideas into an articulate representation of the commonalities between Pop Art and design, we are thus indebted to our highly dedicated and professional partners and staff.

Our visions could not have become a reality without the early pledge by Poul Erik Tojner, director of the Louisiana Museum of Modern Art in Humlebaek, to show the exhibition and contribute to its development with high-calibre loans and curatorial advice. Louisiana's curator Kjeld Kjeldsen was a vigorous advocate, and under the leadership of his colleague Anders Kold a collaboration took shape characterized by mutual respect and trust. We also came to cherish Louisiana's curatorial coordinator Arne Schmidt-Petersen as well as the curator in charge of loans, Kirsten Degel, as exceedingly competent and helpful colleagues.

Furthermore, Anders Kold deserves thanks for bringing the Moderna Museet in Stockholm on board as a further partner. We were thus able to include its director Daniel Birnbaum and its curator Magnus af Petersens early on in the planning of the project and arrange important loans from Sweden and a subsequent presentation of the exhibition at the Moderna Museet.

Lending institutions and individuals were uniformly helpful and cooperative, with special mention going to the Museu Colecção Berardo, the Andy Warhol Foundation for the Visual Arts, the Instituto Valenciano de Arte Moderno (IVAM), the art collections of Ruhr-Universität Bochum, the Centre Pompidou, the Israel Museum, the Scottish National Gallery of Modern Art, the Kunstmuseum Wolfsburg, the Muzeum Narodowe w Poznaniu, the Museum für Gestaltung Zürich, Jennifer Bass, Barbara Radice, Volker Albus, Gianni Arnaudo, Gerrit Terstiege, Cuno Affolter, the Galerie Klaus Benden and Mitchell-Innes & Nash.

I am also greatly indebted to my assistant Bettina Korintenberg who maintained personal contact with all correspondents and provided me with untiring and dedicated support day in and day out. As a steadfast companion, she kept track of all the many details and served as a loyal yet critical contributor throughout the entire project. With enthusiasm and absolute precision, our conservator Susanne Graner meanwhile ensured that each work be treated with optimal care and attention together with her fellow staff members Boguslaw Ubik-Perski, Andreas Nutz, Serge Mauduit, Grażyna Ubik and Luise Lutz. In addition, it was a particular pleasure to work with Matthias Schnegg, Isabel Jung and Joseph Kennedy of groenlandbasel on the staging of the exhibition. With their intuitive understanding and sensitivity, they took mere ideas and gave them the desired shape, which Thomas Schmidhauser and our workshop team then technically executed to perfection.

I would also like to convey my thanks to the authors and especially the translators as well as the editors Gudrun Altfeld and Ariel Krill for their critical and sensitive treatment of all the texts in this catalogue. They all contributed to the project with great care, intelligence and extensive research. The fact that this book not only coherently implements the exhibition concept but also stands on its own as a compelling independent work is due, above all, to the work of Thorsten Romanus, whose layout imbues the volume with the right mix of strength and serenity befitting the subject matter. In addition, Jörn Strüker and Markus Bocher of GZD supported the publication with great competence.

I am also highly grateful for the assistance provided by the Museo Nazionale della Scienza e della Tecnologia Leonardo da Vinci, the Galerie Gmurzynska, Maria Blaise, Judith Brauner, Jim Brehm, Katharina von Flotow, Sevil Peach and Gary Turnbull, Hubert Kubacki, Tido von Oppeln, Margot Notarius, Marirosa Toscani Ballo, Eames Demetrios and Genevieve Fong, Roland Mönig, Sam Keller, Nina Schleif and Laura Hompesch. The project initially received key encouragement from Alexander von Vegesack who, upon his departure from the Vitra Design Museum, handed over the endeavour to the care and direction of Mateo Kries and Marc Zehnter.

Pop Art Design took me back to the roots of my training in art history and in this regard marks a turning point in my twenty-year career as a curator at the Vitra Design Museum. My thanks go to the museum's entire team and the many individuals who over the years have had such a strong influence on me and, hence, on this exhibition and book.

Mathias Schwartz-Clauss
Curator
Vitra Design Museum

Robert Venturi and Denise Scott Brown,
The Mint Hotel and Casino, rooftop terrace,
Las Vegas, 1968
Photograph from the Las Vegas study
Courtesy Museum im Bellpark Kriens from
the 'Las Vegas Studio' project
© Venturi, Scott Brown and Associates, Inc.,
Philadelphia

Richard Hamilton, *Just What Was It
That Made Yesterday's Homes So Different,
So Appealing?*, 1993
Collage electronically restored and printed
on a Canon colour laser printer (based on
*Just What Is It That Makes Today's Homes So
Different, So Appealing?* of 1956)
46.8 x 42 x 3 cm
Courtesy Alan Cristea Gallery, London

Charles and Ray Eames, *DKR*, 1951
Herman Miller Inc., Zeeland, MI, USA
Chair
Lacquered steel wire, two-piece vinyl pad,
plastic
81 x 48 x 53 cm
Vitra Design Museum

Charles and Ray Eames,
Giant House of Cards, 1953
Tigrett Enterprises, Chicago, IL, USA
Card game
Printed card stock
20 playing cards, 27.8 x 17.8 cm (each card)
Vitra Design Museum

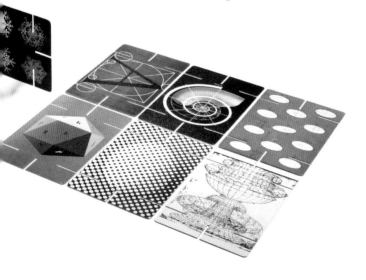

James Rosenquist,
I Love You With My Ford, 1961
Oil on canvas
210 x 238 cm
Moderna Museet

Richard Hamilton,
Hommage à Chrysler Corp., 1958
Illustration for the magazine
Architectural Design 28, no. 3, 1958
30.5 x 23 cm
Vitra Design Museum

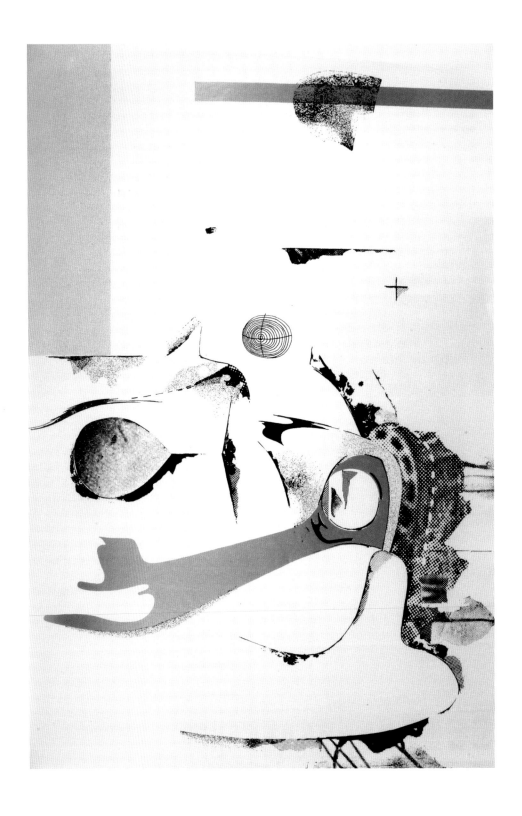

Achille and Pier Giacomo Castiglioni,
No. 200 / Sella, 1957/1983
Zanotta SpA, Nova Milanese (MI), Italy
Stool
Chrome-plated and lacquered steel,
lacquered cast iron, leather, copper
73 x 28 x 32 cm
Alexander von Vegesack, Lessac

Robert Rauschenberg, *Tideline*, 1963
Oil and silkscreen print on canvas
213 x 152.5 cm
Louisiana Museum of Modern Art
Long-term loan
Museumsfonden af 7. december 1966

George Nelson, *Block Clock / No. 2285c*, 1950
Howard Miller Clock Co., Zeeland, MI, USA
Wall clock
Lacquered metal, lacquered wood, clockwork
29.5 x 29.5 x 8 cm
Vitra Design Museum

Jasper Johns, *Green Target*, 1957
Encaustic and newspaper on canvas
25.4 x 25.5 cm
Louisiana Museum of Modern Art
Donation Elena and Nicolas Calas

Judy Chicago, *Car Hood*, 1964
Sprayed acrylic on Corvair car hood
109 x 125 x 11 cm
Moderna Museet
The Second Museum of Our Wishes

Andy Warhol, *You're In*, 1967
Spray paint on glass bottles in printed
wooden crate
23 x 43.2 x 30.5 cm
The Andy Warhol Museum, Pittsburgh,
Founding Collection

Anonymous, *Mod. 44*, 1947–51
The Vendo Company, Kansas City,
MO, USA
Vending machine
Lacquered sheet steel, cast aluminium
148 x 41.5 x 53.5 cm
Vitra Design Museum

Simon International,
Omaggio ad Andy Warhol, 1973
Gavina SpA, Bologna (BO), Italy
Stool
Paint drum with silkscreen,
fabric upholstery
45 x 31 x 31 cm
Vitra Design Museum

Andy Warhol, *Close Cover Before Striking*, 1962
Acrylic and sandpaper with chalk on canvas
183 x 137.5 cm
Louisiana Museum of Modern Art

John McHale, magazine cover,
Architectural Review CXXI, no. 724, May 1957
(*Machine Made America*)
Offset printing
31 x 25 x 1.5 cm
Vitra Design Museum

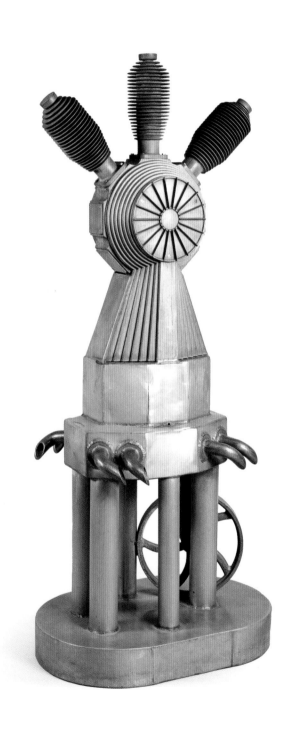

Eduardo Paolozzi,
The Bishop of Kuban, 1962
Cast aluminium
210 x 93 x 60.7 cm
Scottish National Gallery
of Modern Art

Anonymous, film poster, *Forbidden Planet*
(dir. Fred M. Wilcox's), 1956
Colour lithograph on paper
104 x 69 cm
Vitra Design Museum

Anonymous, *High Wheel Robot*, 1965
Yoshiya, Japan
Toy robot
Tin, plastic
27 x 11 x 10 cm
Fifo Stricker

Charles and Ray Eames,
A Communications Primer, 1953
16-mm film, digitized
22 min 30 sec, colour
Courtesy Eames Office

Tomás Maldonado (Ulm School of Design)
and Ettore Sottsass, *Elea 9003*, 1959
Olivetti SpA, Ivrea (TO), Italy
Central console of mainframe computer
Aluminium, plastic, steel
155 x 125 x 100 cm
Museo Nazionale della Scienza e della
Tecnologia Leonardo da Vinci

33

fig. 1
Roy Lichtenstein, magazine cover,
Newsweek, 25 April 1966

Just What Is It That Makes Pop Art So Different, So Appealing?
A Success Story

Tobias Lander

fig. 1

fig. 2
Andy Warhol, *Campbell's Soup Cans*, 1962
Synthetic polymer paint on thirty-two
canvases
50.8 x 40.6 cm (each canvas)
The Museum of Modern Art, New York
Gift of Irving Blum, Nelson A. Rockefeller
Bequest, gift of Mr. and Mrs. William A.M.
Burden, Abby Aldrich Rockefeller Fund,
gift of Nina and Gordon Bunshaft in honour
of Henry Moore, Lillie P. Bliss Bequest,
Philip Johnson Fund, Frances Keech Bequest

fig. 2

I t is quite telling that the word 'Pop' can be understood not only as an abbreviation of 'popular' but also as the sound of a shot or an explosion, for from today's point of view Pop Art burst onto the art scene with nothing less than a veritable bang (fig. 1). Art viewers suddenly found themselves confronted with lurid neon, candy-coloured images that evoked the advertisements spread across big-city billboards. Comic strips – a genre that until then had been condemned in influential campaigns as trashy literature – catapulted to newfound status as an art-worthy subject. Coca-Cola bottles and Campbell's Soup cans made their way from grocery store shelves to the canvas (fig. 2) and hamburgers mutated into sculptures and seating for pin-up girls (fig. 24), while the garishly made-up visage of Marilyn Monroe cast a vibrant glow over it all with her knowing smile → p. 168. A new generation of artists transported the trivial motifs of their urban environment – seemingly untransformed – into the hallowed halls of art, if not simultaneously recasting the gallery as an American supermarket.[1] They conveyed an utter lack of pretension and deliberately blurred the boundary between art and life. Virtually overnight, Pop Art knocked the hitherto prevailing art movement of Abstract Expressionism off its pedestal and, according to Tom Wolfe, it was as if the public had been expectantly awaiting the appearance of just such everyday imagery:

> It was the thaw! It was spring again! The press embraced
> Pop Art with priapic delight. That goddamned Abstract
> Expressionism had been so solemn, so grim ... 'Shards of
> interpenetrated sensibility make their way, tentatively, through
> a not always compromisable field of cobalt blue – ' How could
> you write about the freaking stuff? Pop Art you could have
> fun with. . . .
>
> In short . . . the culturati were secretly *enjoying the
> realism*! – plain old bourgeois mass-culture high-school

goober-squeezing whitehead-hunting can-I-pop-it-for-you-Billy realism! They looked at a Roy Lichtenstein blowup of a love-comic panel showing a young blond couple with their lips parted in the moment before a profound, tongue-probing, post-teen, American soul kiss, plus the legend 'WE ROSE UP SLOWLY. . . AS IF WE DIDN'T BELONG TO THE OUTSIDE WORLD ANY LONGER . . . LIKE SWIMMERS IN A SHADOWY DREAM . . . WHO DIDN'T NEED TO BREATHE . . .' and – the hell with the *sign systems* – they just loved the dopey campy picture of these two vapid blond sex buds having their love-comic romance bigger than life, six feet by eight feet, in fact, up on the walls in an art gallery.[2] (fig. 3)

The contrast to Abstract Expressionism, ossified in academic formalism and sapped of its former ability to spark enthusiasm within the art crowd, was certainly a key factor in Pop Art's success. As the banal imagery of Pop artists opened up their works to a wider audience, viewers uninitiated in the discourses of the art world presumably approached the familiar likeness of a soup can with much less trepidation than the often hermetic works of abstraction. To grasp the significance of this paradigm shift, one must bear in mind that modernist-era Western culture no longer valued the ease with which a work could be understood. On the contrary, incomprehensibility was seen as a criterion of quality for complex and original works of art, leading the viewer to accept the intermediary role of experts and rely on their interpretation in order to understand and experience such works. The provocation of Pop artists now consisted in offering broadly understood motifs that tore down the social barrier between educated, art-indoctrinated viewers and the cultural underclass. 'People want all the prerogatives of education without going to the trouble of being educated', came the prompt reaction of bypassed art critics whose expert knowledge, so readily consulted during abstraction's heyday, was apparently no longer required.[3] The 'picture-worthiness' of the banal devalued the interpretative function and threatened the institutional status of a caste of critics who understood the elite in art as a normative value. In 1964, *Life* magazine published an article on Roy Lichtenstein entitled 'Is He the Worst Artist in the U.S.?', and many established critics would have undoubtedly replied in the affirmative.[4] Yet the public – especially the well-heeled collectors – disregarded such criticism, for the possibility of anti-intellectual perception offered liberation from their 'own secret fear of the incomprehensible in the normally elitist art world'.[5]

The Pop artists fuelled this clash of high and low in art by explicitly positioning themselves in contrast to Abstract Expressionism. An early beacon of this liberation from the parent generation was signalled by Robert Rauschenberg's para-digmatic erasing of a drawing by Willem de Kooning (1953); its irreverent culmination might be seen in Andy Warhol's copying of Jackson Pollock's drippings by urinating on a metallic ground in his *Oxidation Paintings* (1977–78). Roy Lichtenstein's *Brushstrokes* put themselves at the heart of this debate as parodistic travesties of expressionist painting. Yet although their smooth pictorial surface is diametrically opposed to the irregularly applied one of Action Painting, this group of works by Lichtenstein cannot simply be put down to the sensation of painterly negation. After all, he undeniably pays his respects to the brushstroke as he captures its character with the graphic means of comic strips. In *Yellow*

fig. 3

Brushstroke → p. 164, for example, the appearance of splashes and drips on the left suggests a brush freshly dipped in paint while, moving across to the right, the brushstroke loses more and more of its density before thinning out at the edges, as if the brush were lifted from the canvas. In a figurative sense, Lichtenstein extracts an individual trail of paint from gestural painting and makes it the defining subject; and although his *Brushstrokes* never entirely shed the appearance of caricature, they assert themselves as an elementary structural component of the brushwork that the second generation of Abstract Expressionists had stripped of aggressiveness and rawness and degraded as ornament.[6]

Tom Wesselmann's *Landscape No. 4* (fig. 4) also wades into the feud between American abstraction and Pop realism, even though the painting looks at first glance more like an advertising poster for a new car. Under a medium-blue sky, a black sports coupé rolls along against the backdrop of snow-covered Mount Hood in Oregon. Behind the grey asphalt strip of roadway, Lost Lake stretches out as a band of light blue. The prominent peak is familiar to art lovers from paintings by Albert Bierstadt, and it is characteristic of Pop that Wesselmann supplies the very same view one century later. In contrast to his predecessor, however, Wesselmann renders natural phenomena like the sky or the water surface in a wholly unmodulated manner. His blue does not serve as an indicator of shadow or distance but as conspicuous labelling. In particular, the contrast of the light

fig. 4

fig. 5

blue lake with the dark shoreline emphasizes the stringent horizontal arrangement of the linear picture elements, which bluntly cite works of Colour Field painting. Yet the relation to Colour Field painting is less a matter of motifs than an aspect of the history of ideas. It was the Abstract Expressionists and Colour Field painters who saw themselves as salvaging the much-vaunted sublimity of nineteenth-century American painting and bringing it into the modernist era. Artists like Barnett Newman und Clyfford Still understood their megalomaniac fields of colour as an abstract equivalent of the American landscape and shifted the national frontier myth to the domain of art with the battle cry 'The Sublime is Now!'[7] Thus, when Wesselmann references the heroes of American abstraction, he pays them respect with a sardonic smile. The existentialism of Colour Field painters, their desire to be deep at all costs, their dreams of breaking with European tradition and their psychologization of colour spaces are foreign to the Pop artist. Above all, however, Wesselmann does not believe in the primacy of abstraction. He short-circuits the typical colour fields with the naturalistic representation of the mountain, essentially doubly citing the postulated sources of the sublime. Spoiled by the profane realism that besets the pure fields of colour, his quotation of a pioneering pictorial achievement simultaneously serves as a signal of its displacement.

This distance from the abstraction that preceded them can be found in varying degrees in nearly every Pop work. While Abstract Expressionist painting titans wrestle with their inner compulsions in tempests of paint, Pop artists reject the notion of a subjective pictorial language that can shed light on the artist personality. In place of the legible traces of the action painter's physical struggle with the canvas, most Pop artists present smooth surfaces with no sign of authorship. The pathos of the older generation is met with irony in the works of their successors and the well-maintained attitude of the artist-genius

fizzles out under Pop's typical reduction of artistic intervention – through the selection of found motifs, the use of modern reproduction techniques or even the delegation of artistic activity to a collective, such as in Warhol's Factory. The large canvas propagated by their elders as a means to the sublime is filled by Pop artists with blown-up comic strips or – in reference to the Pollockian 'all over' – with hundreds of Campbell's Soup cans, while the ambience of contemplation created by Rothko in quasi-sacred spatial compositions is countered in the art of his successors by the din of the city. Yet it is an established convention of the avant-garde to stress aspects that divide over those that unite as a means of drawing attention to the novelty of their own concept. In the case of Pop Art, however, this stance requires far-reaching ignorance of works by such hinge figures as Robert Rauschenberg → p. 25 or Jasper Johns → p. 26. The suddenness of the stylistic break is a construct. After all, there are works that can be classified as Pop Art in view of the motifs they harbour without denying their debt to the formal inventions of Abstract Expressionism – Claes Oldenburg's coarsely modelled objects covered with expressive smears of colour, for instance (fig. 5). Yet even beyond Abstract Expressionism, Pop artists were aware of their art-historical position. Hieratic presentations of consumer goods, such as Warhol's *Campbell's* series, had already been explored back in 1924 in Stuart Davis's *Odol* (fig. 8), and sign painters like Robert Indiana → p. 101 intentionally sought an affinity with such incunabula of American Cubism as Charles Demuth's *I Saw the Figure 5 in Gold* (fig. 7). Other artists drew on the disparate motif combinations of Surrealism – for example, James Rosenquist's composite of a pair of lovers whispering sweet nothings, the radiator grill of a car and spaghetti with tomato sauce in *I Love You With My Ford* → p. 22. The appeal of this painting is due in large part to Isidore Ducasse's principle of the '*rencontre fortuite sur une table de dissection d'une machine à coudre et d'un parapluie*'.[8] In a 1934–35 gouache, Salvador Dalí interpreted the face of actress Mae West as a

fig. 7

fig. 6

fig. 8

fig. 9
Roy Lichtenstein, *Portrait of Ivan Karp /*
Portrait of Allan Kaprow, 1961
Oil on canvas
61 x 51 cm (each painting)
Private collection

fig. 10
Tom Wesselmann, *Great American Nude No. 57*, 1964
Synthetic polymer on composition board
121.9 x 165.1cm
Whitney Museum of American Art, New York
Purchased with funds from the Friends of the
Whitney Museum of American Art
Photo: Bill Orcutt

fig. 9   fig. 10

theatrically staged room with a couch whose back assumes the curve of the Hollywood star's upper lip while its seat comprises her lower one. Shortly thereafter, a small number of these couches actually went into production.[9] The Surrealist apparently understood his design as Pop *avant la lettre*, since in 1971 he placed such a lips sofa, upholstered in glossy pink → p. 170, outside his house in Port Lligat and hung neon-lit signs of the tyre company Pirelli's logo above it (fig. 6), thus tapping into the aesthetic of Pop Art. Dalí's *Mae West Lips Sofa* makes it possible to own and even sit on an unattainable film star – an aspect that evokes the erotic play of submission and domination, which, in turn, connects Dalí's couch with Allen Jones's *Chair* → p. 173. All of Jones's women-as-furniture pieces – a trio that includes a table and hat stand alongside the chair – attest to the same fascination with life-size female dolls manifested decades earlier in the mannequins made by various artists at the 1938 *Exposition Internationale du Surréalisme*. And when an anonymous Pop artist says 'We paint Coke bottles instead of wine bottles',[10] he not only plays with the humble origins of his motif but also links it to René Magritte and his *Femmes-bouteilles* (fig. 11). Yet Pop's characteristic choice of an industrial form that already unmistakably mimics the erotic contours of the female body obviates the need for a nude painting on the bottle à la Magritte – even if Charles Frazier adopted the 'more is more' motto of Pop by augmenting the Coca-Cola bottle with a pair of mighty breasts (fig. 13).

Closely related to Surrealism, Dadaism, too, lies in the ancestral line of Pop Art. For instance, the aesthetics of assemblage place a umber of Combine paintings by Rauschenberg and some early works by Johns in the tradition of Kurt Schwitters, and 'Neo-Dada' was a widely applied label for the new strain of American figuration before the term 'Pop Art' gained currency.[11] Above all, however, the influence of Dadaism is rooted in the 'personality of choice', to use Louis Aragon's description of the idea of transferring a found object into

the sphere of art.[12] In particular, Marcel Duchamp is recognized as a forerunner of Pop, with Johns's *Painted Bronze* (fig. 12) and Warhol's *Brillo Boxes* → p. 167 exuding the spirit of revolutionary ready-mades. Yet even if prominent art philosophers erroneously insist here on the indistinguishability of model and copy, these Pop works are not ready-mades but rather their quotations.[13] Referring to the idea of the ready-made without being ready-mades themselves, they discus the role of the artist and the possibilities of painting in the indifferent zone between original and copy, reality and perception.

These relations to established positions bear witness to a seriousness of artistic purpose that seems to resist Richard Hamilton's definition of Pop Art as 'Popular (designed for a mass audience); Transient (short-term solution); Expendable (easily-forgotten); Low cost; Mass produced; Young (aimed at youth); Witty; Sexy; Gimmicky; Glamorous; Big business.'[14] Hamilton's manifesto is trotted out in nearly every text on Pop Art, yet upon closer inspection the listed characteristics of Pop do not hold up in their entirety. To be sure, the movement targets a mass audience with its selection of motifs and it is often 'gimmicky' as well. However, it is by no means 'mass produced' and even in Warhol's Factory was created in controlled quantities. Moreover, it is not transient nor is it geared towards short-term solutions, expendability or imminent oblivion, but rather possesses an appeal that extends up to the present. As will be shown, the iconographic and conceptual ties between subsequent generations of artists and Pop Art are nearly omnipresent. Continuing to work down Hamilton's list, Pop Art is by no means cheap – not in terms of the utilized materials, which range from latest-generation Magna acrylic resin paints to fragments of industrial diamonds, and certainly not with regard to its market value, which has multiplied in record time. Given the rapid commercialization of the works, Hamilton's estimation of Pop Art as 'big business' indeed applies without qualification. The assertion that

fig. 11
René Magritte,
Femme-bouteille, 1945
Oil on bottle
30 x ø 7 cm
Private collection

fig. 12
Jasper Johns, *Painted Bronze*, 1960
Oil on bronze
14 x 20.3 x 12.1 cm
Museum Ludwig, Cologne
Ludwig Donation

fig. 13
Charles Frazier,
American Nude, 1963
Bronze
19.6 x ø 6.8 cm
Private collection

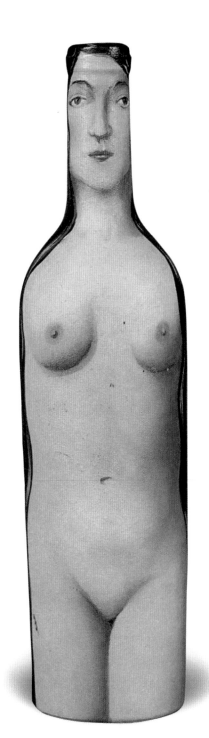

fig. 11

Fig. 12

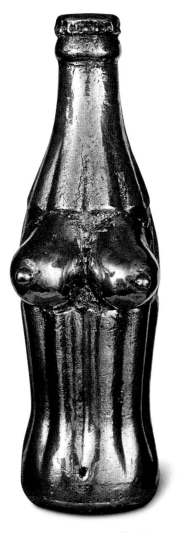

Fig. 13

fig. 14

fig. 14
Eduardo Paolozzi,
Real Gold, 1950
Collage
35.6 x 23.5 cm
Tate, London

Pop Art aims at youth also seems apt, as is exemplified in its embrace of comics, the quintessential reading material of the young. Yet curiously, the Pop artists who adopted this motif frequently referred back to the classics of the genre. From Mickey Mouse to Superman, many of the comic strip characters employed by Pop artists were first created in the 1930s. Rather than evoking the youthful attitudes and lifestyle of the early 1960s, the artists harked back to the comics of their childhood years – a choice that lends a nostalgic flair to this motif. The claim that Pop Art is glamorous and sexy is beyond dispute in view of the actress portraits by Warhol and the consumer pin-ups by Mel Ramos, yet the mannequin furniture of Allen Jones and the faceless Wesselmann nudes (fig. 10) are tinged by an undertone of disrespect that is more sexist than sexy. The same applies to Hamilton's characterization of Pop as witty. Considering the accident victims shown in Warhol's *Car Crashes* (1962–64), the question has to be asked if wit can really be called a universal Pop trait. Lichtenstein's double portrait of his colleague Allan Kaprow and gallery owner Ivan Karp, on the other hand, unquestionably evinces a sense of humour, consisting as it does of two absolutely congruent paintings of two individuals who scarcely resembled one another in real life (fig. 9). In selecting a stereotype of a smart and self-assured man of the 1960s to depict both his subjects, the artist reveals the superficiality of modern visual media – from advertising to feature films – and its incapability of offering anything more than a mere simulation of identity. Instead of a quickly fizzling joke, we experience here the cognitive power of irony, whose significance for all of Pop Art can hardly be overestimated.

Why is it that Hamilton's description of Pop Art comes up short in retrospect? One reason is the diversity of different artistic approaches that developed independently from one another but were grouped under the heading 'Pop Art'. Originating in the mid-1950s with the Independent Group, which met informally at London's Institute of Contemporary Arts, the term initially described objects pertaining to popular culture and not artworks that took these objects as their theme. For the artists of the group, one of whom was Hamilton, the found object was more significant than large-format reproduction and the incorporation of trivial culture into the concept of art, and the changes in society and the world were more important than the gallery-friendly representation of everyday life. Thus, when Hamilton spoke of Pop Art, he was thinking of commercial mass culture. Nevertheless, the boundaries of art had become blurred. With their sheer mass of prominently presented American magazine titles and advertisements, works by Hamilton's colleague Eduardo Paolozzi (fig. 14) came across as if they were display panels on the theme of 'U.S. cultural hegemony in postwar Europe' due to the fact that the artist found most of his material in the rummage bins of Parisian booksellers. By dint of their collage aesthetic, however, these pieces unquestionably laid claim to being art. With *Just what is it that makes today's homes so different, so appealing?* of 1956 → p. 181, Hamilton himself presented a nearly complete early iconography of Pop (including the word 'Pop') and thus created an incunabulum of Pop Art. By the time of the legendary Symposium on Pop Art, held at the Museum of Modern Art in 1962, the term had caught on as a collective label for New York Pop artists, leading to a shift in its meaning. Under this preferred designation – highly favoured by the market as well – positions were now grouped together and charged with a related artistic impetus, irrespective of their temporal and spatial distance from one another. The characteristics of the artwork itself were now more important than the sociological view of everyday culture. Accordingly, Hamilton's catchphrases offer a very good description of Pop Art as understood by the Independent Group – although they have little in common with the typical strain of hardcore New York Pop.

fig. 15
Mimmo Rotella, *Marilyn*, 1962
Decollage on canvas
133 x 94 cm
Private collection

fig. 15

fig. 16
Robert Indiana, *LOVE*, 1966
Oil on canvas
183 x 183 cm
Indianapolis Museum of Art

fig. 16

Considering the stylistic heterogeneity of Pop artists – from the collages of Paolozzi and Hamilton through the almost sterile, unmodulated fields of colour in Lichtenstein's blown-up comic strip images to performative art actions such as Oldenburg's *The Store* → p. 124 – it seems only logical that the term 'Pop Art' has remained vague.[15] What ultimately functions as the lowest common denominator of all these divergent forms of artistic expression is popular culture as a frame of reference. The overall movement was shaped not only by the artists in the centres of London and New York but also by those on the American West Coast and in continental Europe. There were Pop artists working in isolation, such as the Paris-based Swiss Peter Stämpfli → p. 166, as well as entire movements that acted with similar aims along the fringes of Pop Art, such as the *nouveaux réalistes* → p. 176. In addition, pictorial inventions were absorbed from other quarters, such as the psychedelic style of late-1960s poster design that emanated from the hippie culture of San Francisco but suddenly itself became Pop → p. 65. Moreover, Pop artists often sought proximity to simultaneously emerging movements such as Minimal and Op Art. It comes as no surprise, therefore, that Pop Art consists of a variable number of artists depending on the perspective from which it is considered. In 1966, Lucy L. Lippard named Andy Warhol, Roy Lichtenstein, James Rosenquist, Claes Oldenburg and Tom Wesselmann as belonging to the inner core of Pop; yet she also included European artists such as Konrad Klapheck → p. 150, Gerhard Richter and Enrico Baj. In 1985, Henry Geldzahler ranked George Segal and Jim Dine among the masters, while Tom Wesselmann had to content himself with the attribute 'still important in the Pop context' and artists such as David Hockney and Mel Ramos with being relegated to the periphery of the movement.[16] Countless other examples can be cited: from Rauschenberg and Johns, at times addressed as full-fledged Pop artists and other times as precursors of the movement, through artists such as

John Chamberlain and George Segal, whose Pop-like affiliation with everyday life was always paired with elements of established tradition, to *affichistes* like Mimmo Rotella, who made a direct link to American Pop Art with his banal yet glamorous décollages of cinema posters even though he sailed under the flag of *nouveau réalisme* (fig. 15). A particularly tragic aspect in this connection is the treatment of female Pop artists. These were largely ignored, initially by those critics who 'carved out the criteria of Pop Art in the mid-1960s as an Anglo-Saxon movement in the hands of a few male artists', and then – as misogynist sexism began to infuse the Pop Art discourse – by feminist art criticism (figs. 22–24).[17]

For Hamilton, Pop Art is synonymous with mass culture, which is why his definition tends to apply more to pop music and its goal of affordable mass entertainment with no claim to eternity. This validity might also extend to the famed album covers designed by Pop artists → p. 54-57, as they are largely tied to the same distribution channels. As an art movement, however, Pop Art was never part of everyday culture. With a few exceptions, it did not produce works of art for broad sections of the population – even the multiples never constituted high-volume mass art but merely a less expensive variant of so-called high art. The democratization of art by Pop Art was only a semblance. First and foremost, the whiff of the everyday and the ordinary served to give the movement a position within cultural discourses and ultimately in institutions. Oldenburg dreamed of an art 'that does something other than sit on its ass in a museum'; yet once accepted by the elite art world, Pop works were soon firmly entrenched on their haunches in museum settings.[18] The intellectual aspirations of Pop Art further set it apart from the masses. As genuine as the offer of low-threshold access might have been in terms of the widely comprehensible Pop motifs, on a second level Pop Art has always remained an art in need of interpretation. It insists, for instance, on the distinction between

fig. 17
Richard Prince,
untitled (Cowboys), 1987
Ektacolor photograph
50.8 x 61 cm
Courtesy of the artist

fig. 18
Rosalyn Drexler,
Death of Benny "Kid" Paret, 1963
Oil on paper on canvas
35.2 x 45.7 cm
Private collection of the artist

fig. 17

form and content in its symbolically and emotionally charged motifs – 'I am calling attention to the abstract quality of banal images' (Lichtenstein)[19] – and provided important impulses for Conceptual Art. With respect to Warhol's soup cans, for example, Marcel Duchamp ignored their trivial motifs and commented that 'what interests us is the *concept* that wants to put fifty Campbell's soup cans on a canvas'.[20] Artists like Jasper Johns and Jim Dine followed related tendencies of Conceptual Art – such as those of Joseph Kosuth – with their experiments on the relations between image and copy. Ed Ruscha, in turn, sought to do justice to the significance of words and lend them adequate visual expression → p. 139, thereby engaging with one of the hotspots of philosophy and linguistics. Insights from the psychology of perception, like the relationship of figure and ground, were explored by both Warhol and Robert Indiana – the former with his *Flowers* → p. 158, the latter in the variations of his

famous *LOVE* logo (fig. 16), in which the letters vie with the colour fields of the intermediary spaces. Claes Oldenburg's soft sculptures → p. 161, on the other hand, elude the primacy of composition through their variability of form conditioned by the soft material and hence question the classical concept of sculpture. In addition, Pop Art investigates aspects of modern media, as with Rosalyn Drexler who in 1963 explored the voyeuristic character of a fatal boxing match shown on TV by capturing individual frames from the broadcast

fig. 18

on canvas (fig. 18). Warhol, in particular, stretched the typical media-specific possibilities when he created a static series of images suggesting cinematic progression (*Baseball*, 1962) or, the other way around, when he filmed hours of continuous footage of a single view of the Empire State Building whose lack of action counteracts the characteristic properties of the medium (*Empire*, 1964). Above all, however, Pop Art examines sociocultural conditions, from the flood of images in the mass media through the production process of modern consumer goods, which is likewise quoted in Warhol's assembly line-like sequences of individual motifs, to changing patterns of consumption. With his *TV Dinner* (fig. 21) from 1965, for instance, Robert Watts turned his attention to hypermodern convenience food meant to be consumed while watching television. In this work, he pasted black-and-white photos of the meal's components – the aluminium tray of food (roast turkey with mashed potatoes and cranberries), the cutlery and a filled glass – onto individual wooden boards; only the peas were affixed three-dimensionally and tinted bright green. Watts's meal is a symbolic reference to the cliché of the American family idyll on Thanksgiving and, as a simulation of an already simulated culinary tradition, reveals the discrepancy between aspiration and reality. Mere nutritional intake has replaced the social act of dining.

This example leads us to the still-relevant discourse on the critical content of Pop Art – not the critical self-reflection on the medium of painting, as evident in works like Lichtenstein's *Brushstrokes*, but rather the reaction of artists to the social and political upheavals of their time: for instance, Warhol's treatment of the nuclear threat (*Atomic Bomb*, 1965), racial unrest (*Red Race Riot*, 1963) and the mass media's depersonalization of death in his *Disaster* series (1963–64).[21] The ability of Pop's visual language to convey political statements is demonstrated

ambivalence since it combines the heightening of the female sexual aura with a phallic form, especially when it can be mechanically extended, as in Oldenburg's example, and made erect to full size. Thus, Oldenburg's subversive *Lipstick* is an anti-war monument that pokes fun at the male hero obsession.

In his trademark-inspired pastiche *ESSO LSD* → p. 147, the Icelander Öyvind Fahlström lamented consumer addiction in adapting the

fig. 19

by James Rosenquist's *F-111* (fig. 19), in which the fighter jet of the same name and an atomic bomb explosion are interspersed with images of consumer goods: car tyres, light bulbs and his trademark spaghetti. The artist originally wished to sell the painting as fifty-one separate fragments and thus expose the complicit participation of the individual, all the way down to the deployment of a fighter-bomber during the Vietnam and Cold War era.[22] Claes Oldenburg augmented the amalgamation of everyday American myths and implements of war with the issue of sexuality. In his grand piece entitled *Lipstick* (fig. 20), he attached a giant red tube of lipstick onto a base modelled after the chassis of a tank. Per se, lipstick possesses an interesting

three letters of the drug to the Esso logo. Such unambiguously critical statements are far from the rule, however, as Pop works tend to impart an impression of indifference vis-à-vis the realities of consumer society. Pop Art does not explicitly exalt Western consumer economy, nor does it call into question the materialistic promises of happiness. In fact, the question of whether Pop Art is apolitical, pro-consumption or critical of capitalism seems to primarily depend on the political convictions of the interpreter.[23] Nevertheless, there are good reasons not to dismiss its laconic presentations of commodities as merely affirmative. In 1962, Andy Warhol reproduced thirty-two Campbell's Soup cans on individual canvases, corresponding to the number of

fig. 20
Claes Oldenburg, *Lipstick (Ascending) on Caterpillar Tracks*, 1969 (installed on Beinecke Plaza at Yale University, 1969/70)
Cor-Ten steel, aluminium, cast resin, polyurethane enamel
716 x 758 x 333 cm
Yale University Art Gallery, New Haven
Gift of Colossal Keepsake Corporation

fig. 21
Robert Watts, *TV Dinner*, 1965
Wood, laminated photographs, latex, paint
17.8 x 22.9 x 3.2 cm
Walker Art Center, Minneapolis

fig. 20

fig. 21

fig. 22
Patricia Waller, *Buffet*, 1999
Crochet work, 8 parts
Wool, cotton filling, plastic, wood
Courtesy Galerie Deschler, Berlin

fig. 23
Jann Haworth, *Donuts, Coffee Cups & Comics*, 1962
Various textiles, kapok
Private collection of the artist

fig. 24
Mel Ramos, *Virnaburger*, 1965
Oil on canvas
152.4 x 127 cm
Museu Colecção Berardo, Lisbon

fig. 25
Erró, *Foodscape*, 1964
Oil on canvas
201 x 302.5 cm
Moderna Museet, Stockholm

fig. 22

fig. 23

fig. 24

fig. 25

fig. 26

commercially available varieties, from Turkey Noodle to Tomato (fig. 2). Hence, those wishing to acquire one of the paintings intended for individual sale formed their preference solely on the absurd basis of the labelled contents. Artistic taste, unable to distinguish and rank the otherwise identical soup cans, is replaced here by a preference for a particular soup flavour. What finer example could there be of the commoditized nature of art?

The famous debate that took place at the 1959 American National Exhibition in Moscow lends a political dimension to Warhol's cans. United States Vice President Richard Nixon and Soviet Premier Nikita Khrushchev discussed the relative merits of their economies, whereby Nixon persistently emphasized that a system's strengths can be measured in household technology and the general access to goods. In a pivotal statement at this so-called Kitchen Debate, Nixon linked consumer choice to the free selection of a political ideology: 'Let the people choose the kind of house, the kind of soup, the kind of ideas that they want.'[24] It merits at least some degree of consideration that Warhol adopted the motif of Campbell's Soup cans after the purchase of soup, of all things, had been put on a par with the democratic freedom of choice. Against the background of this contest of ideologies, Warhol's soup can appears as a metaphor for a 'free' Western world that is based on the societal consensus of consumption.

The postmodern 'anything goes' made certain practices a matter of course: the adoption of existing, familiar images from everyday life, the associated dismantling of the creative artist and the exposure of art's market value. Pop concepts such as the melding of high and low, the examination of consumer society and the mass media, quotations of art and the use of the latest reproduction techniques can be found in a multitude of post-Pop artistic expressions. Haim Steinbach's arrangements of everyday objects renew the often-mentioned relationship between Pop and Minimal Art; the surrealistic confrontation of disparate pictorial elements makes David Salle an heir of Rosenquist's; and the interaction of image and word in the works of Jasper Johns, Jim Dine and Ed Ruscha paved the way for artists like John Baldessari. Les Levine, Jenny Holzer and Barbara Kruger employ the aesthetic and technique of advertising to disseminate their slogans. Richard Prince's *Cowboys* correspond to the clichés of masculinity cultivated in cigarette advertising (fig. 17), while Cindy Sherman alludes to the myth of Hollywood in her *Untitled Film Stills*. Jeff Koons' Neo-Pop reproduces the brash kitsch of mass culture (fig. 26) and aims squarely at high-impact public sensation with such groups of works as *Made in Heaven* (1990), in which the artist and the porn queen Ilona Staller celebrate various sex practices in giant photographs and life-size sculptures. Sensation is likewise guaranteed in the case of Damien Hirst, especially in his 2007 platinum cast of a human skull fitted with diamonds, this material overkill alone creating presumably the most expensive work by a contemporary artist. As with Hirst, Erwin Wurm's *Fat Car Convertible* (2005) is linked

fig. 27

fig. 28

fig. 28
Daniel Pflumm,
untitled (Tic Tac), 2001
Light box
72 x 85 x 15 cm
Courtesy Daniel Pflumm
and Galerie Neu, Berlin

to Pop Art through its expansively applied irony. The red Porsche convertible disappears beneath the bulges and folds of its obesely bloated bodywork. Wurm gives literal expression to the notion of a 'fat ride', for aside from Porsche's motor sports credentials, the luxury car is instantly recognized as a status symbol. With his light boxes based on the logos of well-known companies, Daniel Pflumm revives the view of our consumer world exercised by Pop Art (fig. 28); first and foremost, however, he examines the aesthetic value of standardized signals, which makes him seem more indebted to universal icons like Johns's *Targets* than the explicitly political illuminated signs of Fahlström → p. 26 and 147. Rosemarie Trockel's knitted repetitions of familiar symbols and Patricia Waller's crochet pieces (fig. 22) renew a gender-specific discourse initiated earlier by Jann Haworth with her stitched-together fabric sculptures (fig. 23). The oppressive mass of commodities in Andreas Gursky's *99 Cent* looks like a descendent of Erró's *Foodscape*, in which a gargantuan sea of food threatens to engulf the viewer (fig. 27 and 25); while the works of Michel Majerus, the Luxembourg artist who died at a young age in 2002, create a resonance chamber for the accelerated circulation of mass media images based on his findings from the World Wide Web and transport Pop's characteristic usurpation of visual icons into the Internet era. In short, there is scarcely an artist working today who does not profit in one way or another from the innovations of Pop Art.[25] Above all, it is the strategy of channelling art through the familiar conduits of everyday culture that makes Pop Art so interesting. It is not confined to mere citation – Pop Art does not culminate in blithe detachment but retains a sceptical attitude towards the subject, albeit one that can only rarely be precisely defined. It is this very interpretative uncertainty that incites a questioning of sociocultural realities without patronizing the viewer. As an anti-intellectual art that taps into the mythology of the everyday via Hollywood stars, comic strips and Coca-Cola,

it offers low-threshold access. As an art dependent on interpretation that functions on various meta-levels and works with a multitude of associations, Pop Art appeals to the intellect. It is a clever art that viewers can find decorative without needing to feel ashamed; and, to paraphrase Richard Hamilton, *that is just what makes Pop Art so different, so appealing*.

★

Endnotes

1 See Christoph Grunenberg, 'The American Supermarket', in Christoph Grunenberg and Max Hollein, eds., *Shopping: A Century of Art and Consumer Culture*, exhibition catalogue, Schirn-Kunsthalle Frankfurt and Tate Liverpool (Ostfildern-Ruit: Hatje Cantz, 2002), 170–177.

2 Tom Wolfe, *The Painted Word* (New York: Bantam Books, 1999), 69–70, 72–73; originally published by Farrar, Straus and Giroux in 1975.

3 Hilton Kramer, quoted in Peter Benchley, 'Special Report: The Story of Pop', in Steven Henry Madoff, ed., *Pop Art: A Critical History*, Documents of Twentieth Century Art (Berkeley and Los Angeles: University of California Press, 1997), 149; originally published in *Newsweek*, 25 April 1966.

4 Dorothy Seiberling, 'Is He the Worst Artist in the U.S.?', in Madoff, *Pop Art*, 195; originally published in *Life*, 31 January 1964. The title plays on an article published in the same magazine 15 years earlier: 'Jackson Pollock: Is He the Greatest Living Painter in the United States?', *Life*, 8 August 1949, 42–45.

5 Zdenek Primus, 'Pop-Art: Art for the Sixties', in Zdenek Primus, ed., *Much Pop, More Art: Kunst der 60er Jahre in Grafiken, Multiples und Publikationen / Art of the 60s in Graphic Works, Multiples and Publications*, exhibition catalogue (Stuttgart: Amerika Haus Stuttgart and Mercedes-Benz AG Stuttgart, 1992), 21–24.

6 See Diane Waldman, *Roy Lichtenstein*, exhibition catalogue, Salomon R. Guggenheim Museum New York and other locations (Ostfildern: Gerd Hatje, 1994), 148–163. 'Abstract Expressionism was often diluted in the hands of its successors. Even by the time of Pollock's death, in 1956, it was clear that much of Abstract Expressionism had become stale and academic and was spawning hordes of imitators' (Lisa Phillips, *The American Century, Part 2: Art & Culture, 1950–2000*, exhibition catalogue, Whitney Museum of American Art New York [New York: W. W. Norton & Company, 1999], 42. See, for example, Lee Krasner's painting *The Seasons* (1957) (Phillips, *The American Century*, 43).

7 See Tobias Lander, *Piet Mondrian, Hans Hofmann, Willem de Kooning: Europäische Künstler in den USA – Amerikanische Künstler aus Europa* (Freiburg: Rombach, 2003), 52–56, especially nn. 100 and 105.

8 Isidore Ducasse [Comte de Lautréamont, pseud.], 'Les chants de Maldoror, chant VI, strophe 3' (1869), in Lautréamont/Ducasse, *Œuvres complètes* (Centre de recherches Hubert de Phalèse and the Université de la Sorbonne Nouvelle, Paris III), http://www.cavi.univ-paris3.fr/phalese/MaldororHtml/Oeuvres/MaldororChant6Strophe3.htm.

9 Karin von Maur, *Salvador Dalí, 1904–1989*, exhibition catalogue, Staatsgalerie Stuttgart and Kunsthaus Zurich (Stuttgart: Gerd Hatje, 1989), 182; Gilles Néret, *Salvador Dalí, 1904–1989* (Cologne: Taschen, 1999), 40–41.

10 Benchley, 'The Story of Pop', 149.

11 Clement Greenberg, 'After Abstract Expressionism', in John O'Brian, ed., *Clement Greenberg: The Collected Essays and Criticism*, vol. 4 (Chicago: University of Chicago Press, 1993), 133; originally published in *Art International* 6, no. 8 (25 October 1962).

12 Louis Aragon, 'The Challenge to Painting' (1930), in David Evans, ed., *Appropriation* (London and Cambridge, MA: Whitechapel Gallery and MIT, 2009), 28.

13 See, for example, Arthur Coleman Danto, *Beyond the Brillo Box: The Visual Arts in Post-Historical Perspective* (Berkeley, Los Angeles and London: University of California Press, 1998), 5.

14 Richard Hamilton, 'Letter to Peter and Alison Smithson' (16 January 1957), in Madoff, *Pop Art*, 5–6.

15 For a discussion of Oldenburg's *The Store*, see, for example, Paul Schimmel, 'Leap into the Void: Performance and the Object', in Paul Schimmel and Russel Ferguson, eds., *Out of Actions: Between Performance and the Object, 1949–1979.*, exhibition catalogue, The Museum of Contemporary Art Los Angeles and other locations (New York and London: Thames and Hudson, 1998), 17–120.

16 Lucy R. Lippard and other locations, *Pop Art*, 3rd ed. (1970; repr., London: Thames & Hudson, 2001), 69, 188–89 and 193; Henry Geldzahler, *Pop Art, 1955–70*, exhibition catlogue, Art Gallery of New South Wales Sydney and other locations (Sydney: International Cultural Corporation of Australia, 1985), 11–12.

17 Kalliopi Minioudaki, 'Der andere Pop: Die Verdrängten zweier Diskurse kehren zurück', in Gerald Matt and Angela Stief, eds., *Power Up: Female Pop Art*, exhibition catalogue, Kunsthalle Wien et al. (Cologne: DuMont, 2010), 135.

18 Claes Oldenburg, 'Statement', in Madoff, *Pop Art*, 213; originally published in *Environments, Situations, Spaces*, exhibition catalogue (New York: Martha Jackson Gallery, 1961). See Walter Grasskamp, 'Schönheit und Müll: Streifzug durch die zahlreichen Paradoxien des Pop', *Neue Zürcher Zeitung*, no. 218 (18/19 September 2004): 68.

19 Roy Lichtenstein, quoted in Benchley, 'The Story of Pop', 149.

20 Marcel Duchamp, quoted in Peter Gidal, *Andy Warhol: Films and Paintings* (London and New York: Studio Vista and Dutton Pictureback, 1971), 27.

21 See Tobias Lander, 'Triumph der Ohnmacht', in *Gewalt, Angst und Politik*, Respektive: Zeitbuch für Gegenblicke 2 (Zurich: Medienverein Respektive, 2011), 160–173; Tobias Lander, 'The American Way of Death: Die Disasters von Andy Warhol', in Anna Pawlak and Kerstin Schankweiler (eds.), *Ästhetik der Gewalt – Gewalt der Ästhetik*, Schriftenreihe der Guernica-Gesellschaft 19 (Weimar: Verlag und Datenbank für Geisteswissenschaften, forthcoming).

22 G. R. Swenson, 'The F-111: An Interview with James Rosenquist', in Suzi Gablik and John Russell, *Pop Art Redefined* (London: Thames & Hudson, 1969), 106–7; originally published in *Partisan Review* 32, no. 4 (Fall 1965).

23 Catherine Dossin sees the anti-consumerist, anti-capitalist interpretation of Pop Art as a misunderstanding on the part of German critics influenced by the Frankfurt School. It was not until the 1970s that the 'correct' (in her opinion) view of Pop Art, as an art in praise of capitalist society, finally gained acceptance in Germany. While very much open to argument, this opinion of Dossin's demonstrates that the debate surrounding the critical approach of Pop continues even today. Catherine Dossin, 'Pop begeistert: American Pop Art and the German People', in *American Art* 25, no. 3 (Fall 2011): 100–111.

24 Recorded using pioneering colour videotape technology and printed in its entirety in all the major American newspapers, the debate was certainly familiar to Warhol. 'The Kitchen Debate', 24 July 1959 (transcript), in *TeachingAmericanHistory*, http://teachingamericanhistory.org/library/index.asp?document=176.

25 For a discussion of the reception of Pop Art, see Dan Cameron, 'Neo-this, Neo-that: Approaching Pop Art in the 1980s', in Marco Livingstone, ed., *Pop Art: An International Perspective*, exhibition catalogue, Royal Academy of Arts London and Museum Ludwig Cologne (New York: Rizzoli, 1992), 260–266; Marco Livingstone, 'Eat Dirt Art History: Neo-Pop in the 1980s', in *Pop Art: A Continuing History*, 2nd ed. (London: Thames & Hudson, 2001), 220–248; Sandra Danicke, 'Pop ist überall', in *Art: Das Kunstmagazin* (June 2010), 52–64.

Jack Wolfgang Beck, book cover, Don Wallance,
Shaping America's Products, New York, 1956
Offset print
27 x 20.5 cm
Alexander von Vegesack, Lessac

Ray Eames, magazine cover,
Arts & Architecture, July 1943
Offset print
25.4 x 32.7 cm
Vitra Design Museum

Gianni Arnaudo, stationery design
(unrealized), Studio 65, 1972
Offset print
29.6 x 21 cm
Gianni Arnaudo

Wolf Vostell, catalogue cover, *Kunst der
sechziger Jahre: Sammlung Ludwig im Wallraf-
Richartz-Museum / Art of the Sixties: Sammlung
Ludwig at the Wallraf-Richartz-Museum*,
edited by Gert von der Osten and Horst Keller,
4th rev. ed., Cologne, 1970
Transparent embossed PVC, printed paper,
metal
20 x 30 cm
Thorsten Romanus

Alexander Girard, poster announcing
the opening of Herman Miller's
Textiles & Objects store, New York, 1961
Silkscreen
50.8 x 66 cm
Vitra Design Museum

Loretta Li, cover design
for John Rublowsky and Kenneth Heyman's
book *Pop Art*, New York, 1965
Offset print
28 x 22 cm
Vitra Design Museum

Richard Hamilton, poster insert,
The Beatles, *The Beatles (The White Album)*,
Apple, 1968
Offset print
87 x 58 cm
Mathias Schwartz-Clauss

**Peter Blake, Robert Fraser, Michael
Cooper and Jann Haworth**, album cover
and insert, The Beatles, *Sgt. Pepper's Lonely
Hearts Club Band*, Parlophone/EMI, 1967
Offset print
31.2 x 31.2 cm
Mathias Schwartz-Clauss

Anonymous, *NIVEA Creme*, 1959–70
Beiersdorf Hamburg, Germany
Tin container
1.5 x ø 7.5 cm
Werkbundarchiv, Museum der Dinge, Berlin

Andy Warhol, album cover,
The Velvet Underground,
The Velvet Underground & Nico, Verve, 1967
Offset print
31.5 x 31.5 cm
Vitra Design Museum

Andy Warhol, *Campbell's Soup Can (Tomato)*,
1964
Shopping bag for *The American Supermarket*
gallery project, Bianchini Gallery, New York
Silkscreen print on paper bag
48.9 x 43.2 cm
The Andy Warhol Museum, Pittsburgh

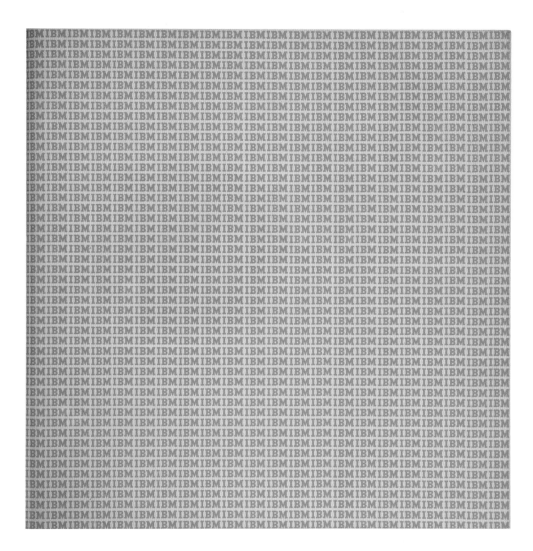

Alexander Girard, magazine cover,
AIA Monthly Bulletin 27, no. 3,
Michigan Society of Architects, March 1953
Offset print
28.5 x 39.5 cm
Vitra Design Museum

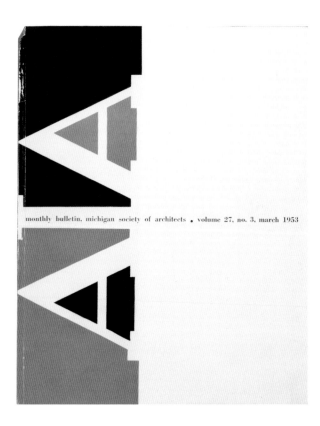

Paul Rand, IBM logo, 1956
From Paul Rand, *The Trademarks
of Paul Rand: A Selection*, New York, 1960
Silkscreen
24.2 x 24.2 cm
Vitra Design Museum

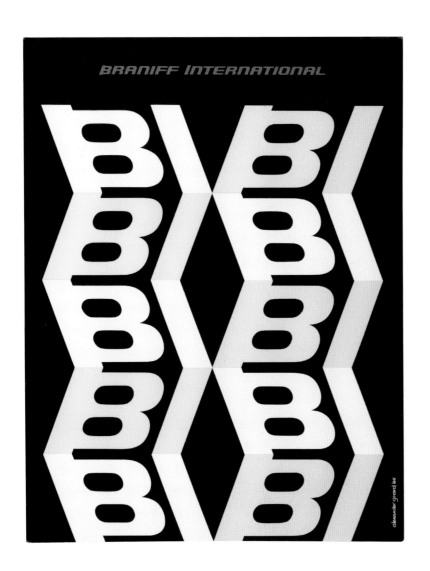

George Nelson Associates, Inc.
(Don Ervin), official logo,
American National Exhibition, Moscow, 1959
Silkscreen
26 x 32.8 cm
Vitra Design Museum

Alexander Girard, promotional poster,
Braniff International, 1965
Offset print
50.5 x 65.5 cm
Vitra Design Museum

George Nelson Associates, Inc.
(Don Ervin), film poster design
(unrealized), *The Misfits* (dir. John Huston), 1961
Silkscreen
27 x 31.8 cm
Vitra Design Museum

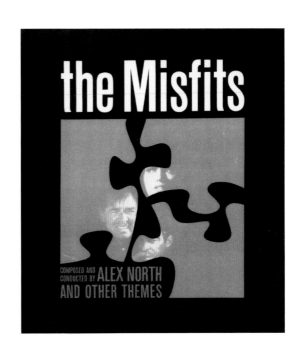

Wojciech Zamecznik, film poster,
Pociąg (*Night Train*) (dir. Jerzy Kawalerowicz), 1959
Offset print
84.5 x 127.5 cm
Muzeum Narodowe w Poznaniu

Saul Bass, stills of opening credits,
North by Northwest (dir. Alfred Hitchcock), 1959
Private Collection

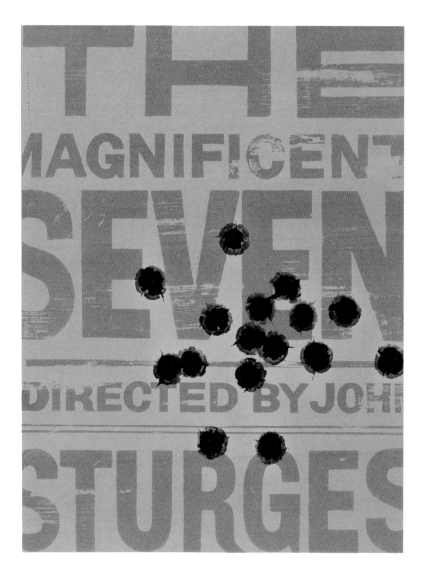

Saul Bass, film poster design (unrealized),
The Magnificent Seven (dir. John Sturges), 1960
Offset print
28 x 43 cm
Private collection

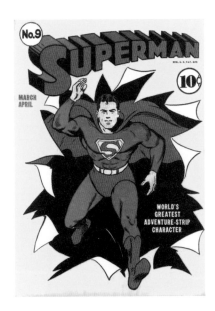

Fred Ray, comic book cover,
Superman, no. 9, March/April 1941
Offset print
26.2 x 19 cm
Courtesy Paul Gravett, London

Milton Glaser, poster insert, Bob Dylan,
Bob Dylan's Greatest Hits, Columbia, 1966
Offset print
83.5 x 55.7 cm
Gerrit Terstiege

Guy Peellaert, comic strip illustration,
Les Aventures de Jodelle, Paris, 1966
Offset print
33 x 32 x 2 cm
Bibliothèque Municipale de Lausanne

Ettore Sottsass, magazine cover,
Avantgarde – Pianeta fresco 2/3, edited by
Fernanda Pivano and Ettore Sottsass,
Milan, 1968
Front and back cover
Colour lithograph
28 x 21.5 x 1 cm
Alexander von Vegesack, Lessac

Victor Moscoso, concert poster,
The Chambers Brothers, 1967
Offset print
56 x 35.5 cm
Museum für Gestaltung Zürich,
Poster Collection

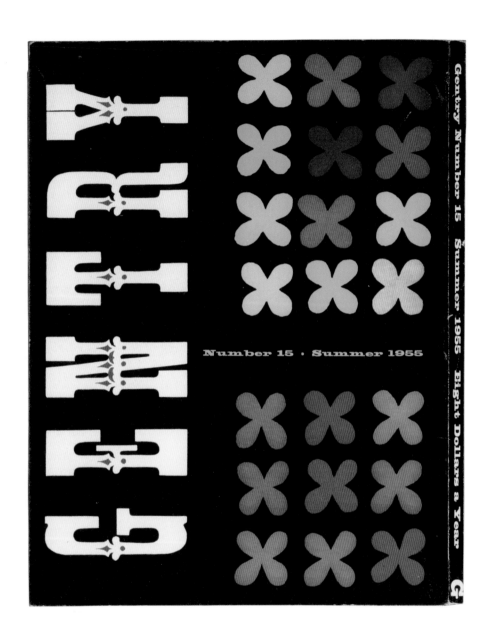

Alexander Girard, magazine cover,
Gentry, summer 1955
Back cover
Offset print
28.5 x 39.5 cm
Vitra Design Museum

Studio 65, promotional poster,
Babilonia 72 exhibition stand, 1972
Offset print
70 x 70 cm
Gianni Arnaudo

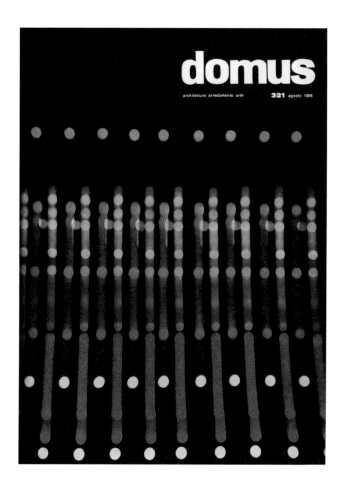

William Klein, magazine cover,
Domus: Architettura Arredamento Arte, no. 321,
August 1956
Offset print
23.5 x 32 cm
Vitra Design Museum

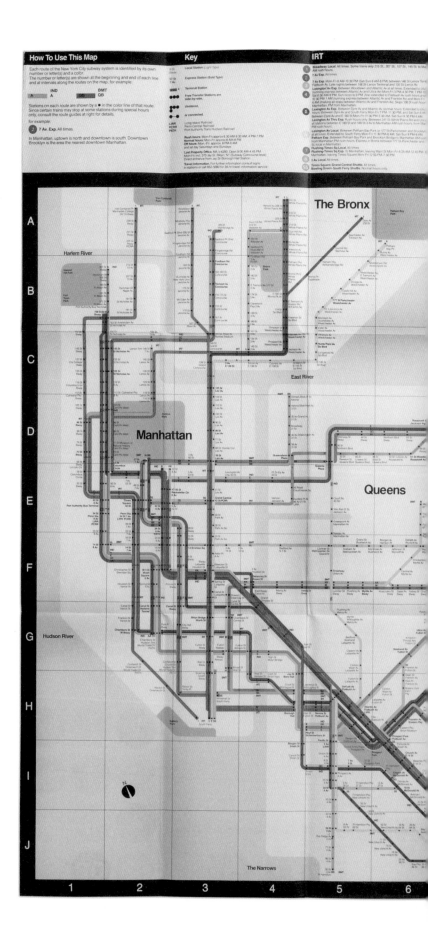

Massimo Vignelli, diagram of the New
York subway system, designed in conjunction
with its graphic signage system, 1972
Offset print
45.5 x 53 cm
Vitra Design Museum

Anders Österlin, catalogue cover,
The Machine as Seen at the End of the Mechanical Age,
edited by Pontus Hultén,
Museum of Modern Art, New York, 1968
Based on a photograph by Alicia Legg
Embossed and enamel-painted aluminium boards
21.7 x 24.3 cm
Vitra Design Museum

fig. 1
Lucian Bernhard, poster (no text), ca. 1925
Lithograph, 91 x 71 cm
Museum für Gestaltung Zürich, Poster Collection
Franz Xaver Jaggy

From Mad Men to Pop Artists: The Nexus of Advertising and Pop Art

Steven Heller

fig. 1

fig. 2

fig. 2
Leslie Ragan, poster,
The New 20th Century Limited, 1938
Lithograph
104 x 68 cm
Museum für Gestaltung Zürich, Poster Collection
Franz Xaver Jaggy

The seeds of Pop Art were sown around the end of the nineteenth century and grew extensively throughout the early twentieth until reaching maturity in the 1960s. This assertion is not found in most art history books. For although Pop Art has always been defined as a reaction to commercial advertising in the United States, it has seldom been noted that the late nineteenth century saw the first rumblings from which its precursor – advertising art – exploded as a new art form.

Advertising art was always of a paradoxical nature. In an article published in 1930 entitled 'Art as a Means to an End', advertising pioneer Earnest Elmo Calkins argued that, unlike anything else in the realm of aesthetics, art is subject to such constant scrutiny that each fresh innovation 'adopted by the radicals' is in turn resisted by the conservatives, then tolerated, and finally copied until 'it too becomes old stuff' and the vanguard are already in full cry after something newer'.[1] This has a familiar art-historical ring, yet Calkins's statement appeared in the premiere issue of *Advertising Arts* magazine and addressed – in a rather sophisticated way – what until then was derisively called 'commercial art'.

The path from late-nineteenth-century advertising art to mid-twentieth-century Pop Art winds its way through this unique professional magazine, which sought to integrate modern art into the stodgy mainstream of commercial culture. While other trade journals promoted the status quo, *Advertising Arts* – a perfect bound monthly supplement of the weekly trade magazine *Advertising and Selling* – proposed ways to incorporate new design fashions and progressive ideas into conventional practice. The magazine became the vortex of cutting-edge American graphic and industrial design of the era.

Advertising Arts is not to be confused, however, with the radical European design manifestoes issued by the Constructivists, the Futurists or the Bauhaus, which gave rise to the New Typography and revolutionized graphic design and printing practices. In the 1920s, the United States did not have an avant-garde rooted in utopian principles underscored by socialism. Rather, it was unapologetically capitalist – and advertising, after all, is capitalism's tool for influencing the consumer. Yet although commercialism was far more advanced than in Europe, American marketing strategies were much more conventional and word-based. In Europe 'publicity' was more image-oriented and modern avant-garde design was an alternative to the antiquated aesthetics of bourgeois culture and politics. Conversely, in the United States modernistic design was the product of the commercial concept known as 'styling the goods' or 'planned obsolescence', introduced by Calkins as a somewhat devious method of encouraging consumers to 'move the goods' despite the ravages of a worldwide economic depression.

Conservative ad men argued that the fancy advertising images advocated by Calkins were elitist distractions, unresponsive to the tastes of ordinary consumers and therefore doomed to fail. Calkins, they claimed, had taken his own class values for a reflection of society as a whole. Yet Calkins felt that 'artistic advertising' could be a democratizing force in terms of the middle classes. Indeed, his approach was to exclusively target an economic class that he termed 'people of taste' rather than attempt to induce unattainable longings in the so-called have-nots.

Advertising Arts supported Calkins's mission and served as a blueprint for how modernity was marketed as a style – in print, on packages and as industrial wares. For their part, the writers – which included influential graphic and industrial designers such as Lucian Bernhard, Norman Bel Geddes and Rockwell Kent – passionately advocated the new. In an article entitled 'Modern Layouts Must Sell Rather Than Startle', for example, design pundit Frank H. Young wrote: 'Daring originality in the use of new forms, new patterns, new methods of organization and bizarre color effects is the keynote of modern layout and is achieving the startling results we see today.'[2] And despite some grand oratory regarding the sanctity of art – including Rockwell Kent's statement, '[Art] is the concept of the visual mind. It is concerned with images and not ideas. Art is imagination'[3] – it was evident that the magazine was devoted to an art whose purpose was to entice consumers to purchase products, whether they needed them or not.

As for its connection to Pop Art, two points are perhaps worth mentioning. First, *Advertising Arts* promulgated a design style often called Streamline (fig. 2). This was a futuristic mannerism based on sleek aerodynamic design. Planes, trains and cars were given a swooped-back kinetic appearance; typefaces and illustrations were designed to the same effect; and consequently the airbrush became the medium of choice. All futuristic gestures, be they practical or symbolic, were encouraged. Thus, it is not surprising that many of the Pop artists that adopted the airbrush in their work – Andy Warhol, James Rosenquist, Tom Wesselmann, Roy Lichtenstein and others – were those that had previously toiled in the commercial arts: they were simply used to producing advertising's smooth, streamlined veneers.

Second, if art history read true, Lucian Bernhard – the German artist and master of the 'object poster' (*sachplakat*), who designed in the United States some of the most emblematic typefaces of the 1920s and '30s – would be credited as the grandfather of Pop (fig. 1). Bernhard sought to elevate commercial art and announced in an *Advertising Arts* article entitled 'Putting Beauty into Industry' that the new desire for

'beauty in industrial products, only recently started in this country, has not come from the side of manufacturers',[4] thus suggesting that the modern designer must take upon himself the responsibility of recasting American products. His 'object poster' was a celebration of everyday commercial objects – from matchsticks to light bulbs – and, as such, a precursor of the most iconic works of Pop Art.

Advertising Arts was published until the mid-1930s. It ceased to

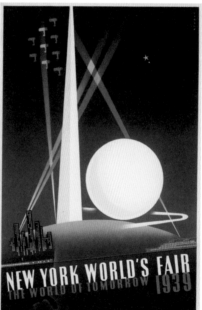

fig. 3

appear before the 1939 New York World's Fair: The World of Tomorrow, where so many of the modern graphic, package and industrial design concepts it had championed were realized (fig. 3). As for its legacy, the magazine undoubtedly raised the standard of design through advocacy of 'the modern' and today arguably serves as a missing link in the genesis of Pop.

Jump to the 1950s: Abstract Expressionism was the vogue and advertising was in the midst of the Creative Revolution, which had a profound impact on American behaviour. It was the era of the Big Idea, when advertising and design were no longer slave to the word but a commixture of word and image – witty, poignant and memorable. The goal was to entertain while triggering desire, and progressive agencies (such as Weintraub, Ogilvy & Mather and Doyle Dane Bernbach (fig. 4) and art directors (among them Paul Rand → p. 58, Helmut Krone, Gene Federico (fig. 5), William Taubin and George Lois) rebelled against no-nonsense, or so-called shirt-sleeve, advertising. While this new breed of ad men took their jobs seriously enough, their work was ironic and satiric: they made sure the American dream was being sold, not romanticized.

© 1962 VOLKSWAGEN OF AMERICA, INC.

Think small.

Our little car isn't so much of a novelty any more.

A couple of dozen college kids don't try to squeeze inside it.

The guy at the gas station doesn't ask where the gas goes.

Nobody even stares at our shape.

In fact, some people who drive our little flivver don't even think 32 miles to the gallon is going any great guns.

Or using five pints of oil instead of five quarts.

Or never needing anti-freeze.

Or racking up 40,000 miles on a set of tires.

That's because once you get used to some of our economies, you don't even think about them any more.

Except when you squeeze into a small parking spot. Or renew your small insurance. Or pay a small repair bill. Or trade in your old VW for a new one.

Think it over.

fig. 4

fig. 5
Gene Federico, *Disraeli: On Education and the Future*,
from Container Corporation of America's
Great Ideas of Western Man advertising campaign, 1956–58
Intaglio print
35.3 x 28 cm
Museum für Gestaltung Zürich, Graphics Collection
Umberti Romito

The Pop artists of the time, on the other hand, were addressing the older, more idealized and heavy-handed ad approaches, and commenting on the clichés of advertising and popular culture, a culture that was epitomized in grand claims of bright transformative futures. Automobile advertisements were the torch bearers. They referred to cars as dream machines, with all the attributes of this brave, new age being summed up in one 1954 Plymouth ad: 'So big… So powerful… So exciting… All-new'. Cars were synonymous with progress – each year's new models were more exciting than those of the last. The veneer was as important as the performance and the two were conflated through futuristic aesthetics inside and out, which included fins, chrome and streamlined dashboard details.

Pop Art was, in its way, a bulwark against this promise of progress. Its proponents focused attention on how commercial products were feeble fetishes. Like the cargo cult tribespeople of the South Seas, consumers gathered around large cans of soup and prayed to their gods of wealth and prosperity. Pop Art was a mirror that said, 'Stop! Look! Think about how much soul is invested in consumption'.

But that, of course, did not stop advertising from hawking and selling modernity. Industry was riding high on the promise of 'the modern'. Lawn-boy was 'Modern America's Power Mower'; Gray PhonAudograph III offered 'Pushbutton Dictation. Modern! Lowest Cost!'; IBM – the THINK corporation – was even 'Getting closer to infinity!'. To Pop artists, these slogans were silly sermons that the gullible public believed.

In addition, advertising and, by extension, Pop Art were impacted by the cold war. The famous Kitchen Debate between United States Vice President Richard Nixon and Soviet Premier Nikita Khrushchev was in essence an advertisement for American consumerism. Commercials were evidence of American superiority. The shear bounty of products – from Surf detergent through the RCA Whirlpool refrigerator-freezer to the Schick power-shave razor ('first in electric shaving') – had to have driven the Soviets tomato red with envy. In such a context, Warhol's *Campbell's Soup Cans* and Oldenburg's giant soft sculptures might have seemed to Soviet eyes as the worst excesses – art that celebrates things rather than glorifies leaders. But these classic Pop works actually embodied mixed emotions: Love for graphic design and product design, on the one hand; rejection of the fetishistic manipulation generated by advertising, on the other.

Finally, Pop Art prefigured yet overlapped the youth revolution of the 1960s. It doubtlessly informed the movement's ethos of opposing mainstream culture's slavish embrace of consumables. By then, the Creative Revolution had become just another manipulative way to sell establishment values; and Pop Art – a high-priced, elitist commodity. The alternative culture of the late 1960s rejected this and all the other rules of art and design; twenty years later it too would become the mainstream sucking on the big capitalist teat.

fig. 5

★

1 Earnest Elmo Calkins, 'Art as a Means to an End', *Advertising Arts*, no. 1 (8 January 1930): 6–8.

2 Frank H. Young, 'Modern Layouts Must Sell Rather Than Startle', *Advertising Arts*, no. 1 (8 January 1930): 25.

3 Rockwell Kent, 'Art Differs From Literature in This', *Advertising Arts*, no. 1 (8 January 1930): 30–32.

4 Lucian Bernhard, 'Putting Beauty into Industry', *Advertising Arts*, no. 1 (8 January 1930): 15–18.

fig. 1
Richard Hamilton, album cover,
The Beatles, *The Beatles (The White Album)*,
Apple, 1968
Embossed card stock

Robert Fraser, album labels,
The Beatles, *The Beatles (The White Album)*,
with the logo of Apple Records, 1968
Offset print

Cover and Content: Appearance and Reality in Pop Music and Pop Art

Diedrich Diederichsen

fig. 1

fig. 2
Andy Warhol, album cover,
The Velvet Underground,
The Velvet Underground & Nico, Verve, 1967
Front cover with and without sticker
Offset print

 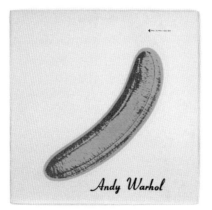

fig. 2

Around 1960 two things occurred that are seldom directly linked to each other. On the one hand, objects of daily use and, in particular, two-dimensional elements of their visual brand identity began appearing in the fine arts: in assemblages, screen prints and wooden objects as well as in paintings. On the other hand, a new genre of graphic design emerged – or, rather, a new task for design. In the late 1940s, Columbia introduced the twelve-inch long-playing (LP) 33⅓-revolutions-per-minute record album. By the mid-1950s, such LP records had become the standard format in the United States, alongside seven-inch singles that played at 45 revolutions per minute and had an average playing time of just under five minutes. Early LPs usually came in plain covers labelled according to the specific section of the record company's catalogue they belonged to, but the industry soon turned to specially conceived and designed album covers. These constituted a new area of work for graphic artists and designers since they involved two-dimensional surfaces without any product-specific constraints – similar, in this respect, to the pages of a magazine or a book – yet simultaneously functioned as packaging, thus situating the task at hand not only in the domain of communication design but also in that of product design.

In general this period saw an increase in the number of graphic design tasks that were not only associated with certain formal standards but had also evolved in close connection with the newly emerging youth and pop culture of the time, which in itself sought liberation from standards of any sort and from standardizations as such. Yet, since this culture was organized from the outset in market terms, some of these new fields of activity developed along the lines of conventional brand and product design. There were, however, many other tasks that had nothing to do with attracting youth to specific products but focused rather on facilitating communication processes within youth culture itself. Such was the case, for instance, with fashion

design, although it had to confront the growing scepticism of youth subcultures towards forms deemed appropriate for them by outsiders. In the case of album covers and concert posters, the main objective was to create photographs, illustrations and design languages through which youngsters would communicate. In this respect, pop music was, from the very beginning, a combination of visual and musical elements. Now that the voices of raucous rock singers and sexy soul stars could be transferred directly into the rooms of young listeners, the constancy and identity of these performers were maintained by images from magazines, television and, above all, album covers. Thus, faces, outfits and visual languages established the stability of the medially precarious correlation between the intimate bedroom experience with the star on the record cover and the socializing pop music experience of concerts and nightclubs.

This new increase in social density and intensity through binding visual languages in youth culture and youth markets drew the attention of the fine arts to the field of design. For the first time, a visual language had taken shape outside official fine arts avenues. In the European tradition, design elements had always emerged from the same workshops, cultural movements and academic environments that produced fine art; and the collages of the Soviet avant-garde and Dadaism were still very much prevalent in American advertising. The situation gradually began to change as the economy started to recognize the importance of certain consumers that had previously been culturally and politically marginalized and labelled as immature or unworthy. This was the case with racially excluded African Americans as well as with other minority groups, women and, in the postwar era, the entire American youth population. Within these culturally and politically disenfranchised markets, new visual languages, such as comic strips, began to develop, gaining the recognition of the wider public during the 1950s. Initially, however, these did not constitute

fig. 3
Martin Sharp, album cover,
Cream, *Disraeli Gears*, Polydor, 1967
Front and back
Offset print

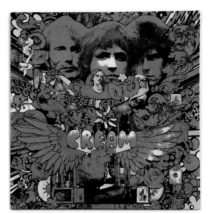

fig. 3

self-contained visual worlds. The first instance of a visual language completely decoupled from the artistic developments of its day appeared in the vocabulary of youth culture, which developed during the first two decades following the Second World War but was initially dismissed and devalued by society at large. It took some time for this to change. The widespread impact of comic book images, close-ups of stars' faces and other standard culture industry ideas had to first take hold among teenagers as they broke free from the cages of Fordist conventionality and developed a new body consciousness. This impact was dramatic and – even if only associated with the new visual languages to a limited extent – merits recognition.

Pop Art was initially less interested in the images stemming from the teen culture of rock 'n' roll and focused instead on the now-legendary cola bottles and other visually unremarkable everyday objects that, in most cases, had actually been designed much earlier. It was less a commentary on specific contemporary images or visual strategies than a demarcation of design as such, thus countering its commonly held conception (at least in the period around 1960) as an unassuming means of communication we avail ourselves of, unaware of the fact that we are actually articulating and communicating, sending out and receiving messages, as we partake in consumer culture, everyday culture, fashion and so on. Today these areas are not only thoroughly demarcated and semiotically overdetermined; their semiotic density also reflects a multitude of assertions regarding social differentiation and identification for which these areas are now called into service. Yet at their inception these strategies undoubtedly adhered to the forms of communication utilized by early youth culture, which for the first time in Western postwar societies articulated the call for an 'exodus' (Paolo Virno) – for the establishment of an autonomous society, in or outside the existing one, that was not based on traditional work-based parameters.

Pop Art reacted to this newly demarcated character of design. The non-artistic visual world had – more or less – suddenly become a world of expression beyond mere communicative functionality. Unlike the discovery of advertising design and newspaper typography in the collages of the first avant-garde, it did not have to be transferred into the domain of art. The new, youth culture-influenced languages of mass culture had become expressive in and of themselves. Granted, the visual vehicles integrated within this culture – comic strips, album covers, concert posters, fashion – had at their outset a communicative function, for they needed to forge the important connection between the private, projecting, dreamy reception of the music experienced with the record player at home and the socializing experiences with peer groups in such new environments as nightclubs, multimedia shows and concerts. Yet what originally merely served as a means of linking two worlds of experience took on a life of its own – not least because it was in the interest of the consumer goods industry. From the social communications systems of youth culture, individual objects could thus be isolated – jeans, T-shirts, particular colours, certain form-fitting clothes – as metonymically associated with a new social experience. All possible visual surface stimuli manifested themselves in this manner and were not only treated by Pop Art but also used in the production of other surfaces.

Much of Pop Art, especially American Pop Art of the 1960s (Roy Lichtenstein, James Rosenquist, Tom Wesselmann), explicitly produced images whose surfaces were entirely dominated by illusionist visual strategies, thus running counter to the modernist call for an anti-illusionistic pictorial surface consisting of the material and the media from which it issued forth. An everyday act that made the idea of 'the surface' even more apparent – as well as the complementary idea of 'the behind' – was the process of removing a record from its cover and putting it back in again. While the album cover was

fig. 4
Carl Lundgren, *Vanessa*, 1967
Poster for the James Cotton Blues Band's
concert at the Grande Ballroom, Detroit
Offset print
33 x 20.3 cm

colourful and laden with meaning, even overloaded with semiotic content, it consisted of pure surface – with a front and a back (one could literally feel the somewhat raw, sticky backside of the printed surface). The more such surfaces circulated as a feature of daily life, the more they fuelled the idea of a 'behind', the desire for its unveiling and the critical conviction, espoused by the student movement, regarding the need for such unveilings in the symbolic topography of the battle against commodities. This very idea was also embraced by psychedelic culture, which for its part gave rise to further intensifications of a cult of contours and drastic colour contrasts.

With its enthusiasm for these intensifications, the culture of psychedelia found inspiration in hidden-object scenes and made use of fraying and blurring and ornamental replications – in the manner of Art Nouveau, collages and traditional ornamental crafts – whose deliberate confusion and opacity contributed more to the dissolution of the contour than to the accentuation typically seen in Pop Art. Psychedelic design of album covers, from Cream's *Disraeli Gears* (fig. 3) to Rick Griffin's drawings for the Grateful Dead, embraced a multiplication of the contour that sought to undermine – but also to aestheticize – the seeing of the figure and the form by means other than abstraction: not on the level of deliberate reflection but through physical and retinal distortion. The two phases of actual so-called psychedelic experience – first, physical reactions such as queasiness and disorientation; then, the aesthetic-religious

fig. 4

transfiguration of the liberation from the coordinates of everyday physical constitution – can be seen in the psychedelic poster art of the American West Coast but also in the psychedelia-inspired art of members of the late or post-Pop Art generation, in particular Sigmar Polke, Peter Saul and Öyvind Fahlström. In this psychedelic version of the interplay between Pop Art and album covers, objects of daily life once again played a prominent role. In most cases, however, they did so neither as mere everyday objects – as in the works of Robert Rauschenberg – nor primarily as objects with specific design qualities – as, at times, in the works of Andy Warhol – but explicitly as a commodity; and that meant, first and foremost, as a criticized, despised commodity. The famous closing scene of Michelangelo Antonioni's *Zabriskie Point*, showing brand products exploding along with the modernist house of the corrupt capitalist and hurtling towards the film's audience in slow motion, served as a model for the appearance of commodities in Fahlström's works as well as on the album covers of Jefferson Airplane (*After Bathing at Baxter's*), The Who (*The Who Sell Out*) and many others.

There was, however, a second quasi-psychedelic form of expression, this time situated in the heart of fine art: Minimalist sculpture. Similar to Pop Art, Minimalism also departed from individual artistic signatures, embraced industrially produced material and accepted the invisibility of production as the new state of affairs.

fig. 5
Andy Warhol, album cover,
The Rolling Stones, *Sticky Fingers*,
Rolling Stones, 1970–71
Front, inner sleeve, back
Offset print and zipper

 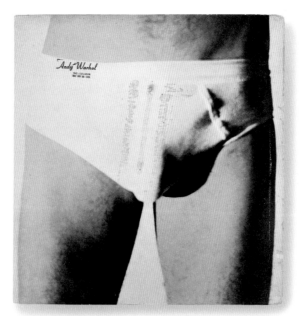 

fig. 5

The difference was that Minimalist artists were not operating on the communicative, outward-facing side of the industrially produced world but took up a search for its inner side, for its material, which in some cases played the metaphysical role of a 'behind' as discussed above. This gave Minimalist sculpture its curious dual form of enlightened revelation of an industrially fabricated, smooth and dead contemporary truth, on the one hand, and the presentation of a mysterious arcane depth – the inner character of something of which only its outside, its veil (as in Mayan culture), is typically visible – on the other. The smooth objects made of plastic or metal thus corresponded to the second stage of psychedelic experience, during which the world is perceived as a series of decontextualized objects that have lost their function and now appear sacred or absurd. Whereas Pop Art seeks to valorize or at least designate everyday life as commodity, banality or context, Minimalism subtracts it from objects in order to establish something behind them, which, as an ambiguous figure between totem and sober form, could be taken to represent a truth of this everyday existence – but only of this specific (capitalist, industrial, commodity-producing) everyday.

With the record album, these two practices – Pop Art and Minimalism – come together in a curious fashion. The colourfully printed Pop Art cover is experienced as pure surface from which record listeners extract a data storage medium that, produced from industrial, monochrome, black plastic, is itself a Minimalist sculpture (fig. 1). Both surfaces are associated with the performance and/or recording of music in multiple ways and through various semiotic relationships: indexically, through the phonographic or photographic recording; iconically, through the graphic design or illustration; symbolically, through the texts and band logo. Yet they tend to detach themselves from their medial relations, assume an independent position and establish new connections – such as in their relationship to and between Pop Art and Minimalism.

Warhol, the most important of Pop artists, recognized this constellation and repeatedly addressed it in his work. Initially in a naïve manner – in as much as he worked as a graphic artist and illustrator and was one of the first professionals called upon to design and illustrate album covers – and then, from the 1960s onwards, in his conceptual reworking of the 'album cover' theme. For the cover of the first LP by the Velvet Underground (*The Velvet Underground & Nico*) (fig. 2) as well as on the cover of *Sticky Fingers* (fig. 5) by the Rolling Stones, he not only sarcastically played with the aesthetics of products and packaging but sought, above all, to simultaneously affirm and deny its superficial character in relation to a desired 'behind', whether real or imagined. In both covers he articulated this relation in an amusing gimmick: on *The Velvet Underground & Nico*, a banana skin sticker could be removed to reveal a peeled banana beneath, while *Sticky Fingers* features an actual jeans zipper that opens onto a pair of cotton briefs and the promise of a penis. Both cases are a suggestive joke about the coveted phallus/penis, a joke that charmingly denounces the metaphysics of appearance and reality, the magical interplay of surface and substance.

★

Images of the Girard family home in Santa Fe, designed by Alexander Girard, to which he and his wife moved in 1953. Most of these photographs of the Girard estate were taken by Charles Eames, although they can no longer be definitively attributed. The same applies for the following images of Herman Miller's showroom in San Francisco, the La Fonda del Sol restaurant in New York and the Textiles & Objects home furnishings store, also in New York.

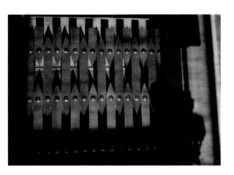

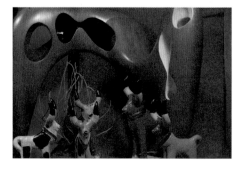

Images of the Herman Miller showroom, designed
by Alexander Girard, San Francisco, 1959

  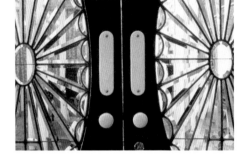 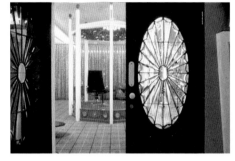

Images of the Herman Miller home furnishings
store Textiles & Objects, conceived and designed
by Alexander Girard, New York 1961

Images of the theme restaurant La Fonda
del Sol, designed by Alexander Girard,
New York, 1959–60

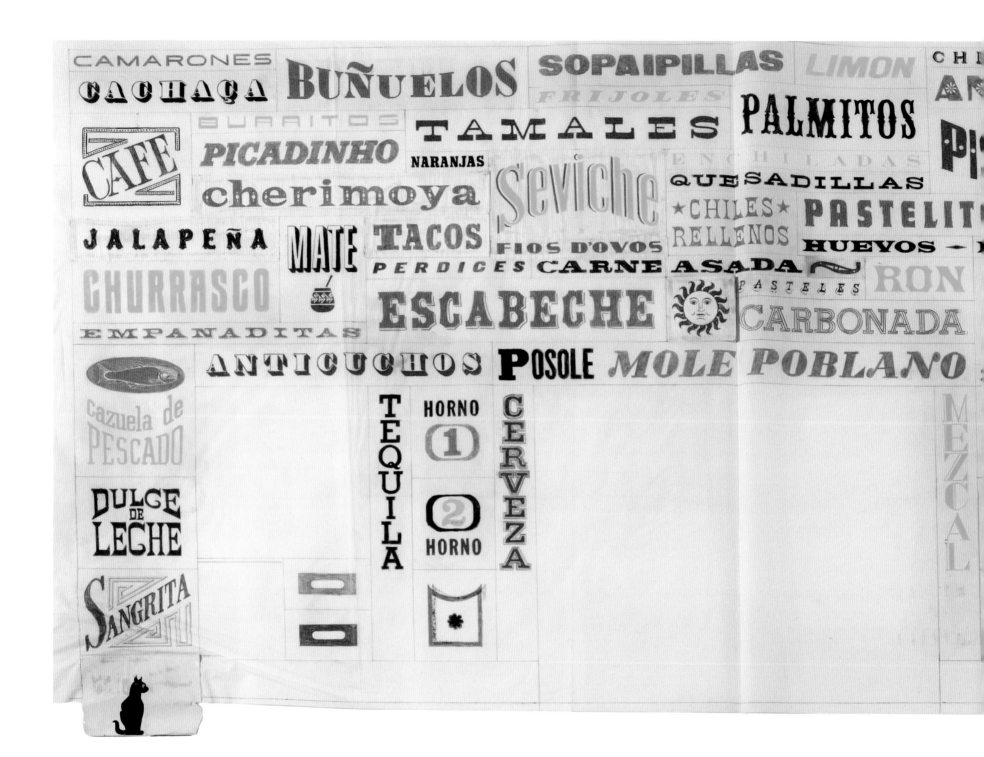

Alexander Girard, mural design for the
restaurant La Fonda del Sol, 1959
Painted tracing paper, lacquered cardboard
107.5 x 220 cm
Vitra Design Museum

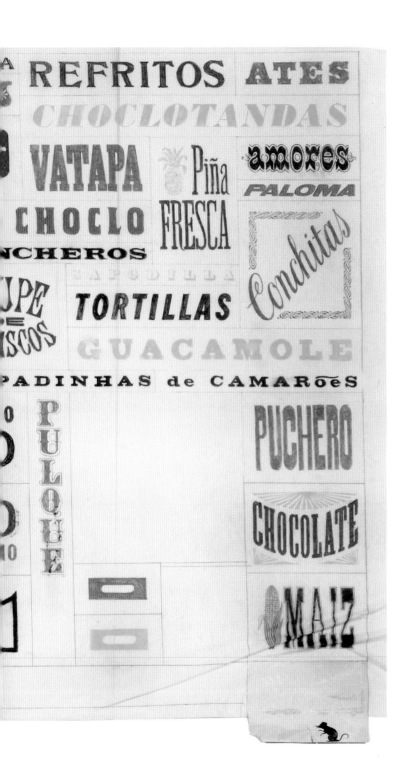

Alexander Girard, tableware for the
restaurant *La Fonda del Sol*, 1959–60
Painted porcelain
9.6 x ø 12.7 cm (toothpick holder)
13.3 x ø 7.5 cm (goblet)
10 x ø 8.5 cm (mug)
8.4 x ø 5 cm (pepper shaker)
8.4 x ø 5 cm (salt shaker)
8.2 x 13.7 x ø 10.5 cm (cup)
8.8 x ø 10 cm (egg cup)
Vitra Design Museum

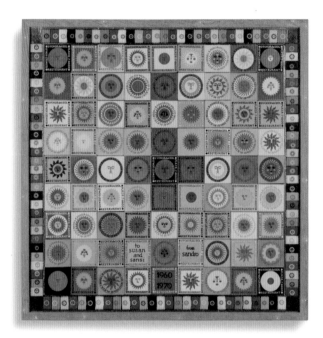

Alexander Girard, *To Susan and Sansi
from Sandro*, 1960–70
Wood, sugar cubes, printed paper,
gold foil
67.5 x 69.5 x 4.7 cm
Vitra Design Museum

Drawer from Alexander Girard's collection
of matchboxes and matchbooks, undated
26.7 x 40 x 2 cm
Vitra Design Museum

Alexander Girard, shopping bag
for the Textiles & Objects store, 1953
Printed paper
48 x 33 x 15 cm
Vitra Design Museum

Andy Warhol, *Torte a la Dobosch*
(from *Wild Raspberries*), 1959
Offset lithograph and watercolour on paper
43.8 x 27.3 cm
The Andy Warhol Museum, Pittsburgh

Alexander Girard, *8 Table Settings*
by Alexander Girard for Georg Jensen Inc., 1955
Shop window decoration
Painted wood
96.5 x 76.5 x 1 cm
Vitra Design Museum

Andy Warhol, untitled, ca. 1958
Three-part folding screen
Silver foil and paint on wood
167.6 x 137 cm
Courtesy Jeffrey Hoffeld Fine Art, Inc.
Loan Jan Cowles

Saul Steinberg, *Eames Chair*, 1950
Ink on paper
28 x 35.8 cm
Vitra Design Museum

Alexander Girard, untitled, 1960
Relief
Lacquered wood, plaster, metal
86.5 x 48 x 3.9 cm
Vitra Design Museum

fig. 1
Robert Indiana, *Chief*, 1962–1991
Wood, oil, iron, iron-rimmed wheels
165 x 61 x 48 cm
Courtesy Galerie Gmurzynska

fig. 2
Ettore Sottsass, untitled
(decoration studies), 1963

'A Menhir in the Middle of a Room': The Spiritual Aspect of Pop

Bettina Korintenberg

fig. 1

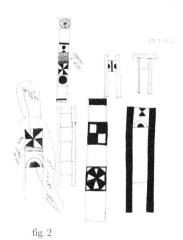

fig. 2

fig. 3

'The *Superboxes* are pop but I don't think I would have thought of them if I hadn't been through India. Even now, no one adopts this idea of using certain colors and staging a tower like a menhir in the middle of a room, which is really a typical way of conceiving space as cosmic and not just as any private space.'[1]

A cosmic-mythical dimension of Pop, as alluded to here by Italian designer Ettore Sottsass, might seem surprising at first, contradicting, as it does, the attributes most typically associated with Pop Art and design. Pop is colourful, shrill and even squeaks occasionally; it is glamour, lifestyle, the cult of celebrity. Pop is a response to the burgeoning culture of consumption and information, liberally drawing on the sources of a fast-paced media world whose influence has spread to nearly all corners of daily life. Cosmological and metaphysical notions appear out of place. And yet Sottsass is not the only one among the ranks of Pop whose work and ideas convey spiritual and mythological themes. This dimension is actually not as far removed from the work of Pop artists as it may seem. After all, these artists re-examined and questioned the things that make up our everyday reality, transforming them into something mysterious and alien – such are the soft sculptures of Claes Oldenburg, for instance, in which commonplace utilitarian objects take on an independent anthropomorphic existence beyond their given functionality. A prime example is offered by his light switches, which, having caved in and become flaccid, droop forlornly from the wall. These designers and artists processed the many impulses that shaped their daily surroundings, all the things they encountered anew each and every day. Robert Indiana's enthusiasm for letters and numbers, for example, was stimulated and inspired by signs, stencils and logos that he found in New York's harbour district; while Billy Al Bengston was highly influenced by the Southern Californian cult of the automobile, the

beauty and durability of the individually decorated lacquered surfaces prompting him to adopt the same technique for his art.

The impulses, however, emanate not only from the immediate everyday environment but also from other cultures and past eras alien to the Western, industrial society that is native to these artists. These influences are wide-ranging and diffuse and it is often difficult to track down concrete precursors and origins. The *Nanas* of French artist Niki de Saint Phalle, for instance, with their simple, compact forms and their unmodulated, colourfully painted characters and symbols, appear as remnants of archaic civilizations; and the colour scheme of Sottsass's *Superboxes* reveals the influence of India while the manner of their presentation is based on the idea of the menhir. In a similar fashion, Indiana's stele-like *Herms* evoke – through the head on their top and their suggestion of a phallus below – the signposts of antiquity after which they are named (fig. 1); while, for his part, American architect and designer Alexander Girard lost his heart to Mexico – a brightly hued world of kitsch and art, a hybrid of ancient indigenous myths and Christian symbols, that shaped much of his work.

The reason for this great diversity of inspirations lies in the way we perceive specific elements of foreign cultures from a distance. In most cases, their culture-bound meaning eludes us. What we perceive and understand – or, rather, what we think we understand – is derived less from intellect than from first-hand sensory experience. This leads into the uncertain waters of the 'semiconscious sphere of the mental and hence' into the 'largely inaccessible yet, in its controlling and orienting function, all the more persistent and enduring sphere of mental programmes, which has a decisive effect on our values and actions'.[2]

Both lines of inspiration – everyday life and encounters with foreign cultures – converged in the shared interest that artists and designers of the 1950s and 1960s showed in them: the fascination with the strong visuality and immediacy of things that produce an intensive

fig. 4
Ettore Sottsass, *Superboxes*, 1966
ABET-Print
Mock-ups for cabinets
plywood and plastic laminate
84 x 30 x 31 cm (each wardrobe)
The Museum of Modern Art, New York
Gift of the manufacturer

fig. 4

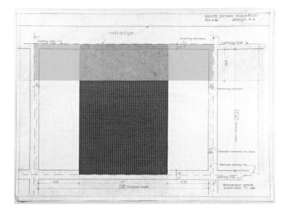

fig. 6

intrinsic effect beyond culturally bound, conventional meanings. Clear colours and shapes play an important role, for colours are decisive in determining how we sense and perceive things – a phenomenon exploited by Pop Art and Pop design. Sottsass found the inspiration for his remarkable colour combinations during his travels to India in 1961: 'India, which communicates and lives through senses, colors, smells, flowers, dances, mudra, mantra, yantra and the carnal intensity of its rites and legends, is what Ettore was never again to forget.'[3] After returning from his journey, he designed the *Superboxes* (1965–1969): towering, monumental wardrobes, with a square base, that rest on a low pedestal and soar upward like stelae. The colours form vertical or horizontal stripes of varying width, thus giving the impression that the wardrobes are actually constructed from blocks of colour stacked on top or adjacent to one another. Their design does not follow the principle of functionality; rather, they organize the space around them and form its spiritual centre (fig. 4, → p. 141).

Of similar force are the close-knit, harshly clashing colour fields of Indiana's sign-like paintings. In these, short words such as 'LOVE' are detached from their actual meaning and translated into a pattern of geometric figures whose architectural structure and flatness are brought to the fore → p. 44. In his oil painting *Seven* of 1968 → p. 132, an ornamentally curved, bright blue '7' takes up the full width and height of the painting, while the surrounding negative spaces create a dynamic pattern in vibrant orange. Coexisting on equal footing, it is impossible to say which is the figure and which is the ground. The two luminous colour zones relate to one another in a constant state of tension, their radiance intensified by the complementary colour contrast. They vie

fig. 5

for attention and primacy in the visual perception of the viewer. It is as if the '7' repeatedly puffs itself up and then recedes again; as if it, or the surrounding orange, pushes outward beyond the borders of the picture; as if one or the other fields of colour lurches out from the painting and forcefully thrusts itself on the viewers. Each of the two parts seems to take on a mysterious life of its own.

In 1961, Alexander Girard designed a poster in a similar formal and aesthetic style for Textiles & Objects, the store he had planned and designed for Herman Miller in Manhattan (fig. 5). The goods on display not only included textiles and furniture but also a colourful variety of folk art from all over the world → p. 86-87. The poster, which was designed to promote the shop, features a rich palette of turquoise, pink and orange on a white background. As with Indiana, giant letters and symbols form large-scale, monumental patterns that seem to speak their own enigmatic language and, in the process, lose their literal meaning. Intensive explorations of colour, colour combinations and their impact can also be found among the numerous studies and sketches for the poster left in Girard's estate (fig. 6). Vivid pink, paired with bold orange, deep raspberry red and cinnamon brown – such combinations also dominate Girard's textile and wall designs as well as his interior design schemes going back to the early 1950s. Mexican folk art fuelled this orchestration of colour. Taking inspiration from it, he made a radical break with the tendency, which was in fashion at the time, to decorate American interiors in muted earth tones of grey, brown and ochre up to a subdued turquoise, and unleashed a veritable visual explosion (fig. 3).

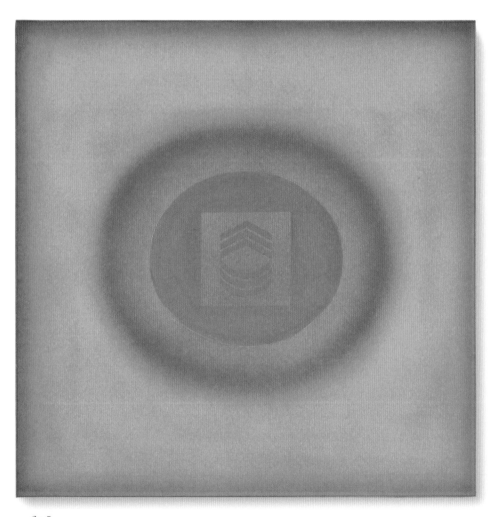

fig. 7

fig. 8

The luminosity of colours was also of interest to the artists of Southern California. Using unconventional materials and technologies – predominantly influenced by the aerospace industry, which had been present in Los Angeles since the Second World War – they probed ways of intensifying the radiance of colours and surfaces. 'Less dependent on particular traditions, the art scene [was] characterized by an openness to experimentation, a close relationship to design and a responsiveness to landscape and climate conditions.'[4]

After the experiences of the war, society found itself on a quest for meaning, in some cases sparking a longing for forms of spirituality outside Western channels. Some turned to Zen Buddhism, which provided a source of inspiration for a good many artists. Others took advantage of the industrial innovations of the day, as manifested in the use of various plastics and varnishes.

The early work of Billy Al Bengston – one of the main figures associated with the Ferus Gallery that was founded in 1957 by Walter Hopps, Edward Kienholz and Bob Alexander – demonstrates the particular mix that characterizes the 'L.A. look': his works operate along the boundary between 'Pop, underground and a healthy dose of spirituality à la L.A.'[5] A persistent focal point of his early paintings is the U.S. Army Master Sergeant insignia – a motif that would preoccupy him throughout the 1960s. In a military context, it is an emblem of power that visibly indicates the rank of its wearer and creates an aura of official authority. The conspicuous display of certain attributes, or the painting of such, is an age-old practice for quickly and easily communicating the function

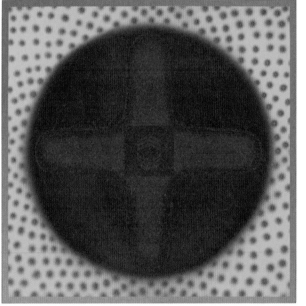

fig. 9

or rank of a member of society and eliciting commensurate behaviour toward this person. By dedicating himself to this one motif over a span of years, modifying it through fading, layering and colouring, Bengston seems to have been literally working away at this demonstrative symbol of power and ultimately almost entirely eliminating its social importance: 'He put the thing through the wringer to such a degree, we're no longer really sure what it means.'[6]

While Bengston's *Sonny* (fig. 7) of 1961 is still conventionally painted with oils, it achieves a chromatic intensity that heralds the even greater vividness of his subsequent works in lacquer. As in all these works, the sergeant stripes are positioned in the centre – here as part of a light purple oval with an almost corporeal appearance that seems to rise up from the golden yellow ground. In *Godzilla's Saddle* of 1962 (fig. 9), the sergeant stripes barely stand out against their surroundings due to the near equivalence of the colours. They are contained inside a cross within a bubble that rises up from a sea of turquoise populated by a multitude of glimmering red-orange dots. Resulting from countless layers of spray paint, applied using car and motorcycle coating techniques,[7] the surface is 'translucent and dense in colour and depth' by dint of meticulous sanding and polishing.[8] The title makes an apparent reference to the atomic mutant Godzilla; and, in general, the work evokes associations with the alien universes envisioned by science fiction as well as the synthetic worlds of the imagination induced by the consumption of hallucinogens – two phenomena that enjoyed a boom during the 1960s. Among fellow contemporary artists, the

fig. 10   fig. 11

perfect, brilliantly gleaming surfaces of Bengston's paintings found many admirers.

Among these was Judy Chicago. She later made her way into the thoroughly male-dominated subcultural art scene of Los Angeles. 'Male domination: You bet your ass' – so goes Bengston's commentary on the so-called art gang[9] represented by the Ferus Gallery at the time – 'Note: This was a male heterosexual gang of comrades who loved chicks and fun even though they wore girdles.'[10] Apparently never a fully-fledged member of the inner circle, Chicago describes her early years along the same lines: 'Here I am, […] figuring out how to make a place for myself in this unbelievably macho environment.'[11] From a family of Jewish intellectuals, she ventured into unfamiliar terrain as she began to pursue her inclination towards manual work with and on material. She trained in auto body painting and finishing techniques and thus muscled her way into this truly masculine domain.

Car Hood of 1964 → p. 27 holds an important position in Chicago's oeuvre. While still clearly influenced by the practices of her male colleagues, the work points ahead to the 1970s when she would join the forefront of the women's movement.[12] In itself, a car bonnet can already be understood as the epitome of masculinity, yet it is all the more so when it becomes an expression of the archaic male striving for strength and power, when the bonnet is celebrated, adorned and fashioned like a warrior's breastplate. As such, the chrome car body constitutes a kind of second skin for its male occupants; and as part of the custom car culture of Southern California, which flourished during the 1950s and 1960s, the metal surfaces of cars and motorcycles were adorned with elaborate paintings. Chicago took the male fetish for the car bonnet and applied the ultimate symbol of femininity to it: a stylized vaginal form in bright orange that acts as the female counterpart to Bengston's sergeant stripes while still evincing certain similar aspects of composition.

Like Chicago, Niki de Saint Phalle also used her art to explore the female body and stereotypical gender roles. Begun in 1964, her colourful *Nana* figures are monuments that present a cheerful, strong and exuberant femininity. Their voluminous forms hark back to those of ancient fertility goddesses, as depicted, for instance, in the *Venus of Willendorf*, the famous Stone Age statuette (fig. 10). Mirthful and uninhibited, the *Nanas* tell of the female condition and of motherhood. They seduce the viewer with their clear, vibrant colours and dynamic movements (fig. 11), their painted patterns revitalizing ancient myths and symbols: 'Periodically throughout history and in all cultures, myths and symbols have been reinvented and recreated. Niki shows us in her very modern way that these myths and symbols are still alive.'[13]

Despite their varied appearance and intentions, all these works share a common gesture: the emphatically sensuous way in which they make contact with the viewer. They exert a direct effect on the perception and avail themselves of entrenched elements of daily life, such as numbers, letters and symbols, that are organized in a clear and simple visual language. In their sensual power of expression, first and foremost a product of their intensive colouration, the works take on a life of their own beyond culturally rooted, conventional assignments of meaning. They initiate a game of changing meanings and effects, which is exactly what lends these Pop works their spiritual and mythical character.

★

Endnotes

1 Ettore Sottsass, as quoted in Barbara Radice, *Ettore Sottsass: A Critical Biography* (New York: Rizzoli, 1993), 61.

2 Thomas Düllo, 'Coolness: Beharrlichkeit und Umcodierung einer erfolgreichen Mentalitätsstrategie', in Thomas Düllo and Franz Liebl, eds., *Cultural Hacking: Kunst des Strategischen Handelns* (Vienna and New York: Springer, 2005), 51.

3 Radice, *Ettore Sottsass*, 61.

4 David Bomford and Thomas W. Gaehtgens, 'Foreword', in Rebecca Peabody et al., eds., *Pacific Standard Time: Los Angeles Art 1945–1980*, catalogue accompanying the exhibition *Pacific Standard Time: Crosscurrents in L.A. Painting and Sculpture, 1950–1970*, J. Paul Getty Museum Los Angeles and Martin-Gropius-Bau Berlin (Los Angeles: Getty Publications, 2012), xviii.

5 Lars Nittve, 'In der Schwebe: Kunst und Anderes in Los Angeles um 1960', in Tobia Bezzola, ed., *Hot Spots: Rio de Janeiro / Milano-Torino / Los Angeles, 1956 bis 1968*, exhibition catalogue, Kunsthaus Zurich (Göttingen: Steidl, 2008), 219.

6 Karen Tsujimoto, 'Malerei als visuelles Tagebuch', in *Billy Al Bengston*, exhibition catalogue (Frankfurt am Main: Galerie Neuendorf, 1993), 17.

7 Bengston took up professional motorcycle racing, which left a lasting influence on his art, both in terms of the visual language as well as the selection of materials and techniques. Formica laminate panels and aluminium sheeting serve as a ground for his paintings, onto which industrial polymer paint and high-gloss nitrocellulose lacquer are applied in multiple layers before being given a final polish—a process brilliantly illustrated by the term 'finish fetish', which was coined at the time by critic John Coplans to describe works like Bengston's.

8 Tsujimoto, 'Malerei als visuelles Tagebuch', 18.

9 Andrew Perchuk and Catherine Taft, 'Floating Structures: Building the Modern in Postwar Los Angeles', in Peabody et al., *Pacific Standard Time*, 49.

10 Billy Al Bengston, e-mail to author, 31 May 2012.

11 Judy Chicago, 'Judy Chicago Speaks about Her Work', April 2011, online video interview, Pacific Standard Time at the Getty Center, http://www.getty.edu/pacificstandardtime/explore-the-era/archives/v9/.

12 The 1972 opening of *Womanhouse*, organized by Chicago together with Miriam Schapiro as one of the first explicitly feminist exhibition projects, would represent a significant milestone on the arduous path towards public awareness of art produced by women.

13 Niki de Saint Phalle, 'Niki by Niki', in Carla Schulz-Hoffmann (ed.), *Niki de Saint Phalle: My Art, My Dreams*, rev. ed. (Munich et al.: Prestel, 2008), 28.

Charles and Ray Eames, installation of
their works, *An Exhibition for Modern Living*,
Detroit Institute of Arts, 1949
Courtesy Eames Office

Gene Moore, shop window with a painting
by Jasper Johns, Bonwit Teller department
store, New York, 1956

Gene Moore, shop window with a painting
by Robert Rauschenberg, Bonwit Teller
department store, New York, 1956

Achille and Pier Giacomo Castiglioni,
installation of a living room and workspace
for the exhibition *Colori e forme nella casa d'oggi*
(Colours and forms in today's home), Villa
Olmo, Como, 1957 (decoration: Giuseppe
Ajmone)

Gene Moore, shop window with paintings by Andy Warhol, Bonwit Teller department store, New York, 1961

Konrad Lueg and Gerhard Richter, *Leben mit Pop – eine Demonstration für den kapitalistischen Realismus* (Life with Pop – A Demonstration for Capitalist Realism) exhibition/happening, Möbelhaus Berges, Düsseldorf, 1963

Ben Birillo and Paul Bianchini,
The American Supermarket, 1964
Project organized by Bianchini Gallery, New York
Photo and © Henri Dauman /
DaumanPictures.com. All Rights Reserved

Emilio Ambasz with Thomas Czarnowski,
installation of the exhibition *Italy: The New Domestic
Landscape* in the Sculpture Garden of the Museum
of Modern Art (MoMA), New York, 1972
The Museum of Modern Art Archives
Photo: Leonardo LeGrand

Lee Friedlander,
New York City, 1963/1978
Silver gelatin print
18.6 x 28.1 cm
Moderna Museet

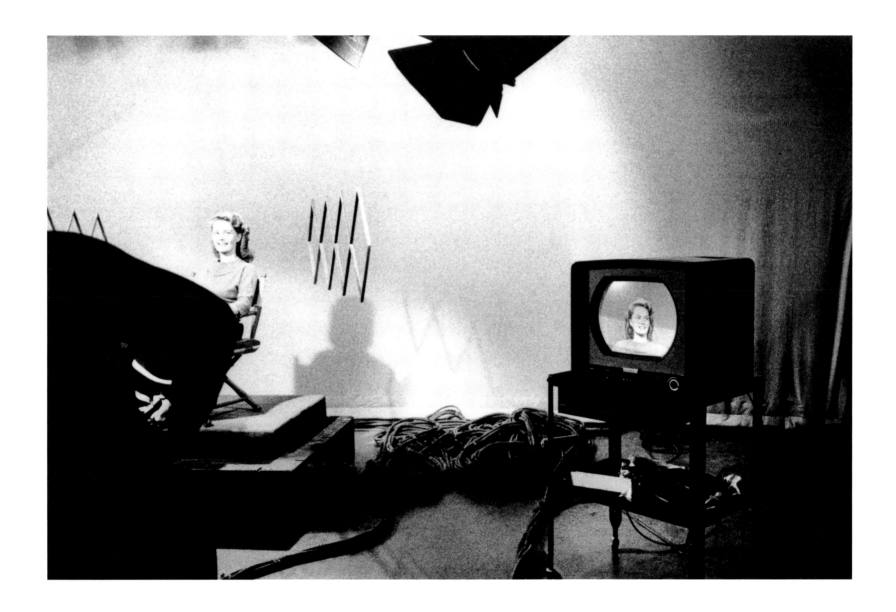

Robert Frank, *Television Studio, Burbank,*
California, 1956
From the series *The Americans*, 1955/66
Silver gelatin print
20.3 x 30.5 cm
The Museum of Fine Arts, Houston
Gift of Jerry E. and Nanette Finger

Charles and Ray Eames,
Glimpses of the USA, 1959
Courtesy Eames Office

The exhibition 'Pop Art Design' shows a
digitally edited summary of the simultaneous
projection, originally presented at the
'American National Exhibition' in Moscow.
4 min 11 sec, colour

William Klein,
Broadway by Light, 1958
Argos Films
Documentary film
10 min 30 sec, colour

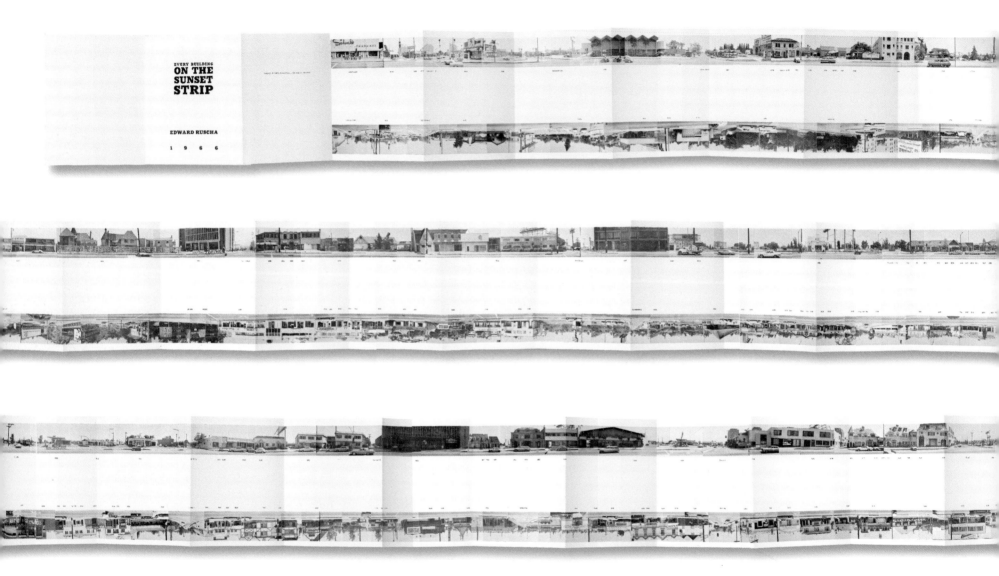

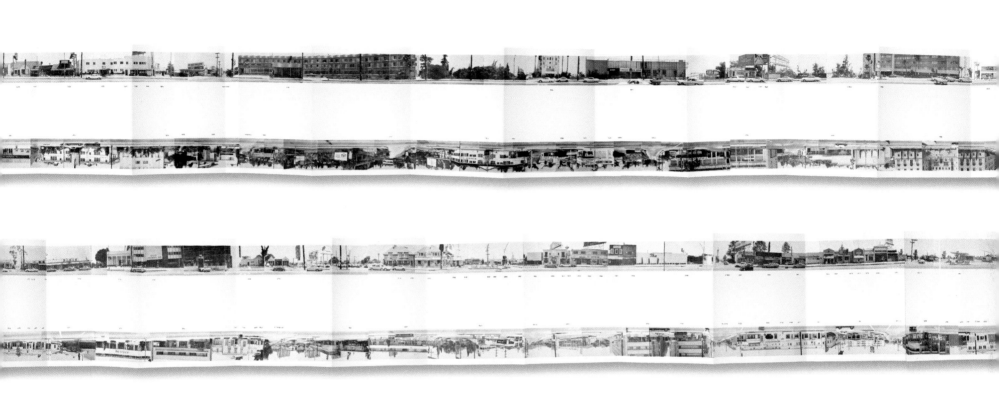

Ed Ruscha, *Every Building on the Sunset Strip*,
1966
Artist book
Offset print on paper
19 x 15 x 2 cm
Louisiana Museum of Modern Art

Gulf gas station, Las Vegas, 1971

Restaurant on the Las Vegas Strip, 1968

Big Donut Drive-in, roadside restaurant, Los Angeles, ca. 1970

Tail Pup, hot dog stand, Los Angeles, ca. 1970

Robert Venturi and Denise Scott Brown, photographs from the Las Vegas study
Courtesy Museum im Bellpark Kriens from the 'Las Vegas Studio' project
© Venturi, Scott Brown and Associates, Inc., Philadelphia

American suburbia, ca. 1968

Gaslite Motel, Las Vegas, 1968

The Big Duck, roadside shop shaped like a duck, Flanders, Long Island, ca. 1970

Lower Strip, from a picture sequence driving north, Las Vegas, 1968

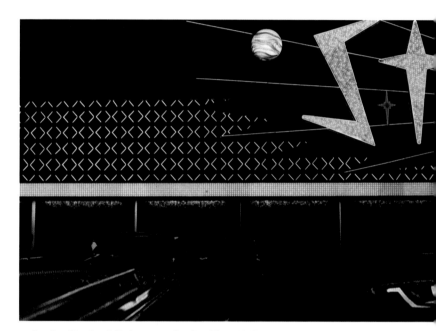

Stardust Hotel and Casino, neon sign, Las Vegas 1968

Las Vegas Strip, ca. 1970

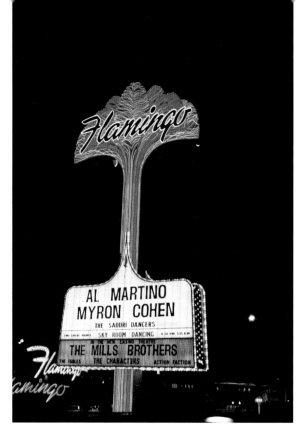

Sign of the Flamingo Hotel and Casino, Las Vegas, 1968

Stardust Hotel and Casino, Las Vegas, 1968

The Mint Hotel and Casino, Las Vegas, 1968

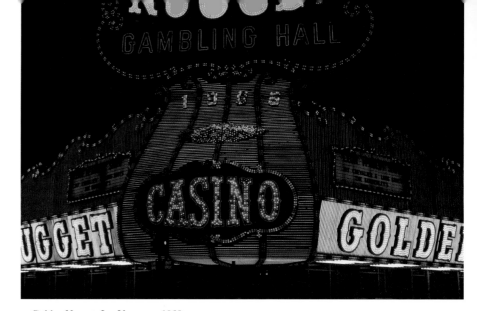

Golden Nugget, Las Vegas, ca. 1968

Fremont Street, Las Vegas, 1968

Aladdin Hotel and Casino, front entrance, Las Vegas, 1968

Fremont Street, view towards Union Pacific Station,
Las Vegas, 1971

Neon signs, Fremont Street, Las Vegas, 1968

Neon fountain, Las Vegas, 1968

fig. 1
Elmgreen & Dragset, *Prada Marfa*, 2005
Adobe bricks, plaster, aluminium frame, glass pane,
MDF, paint, carpet, shoes and handbags by Prada
At the Highway 90 near Marfa, Texas
760 x 470 x 480 cm

The Shop Window and Pop Art: From Precious Elixir to Calmative Potion

Thomas Kellein

fig. 1

fig. 2
Blake Edwards (dir.), film still with
Audrey Hepburn, *Breakfast at Tiffany's*,
1961

fig. 2

The baker puts his loaves in it, the goldsmith his pitchers and goblets. . . . [Yet] the Orient knows nothing of the shop window.
– Karl Ernst Osthaus, 1913

For the banker's son, collector and museum founder Karl Ernst Osthaus, it was still uncharted cultural territory; for us, such a commonplace that irony alone calls our attention to it: the shop window – omnipresent as ever yet today largely eclipsed by the ubiquitous competition of huge, digitally controlled monitors and vinyl film decals. A hundred years ago, window displays could still surprise people and excite their desires. 'Allurement and splendour are required,' wrote Osthaus in 1913, referring to commercial displays in Berlin.[1] Today, if there is any discussion of shop windows, it is mainly because they have unexpectedly shown up in the wrong place – like *Prada Marfa* (2005) by artist duo Elmgreen and Dragset, which landed as if by chance on the Texan prairie (fig. 1). The box-like container of elegant shoes meets the eye as if it were a mirage, and a perpetually shimmering one at that, for this architectural work of art is permanently installed in its remote location.

Not until the arrival of Pop Art and Minimalism did artists begin to use shop windows for exhibiting art – primarily their own, occasionally in a series. In preceding decades, these architectural cubicles in which wares are displayed had slowly but surely developed into aesthetically worthy venues. Decorators had perfected their medium well before museums began presenting temporary exhibitions. When New York art director Gene Moore began in 1950 to hire young artists such as Robert Rauschenberg and Jasper Johns as window dressers, they didn't enter the scene as pioneers but rather as creative disturbers of an already established genre. It was Moore himself who was the pioneer; and when in 1961 Tiffany & Co. appointed him vice president for window display,[2] the management allegedly received

him with the following words: 'A window should never try to sell merchandise'.[3]

As it were, fifty years ago shop windows in New York had such a high cultural status that their commercial function seemed almost secondary. In Truman Capote's 1958 novella *Breakfast at Tiffany's*, adapted into a movie starring Audrey Hepburn in 1961, a woman wearing a pearl necklace and sunglasses takes a taxi to the famous Fifth Avenue jewellery shop in order to drink coffee from a paper cup in front of the window displays (fig. 2). She does not intend to buy anything. She merely wants to dream and dispel her morning melancholy. Thus, temptation and the challenge of resisting it are brought to the foreground in the film's opening scene.

Window dressers in New York as well as in Paris owed their creative success to a love affair with Surrealism. It is not clear to what degree this love originated in Paris. Although in 1950 the theatrically designed windows of Hermès or Schiaparelli in Paris were still superior to American shop windows,[4] already in 1937 Tom Lee produced the first surrealistic *trompe-l'oeil* at Bonwit Teller in New York. In 1939, the window displays he designed in collaboration with Salvador Dalí caused a sensation because they displayed, for the first time, three-dimensional art rather than fashion products. At the time, fashionable department stores such as Macy's, Saks Fifth Avenue and Bergdorf Goodman were in sharp competition with Bonwit Teller. Billboards were scarce and television ads did not yet exist, so shop windows vied with each other for the public's attention. Gradually, the staging of dramatic window displays spread to stores in almost all major Western cities, as if to certify that they were in the business of selling fashion.

In addition to the Surrealists, many European architects and interior designers fled to the United States during the Nazi years, bringing with them their fascination with avant-garde architecture. As a result, American storefronts began featuring artistically displayed

fig. 3

fig. 3
Charles and Ray Eames, Herman Miller showroom, Los Angeles, 1948 Exterior view at night, 1952 Courtesy Eames Office

fig. 4
Marcel Duchamp, *The Bride Stripped Bare by Her Bachelors, Even (The Large Glass)*, 1915–23 Photograph of the still-intact work at the Brooklyn Museum, New York, 1926 Philadelphia Museum of Art Archives Gift of Jacqueline, Paul and Peter Matisse in memory of their mother Alexina Duchamp

furniture and textiles long before European window designers caught up with the trend. In 1948 architects and designers Charles and Ray Eames created the first Herman Miller Furniture Company showroom in Los Angeles (fig. 3), designing a skeletal structure of prefabricated materials within which opaque and transparent windowpanes alternated. Among other things, the couple's design demonstrated that a display window could function as part of a building's structure, thus manifesting a point of view diametrically opposed to that of the Surrealists, who used the shop window as a showcase that is found but never constructed.

In 1958, Alexander Girard, an architect who specialized also in textile design, was commissioned to design the Herman Miller showroom in San Francisco and used earth-coloured textiles to confer an orderly atmosphere upon a former vaudeville theatre and bordello. In 1961 he transformed the Herman Miller showroom in New York into a *gesamtkunstwerk* entitled Textiles & Objects that left nothing to chance.[5]

Surrealistic illusionism and the modern supercool style evolved as complementary trends in the United States. Both played

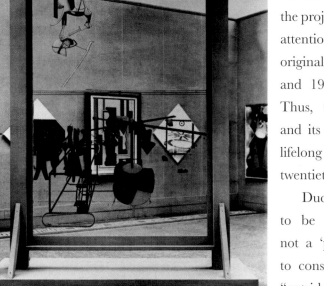

fig. 4

a part in perfecting shop window design as an artistic medium that promises continuous development – similar to painting, sculpture and architecture. Narrative magic and clear structural forms intensified the magnetic effect of shop windows, which had already captivated poets such as Adalbert Stifter in 1850 and photographers such as Eugène Atget in 1900.

Among visual artists, it is above all Marcel Duchamp, travelling between the cultural capitals of Paris and New York, whose most important works can be understood as tributes to the shop window. *The Large Glass*, created between 1915 and 1923 (fig. 4), and the collection of facsimiled documents and sketches entitled *La Boîte verte* (1934) both pay homage to a format that is more indebted to the turnover of goods than to art. Richard Hamilton, one of the founders of Pop Art, whose initial interests lay in exhibition techniques, devoted no less than five years to the typographically faithful translation of the *Boîte verte* texts into English,[6] completing the project in 1960. With similar meticulous attention, he reconstructed the shattered original of *The Large Glass* between 1965 and 1966 for a Duchamp retrospective. Thus, the presentation of merchandise and its underlying organization exerted a lifelong fascination on several artists of the twentieth century.

Duchamp himself originally wanted to be a 'window maker' (*fenêtrier*) and not a 'painter';[7] and *The Large Glass* was to constitute a 'brilliant synthesis of the "outside world" and the inside world of the imagination', as Anne d'Harnoncourt and Walter Hopps put it in 1969.[8] Yet at the time, the issue at hand was not Duchamp's own creations but rather his reception, for without him Pop Art and – through the mediation of Fluxus – Conceptual Art would not have been conceivable. Duchamp had written about the 'obstinacy, ad absurdum, of hiding the coition through a glass pane with one or many objects of the shop window'.[9] Functionally, his technique of mystification had an aim opposite to that of the shop window: In place of the elixir with its erotic promise, the central focus was a secret – which, however, could not be revealed.

In New York in 1930 – historically after Duchamp's *Large Glass* but still before the popularization of Surrealism in American clothing stores – Austrian artist, architect and theatre designer Friedrich Kiesler called for the streets to be regarded as auditoriums and shop windows as theatrical performances.[10] The Surrealists, who came to New York from Paris soon after, prepared the ground for the realization of this idea. For Salvador Dalí, Yves Tanguy and Jean Cocteau, the displays of high-fashion shop windows were a 'ready-made daydream',[11] offering a three-dimensional, widely accessible extension to their work. The first Dalí window at Bonwit Teller appeared in 1936, still without the participation of Tom Lee in its design. Three years later, again at Bonwit Teller, the two men collaborated, dedicating their creations *Midnight Green* and *Narcissus White* (fig. 5) to night and day, respectively.[12] These displays caused such a sensation that the management altered them and removed Dalí's name, to which he responded by personally destroying his work and accidentally shattering the windowpane in the process.[13]

The architectural features of the shop's windowpane – typically, a continuous surface that extends to the edge of the building, its transparency suggesting direct access to the wares behind it – create a surprisingly physical proximity between the viewer and the display. Yet, at the same time, 'coition with the objects' – to use Duchamp's words – is rendered impossible by the glass pane itself. Nevertheless,

fig. 5

the staging techniques developed for shop windows over the decades continually amplify the attraction exerted by the merchandise over the viewer. The windows get bigger and bigger, they can be frequented with family or with friends, by daylight or after dark. Already in the 1920s the dramatic stagecraft of the displays gave a number of artists the idea of showing their own work behind a large glass pane. These were few, however, for window dressers have usually worked separately from painters and sculptors. In 1950 Rauschenberg showed one of his *Blueprints* in a shop window designed by Moore before exhibiting it at the Museum of Modern Art. In 1956 and 1957 Johns hung his *White Flag* and *Flag on Orange Field* in Moore's shop windows before the paintings appeared in his solo exhibition at the Leo Castelli Gallery in 1958.[14] Andy Warhol's famous statement, 'All department stores will become museums, and all museums will become department stores',[15] parodies, perhaps inadvertently, the dream frequently expressed in Germany that department stores might play an educational role.[16] But by 1960 this dream was so spent that the notion of shop windows run by museums or designed by creative artists was almost inconceivable. That may be the reason why Kirk Varnedoe and Adam Gopnik's frequently cited *High and Low* exhibition did not accord the shop window any special significance.[17]

It was Warhol who first took the path from shop window decoration to art and thereby brought about a paradigm shift – around the same time that Moore joined Tiffany & Co. and *Breakfast at Tiffany's* started its run in the movie theatres. Warhol, known at the time only as a decorator and illustrator, designed a window for Bonwit

fig. 6
Christo, *Purple Store Front*, 1964
Wood, metal, enamel paint,
plexiglas, paper, fabric, electric light
235 x 220 x 35.5 cm
Photo: Wolfgang Volz

fig. 7
Claes Oldenburg, *The Store*, 1961
107 East Second Street, New York

fig. 8
Richard Estes, *The Candy Store*, 1969
Oil and synthetic polymers on canvas
121.29 x 174.63 cm
Whitney Museum of American Art,
New York
Purchased with funds from the Friends
of the Whitney Museum of American Art
Photo: Geoffrey Clements

fig. 6

fig. 7

fig. 8

Teller's department store on Fifty-seventh Street in Manhattan → p. 106. Unlike Rauschenberg and Johns, who were commissioned by Moore as creative troublemakers, Warhol was hired as a window dresser. He had already worked with Moore during the mid-1950s, creating display boxes a well as room-filling mobiles using shoes that dangled from invisible threads. But in April 1961, the abrupt change took place: Warhol broke with Surrealism and with Modernism in general, just as he dispensed with his own mother's ornate calligraphy.

Warhol's paradigm shift originated in his decision to start painting within the framework of his work as a window dresser. He produced five paintings, which in retrospect constitute the starting point of his oeuvre as a Pop artist, and displayed them behind the mannequins, either leaning against the wall or, in one case, mounted on a scaffold. Warhol used pre-primed canvas, water-soluble casein paint and wax crayons. He did not sign the paintings as independent works until later. Considered together with Claes Oldenburg's *Store* from the winter of 1961/62 (fig. 7) – a New York gallery exhibition in which the artist sought to sell everyday commodities and food made of painted plaster as if it were a normal store[18] – one can say that American Pop Art, like the aforementioned Audrey Hepburn film, pays homage to a medium that at the time appeared more desirable than traditional painting and sculpture.

After Émile Zola's *The Ladies' Paradise* of 1883, it is the year 1960 that marks the cultural zenith of the shop window. Yet no sooner had this zenith been attained than it was already exceeded. For the shop window could not much longer sustain the constant demonstrations of love and the insatiable appetite for enticement. Artists, already having showrooms of their own, began using the display space as their podium and set about deconstructing it, employing an ironic approach. The intellectual-satirical reflex to the aesthetics of merchandising began in New York with Claes Oldenburg. In Germany, *Life with Pop* → p. 106, a performance piece by Konrad Lueg and Gerhard Richter presented at the Möbelhaus Berges in Düsseldorf, followed suit.[19] For a number of hours, the two artists sat in furniture that was on sale at this pre-existing furniture store and in the evening hung their own works as part of a pronouncedly cool guided tour of the premises. In 1962, the French Fluxus artist Ben Vautier spent fifteen days living in the front window of London's Gallery One as part of the Festival of Misfits. Earlier, in 1958, Yves Klein cleared out the space of Galerie Iris Clert, emphatically purified it with white paint and posted two knights of the Rosicrucian order on either side of the entrance as a ceremonious welcome to the opening of his exhibition *Le Vide*. Christo and Jeanne-Claude, aware of this action when they moved from Paris to New York in 1964, began their American career with a collage of paper-covered shop windows entitled *Store Fronts* (fig. 6).[20]

Jean Tinguely, who began an apprenticeship as a decorator in Basel in 1941 and earned a living as a window dresser well into the 1950s, used the most important artistic 'showroom' in New York – the Museum of Modern Art – for the production of an explosive uproar. When he presented his first self-destructing machine sculpture, *Homage to New York*, in the courtyard of the museum in 1960, his professional origins were no longer on anyone's mind. No artist in 1960 wanted to be known as a window dresser. Rather, it was the admiration of their decorator colleagues that inspired artists to outdo themselves.

As for Warhol, his very first painting, *Advertisement*, is a direct, unmodified appropriation of pre-existing material. His second painting, *Little King*, derives from the eponymous comic strip by Otto Siglow; the third, *Superman*, is an excerpt from *Superman's Girl Friend*, another comic strip. None of the motifs in these works had any biographical connotations for Warhol. Indeed, the originals were just a few days old.[21] *Before and After*, Warhol's fourth painting, features a pair of noses in profile, based on an advertisement for cosmetic

fig. 9
Dan Graham, high school door,
Westfield, New Jersey, 1966
From the series *Homes for America*

surgery. In 1974 the same picture, slightly reworked, was shown in another department store, this time in Japan[22] – a country in which the separation between art museum and department store, a long established convention in the West, was never fully adopted. The fifth painting, *Saturday's Popeye*, is based on a comic strip dated March 1961 – only one month before Warhol's window display.[23]

It was long believed that through its use of the shop window American Pop Art intended to call the very notion of high art into question. Warhol's motifs did not elevate the store display; rather they connected it with themes from everyday life that seemed to be missing from the elegant world of Uptown Manhattan. Streaks and splashes of paint and porous brushwork surely intensified this impression, for the paintings, compared with the original comic strips, look 'trashy' even today. The shop window was well positioned

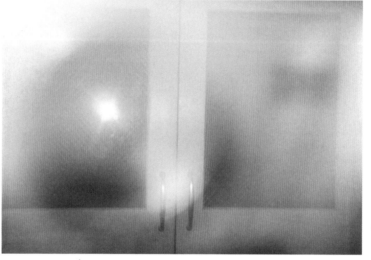

fig. 9

to cope with such a change. Banality revolutionized the art world, which at the time was rather stiffly enamoured of subjective *écriture*. Pop imagery was adopted and developed without calling the claims of high art into question. Virtually at the same time, Roy Lichtenstein started to produce an oeuvre based on comic strip motifs that soon began to forge connections with masterpieces of high art. Thus, from 1960 onward, shop windows, comic strips and commercial art offered artists a language with which to rid themselves of the dominance of existing styles.

For this reason the shop window itself did not fade away – though its nimbus was undermined, both before and after this turning

point. When television became popular in the United States during the 1950s and in Europe during the 1960s, an additional, no less exciting showcase appeared right inside people's homes. And with the continuing growth of cities and increasing motorization, billboards, many times the size of any shop window, began to proliferate. As a result, shop windows gradually lost their exclusive aura, while art, from the mid-1960s onward, began to explore, not to say vivisect, this traditional container for the presentation of goods with almost surgical precision.

Speaking retrospectively of this analytical phase, Dan Graham, who began as an art critic and became the most accomplished window display artist of the second generation, said the following: 'Duchamp had no effect. I think he only influenced Jasper Johns. Duchamp was sort of a gigolo hanging out with very rich older Philadelphia society people, and we were just working people'.[24] In 1965 Graham began photographing the suburban areas of New Jersey, New York and Staten Island, focusing on the theme of *Homes for America*. Among his subjects were the glass doors and windowed hallways of a high school in Westfield, New Jersey. The unspectacular colour snapshots were published and exhibited as a series (fig. 9).[25] To Graham himself, these photographs suggested the route to a 'series of transparent-mirror spaces.'[26] His pictures thematize houses, apartments, rooms and landscapes as patterns, grids and ostensible codes that he refuses to furnish with final interpretations, asking instead that the viewers immerse themselves in these schemata of domesticity. Slides of

fig. 10
Robert Irwin, *Varese Portal Room*
(Varese Window) (detail), 1973
The Solomon R. Guggenheim Foundation,
New York – Panza Collection
Gift 1992
On permanent loan to the Fondo Ambiente
Italiano

fig. 10

windowpanes and facades were projected through a carousel slide projector and lit for five seconds at a time. *Homes for America* gave rise to the more elaborate idea of creating structures made of four rectangular sheets of glass (to which the terms 'showcase' or 'display window' well apply), inside which cameras are installed in such a way as to permit each of them to photograph, mirror and project the wall it is facing. The four resulting images are in turn made to rotate, causing Graham's showcase to revolve around itself and around us in a loop of physical and mental self-referentiality. The distinction between the walls and the supposed contents of the window display is thus eradicated by the continuous cross-fading of the images. Graham's artistic use of the display window thereby abolishes the very function of the commercial shop window.

Artistically, it was about replacing the merchandise with the display window. Graham went on to increase the number of windowpanes in his glass box, creating eight images as a result. His *Project for Slide Projector* was presented at the Nova Scotia College of Art and Design in 1969.[27] From then on, the project was recreated so frequently and in so many places that the viewers and their self-perception became the explicit theme of the work. It is tempting to think of Graham's showcase pavilion as an artist's chapel designed to produce self-reflection. But a display window is a space into which one peers through a sheet of glass. If there is nothing inside, the glass walls themselves and their frames become the focus of attention.

After 1966 Californian art departed from the analysis of perception, empty space, light and (apparent) transparency. At the time, Robert Irwin was working with convex acrylic discs that he hung and secured at a distance from the wall, resulting in images whose architectural immateriality was a product of the light that was shown through them.[28] A little later this approach to the field of vision reached back into art history with the fascinating *Varese Portal Room (Varese Window)* (fig. 10) that Irwin built for the Collection Panza di Biumo in 1974. The visitor enters an empty room with whitewashed walls and a shimmering matt floor and approaches a wide-open window. There is no glass in it. Surprisingly, neither goods nor light-reflecting mirrors are displayed behind the window; instead it offers a view to the Tuscan landscape. Thus the display window returns to its origin. It eliminates itself and becomes nature again. The precious elixir has become a calmative potion.

After the Renaissance, when images of windows furnished a continuous chain of motifs that reached far into the German Romantic period, and after 1960, when Gene Moore, Truman Capote and Andy Warhol succeeded in elevating the shop window to the level of a work of art, artists such as Robert Irwin insist that windows must not be used to showcase merchandise. A window should show us the landscape and the sky, calmly and seriously. For when we are not distracted we can once again take comfort in the world and its natural charms. Artists who experienced the zenith of the shop window around 1960 and who understand what a high level of aesthetic quality can be achieved with the exquisite display of a product, will apparently never be satisfied until one of the most exciting art forms of their generation has been altered in their favour. They simply want to create works that are better than the grandest of shop windows.

★

Endnotes

1 Karl Ernst Osthaus, 'Das Schaufenster', in *Die Kunst in Industrie und Handel*, Jahrbuch des Deutschen Werkbundes 1913 (Jena: E. Diederichs, 1913), 59–60.

2 See Michael Emory, *Windows* (Chicago: Contemporary Books, 1977).

3 Barry James Wood provides important information on Gene Moore in his *Show Windows: 75 Years of the Art of Display* (New York: Congdon & Weed, 1982), 163. See also Judith Goldman, *Windows at Tiffany's: The Art of Gene Moore* (New York: H. N. Abrams, 1980).

4 See illustrations in Walter Herdeg, ed., *International Window Display, Schaufensterkunst, Étalages* (New York: Pellegrini & Cudahy, 1951), esp. 29–47.

5 For illustrations and references of all the window displays mentioned here, see Mildred S. Friedman, ed., *Nelson, Eames, Girard, Propst: The Design Process at Herman Miller*, special issue, *Design Quarterly* (Minneapolis: Walker Art Center), nos. 98/99 (1975).

6 The collection of drafts for *The Large Glass*, issued by Duchamp in 1934 in an edition of 320 copies as *La Boîte verte* (The Green Box), was published in 1960 under the title *The Bride Stripped Bare by Her Bachelors, Even*, using a translation made in 1954 by art historian George Heard Hamilton. In his typographic reconstruction, artist Richard Hamilton reproduced all the metres, underscoring, corrections and red highlighting of the original drafts and Duchamp himself wrote on the last page: 'This version of the Green Box is as accurate a translation of the meaning and form of the original notes as supervision by the author can make it'.

7 For an extended survey of Duchamp's shop window art, see Nina Schleif, *Schaufenster Kunst: Berlin und New York* (Cologne, Weimar and Vienna: Böhlau, 2004), 188–210, especially 189. See also Nina Schleif, 'Die Frage der Schaufenster: Marcel Duchamps Arbeiten in Schaufenstern', in *toutfait.com: The Marcel DuchampStudies Online Journal*, http://www.toutfait.com/online_journal_details.php?postid=1750.

8 Anne d'Harnoncourt and Walter Hopps, 'Étant Donnés: 1° la chute d'eau, 2° le gaz d'éclairage*: Reflections on a New Work by Marcel Duchamp', *Philadelphia Museum of Art Bulletin* 64, nos. 299/300 (1969), 31.

9 Marcel Duchamp, *The Essential Writings of Marcel Duchamp* (London: Thames and Hudson, 1975), 74. In 1937 Duchamp designed a window display for André Breton's Galerie Gradiva in Paris that featured the silhouette of an embracing couple entering a room. In 1943 he conceived the idea of decorating the windows of Denis de Rougemont's store on Fifth Avenue in New York by adorning the ceiling with open umbrellas. In 1945 he contributed a headless mannequin to the design of a showcase at the Gotham Book Mart for André Breton's book *Arcane 17*. The work's name, *Lazy Hardware*, derives from a spigot that was attached to the mannequin's right thigh—a masculine addendum.

10 Frederick Kiesler, *Contemporary Art Applied to the Store and Its Display* (New York: Brentano's, 1930). See also Schleif, *Schaufenster Kunst*, 151–168; and Susanne Breuss, *Window Shopping: Eine Fotogeschichte des Schaufensters* (Vienna: Metro, 2010), 31.

11 Leonard S. Marcus, *The American Store Window* (New York and London: Whitney Library of Design and Architectural Press, 1978), 30.

12 Ibid., 32.

13 For more details, see Schleif, *Schaufenster Kunst*, 177–184

14 Ibid., 211–12.

15 Andy Warhol, as quoted in the epigraph of Mary Portas, *Windows: The Art of Retail Display* (London and New York: Thames & Hudson, 1999).

16 For more details, see Schleif, *Schaufenster Kunst*, 78–99.

17 Kirk Varnedoe and Adam Gopnik, eds., *High & Low: Modern Art and Popular Culture*, exhibition catalogue (New York: Museum of Modern Art, 1990).

18 Claes Oldenburg's *The Store* was open from 1 December 1961 to 31 January 1962 at 107 East Second Street in Manhattan.

19 See Thomas Kellein, ed., *Ich nenne mich als Maler Konrad Lueg* [When I paint my name is Konrad Lueg], exhibition catalogue, PS1 Contemporary Art Center, New York, Kunsthalle Bielefeld and Stedelijk Museum voor Actuele Kunst, Ghent (Bielefeld: Kunsthalle Bielefeld, 1999).

20 Christo's *Store Fronts* were exhibited at the Leo Castelli Gallery in New York in 1964. See Christo and Jeanne-Claude, *Early Works, 1958–1969*, exhibition catalogue, Neuer Berliner Kunstverein at the Martin-Gropius-Bau, Berlin (Cologne: Taschen, 2001).

21 George Frei and Neil Printz, eds., *The Andy Warhol Catalogue Raisonné*, vol. 1, *Paintings and Sculpture, 1961–1963* (London and New York: Phaidon, 2002), figs. 1, 11, 12, as well as pp. 23, 35. 'No works can be documented until early 1961, nor has any record been found that establishes precisely which paintings were made first' (Ibid., 19. See also figs. 11–13).

22 Ibid., fig. 6, as well as p. 26.

23 Ibid., fig. 13, as well as pp. 36–37.

24 Benjamin H. D. Buchloh and Dan Graham, 'Four Conversations: December 1999–May 2000', in Marianne Brouwer, ed., *Dan Graham: Works, 1965–2000*, exhibition catalogue, Museu de Arte Contemporânea de Serralves, Porto and other locations (Düsseldorf: Richter, 2001), 83.

25 See Dan Graham, 'Homes for America', *Arts Magazine* 41, no. 4 (December 1966). The accompanying exhibition, entitled 'Projected Art', was held at the same time at Finch College Museum of Art in New York.

26 Dan Graham, 'Photographs in Motion', in *End Moments* (New York: Dan Graham, 1969), 34.

27 See Brouwer, *Dan Graham: Works*, 106.

28 In order to produce the discs, Irwin employed the services of various workshops, to which he presented himself as a window dresser. See Lawrence Weschler, *Seeing is Forgetting the Name of the Thing One Sees: Over Thirty Years of Conversations with Robert Irwin*, expanded edition (Berkeley: University of California Press, 2008), 105.

Patrick Caulfield, *Dining Recess*, 1972
Oil on canvas
274.5 x 213.5 cm
Arts Council Collection, Southbank Centre,
London

Roy Lichtenstein, *On*, 1962
Oil on canvas
71 x 46 cm
Collection Simonyi

Robert Indiana, *Seven*, 1965
Oil on canvas
61 x 61 cm
Kunstsammlung der Ruhr-Universität
Bochum Campusmuseum

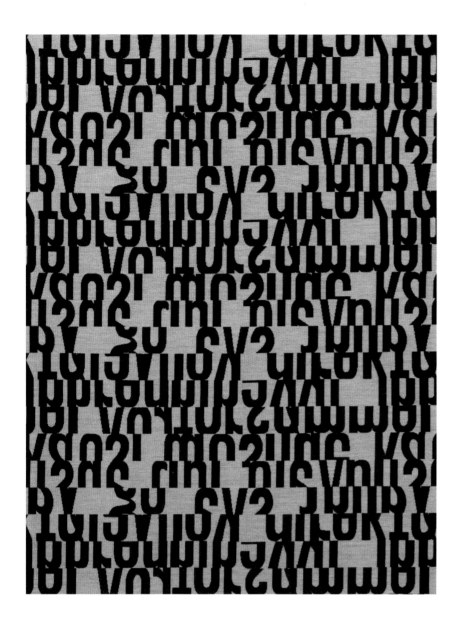

Gunnar Aagaard Andersen, *Letters*, 1955
Kvadrat, Ebeltoft, Denmark
Wall hanging and upholstery fabric
Cotton, wool, nylon
Vitra Design Museum,
Gift of the manufacturer

Alexander Girard, *Alphabet*, 1952
Herman Miller, Inc., Zeeland, MI, USA
Wallpaper pattern
Printed paper
23 x 30.5 cm (per sheet)
Vitra Design Museum

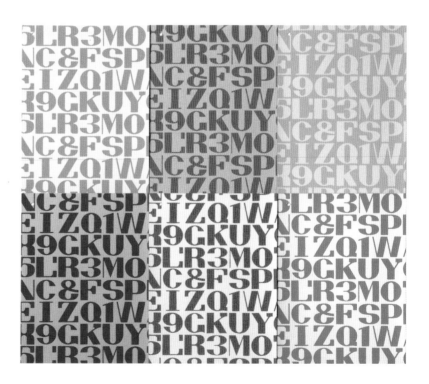

Ettore Sottsass, *Malatesta*
(from the series *Mobili grigi*), 1970
Poltronova Srl, Agliana (PT), Italy
Chair
Glass-reinforced polyester,
foam rubber, vinyl
77 x 41 x 50 cm
Vitra Design Museum

Valerio Adami, *Plein Air NY*, 1968
Acrylic on canvas
249 x 500.4 x 4.7 cm
Institut Valencià d'Art Modern,
Generalitat (IVAM)

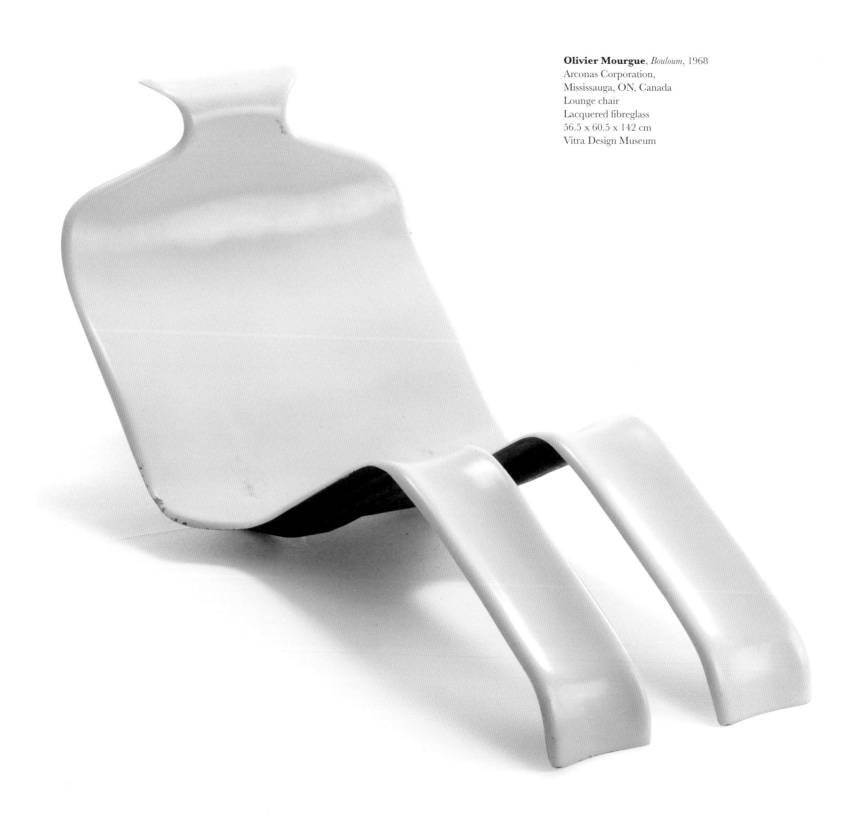

Olivier Mourgue, *Bouloum*, 1968
Arconas Corporation,
Mississauga, ON, Canada
Lounge chair
Lacquered fibreglass
56.5 x 60.5 x 142 cm
Vitra Design Museum

Pierre Paulin, *No. 437*, 1959
Artifort, Maastricht, Netherlands
Armchair
Moulded plywood, chrome-plated tubular
steel, foam upholstery, fabric cover
69 x 83 x 80 cm
Vitra Design Museum

Verner Panton,
Heart-Shaped Cone Chair / K3, 1959
Gebrüder Nehl, Germany
Swivel chair
Steel sheet, foam rubber, fabric cover
90 x 99.5 x 62 cm
Vitra Design Museum

Richard Hamilton,
The Gold Guggenheim, 1965–66
Fibreglass, cellulose, gold leaf
121.8 x 122.4 x 20.5 cm
Louisiana Museum of Modern Art
Long-term loan
Museumsfonden af 7. december 1966

Ed Ruscha, *Honk*, 1964
Graphite powder on paper
53 x 74 cm
Donald B. Marron, New York

Luigi Colani, untitled, 1967
Stacking chairs (two prototypes)
Fibreglass-reinforced polyester,
lacquered
72 x 80 x 76 cm (each chair)
Vitra Design Museum

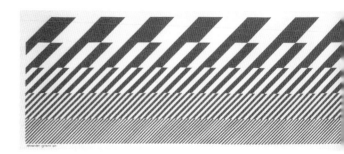

Alexander Girard, *No. 3037 / Diagonals*
(from the *Environmental Enrichment Panel* series), 1971
Herman Miller Textiles, Zeeland, MI, USA
Fabric panel
Printed cotton
68 x 216 cm
Vitra Design Museum

Allan D'Arcangelo, Untitled. 1967
Acrylic on canvas
175 x 213 cm
Estate of Allan D'Arcangelo
Courtesy Mitchell-Innes & Nash,
New York

Superstudio, *No. L 09 / Passiflora*, 1966
Fratelli Francesconi, Roncadelle (BS), Italy
Floor or wall lamp
Methacrylate
27 x 30 x 38 cm
Vitra Design Museum

Marcello Pietrantoni and Roberto Lucci,
Mod. 19041 / Nuvola, 1966
Stilnovo, Milan (MI), Italy
Ceiling or wall lamp
Methacrylate
76 x 146 x 30 cm
Vitra Design Museum

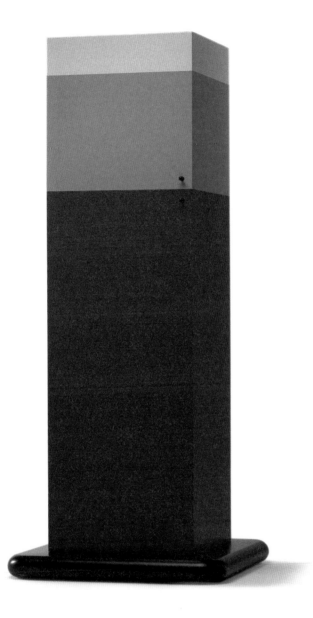

Richard Artschwager,
Chair, 1963
Resopal on wood
94 x 56 x 51 cm
Kunstmuseum Wolfsburg

Ettore Sottsass, *Superbox 'Hotel California'*,
1965/2005
Poltronova Srl, Agliana (PT), Italy
Cabinet
Wood, plastic laminate
205 x 80 x 80 cm
Centro Studi Poltronova per il Design,
Florence

Verner Panton, *Ring Lamps*, 1969/2000
Vitra AG, Basel, Switzerland
Wall lighting units
Lacquered acrylic glass, lacquered metal
62 x 62 x 22 cm (each lamp)
Vitra Design Museum

Anonymous, untitled, 1950–51
Tupper Corporation, Farnumsville, MA, USA
Food storage containers
Plastic
11.3 x ø 24.8 cm (green)
10.5 x ø 22 cm (orange)
8.3 x ø 18 cm (red)
7.6 x ø 16 cm (pink)
Vitra Design Museum

Gino Sarfatti, *No. 604 / Moon '69*, 1969
Arteluce, Milan (MI), Italy
Table lamp
Methacrylate, lacquered aluminum
40 x ø 60 cm
Vitra Design Museum

Eero Aarnio, *Pastilli*, 1967
Asko, Lahti, Sweden
Armchair
Glass-reinforced polyester
50 x ø 90 cm
Vitra Design Museum

Craig Kauffman, *Untitled # 1–7*, 1968–69
Acrylic lacquer on vacuum formed plastic
105 x 230 x 40 cm
Louisiana Museum of Modern Art

Ettore Sottsass, personal telephone for
Italian industrialist Giovanni Agnelli, 1953
Model
Plaster
11 x 25 x 20 cm
Private collection

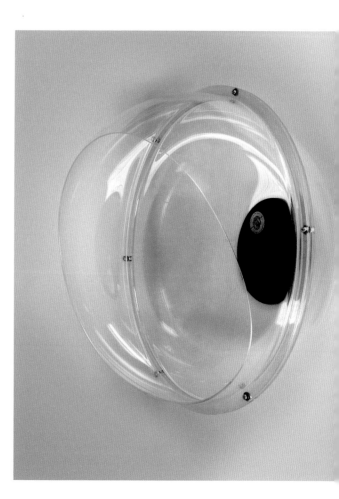

Eero Aarnio, *Bubble Chair*, 1968
Asko, Lahti, Finland
Hanging chair
Acrylic glass, chrome-plated tubular steel,
steel, leather cushions
76,5 x ø 107 cm
Vitra Design Museum

Öyvind Fahlström, *ESSO LSD*, 1967
PVC
89 x 127 x 14.9 cm
Moderna Museet
Gift of Pontus Hultén, 2006

Anonymous, *Telebox* telephone booth, 1972
Jachmann Technik, Germany
Plastic, metal
69 x 47 x 47 cm
Museum für Kommunikation Frankfurt

Claes Oldenburg, *Fagend Study*, 1968
Cast aluminium, hand-painted with enamel
25.4 x 47 x 17.8 cm
Louisiana Museum of Modern Art

Raymond Hains, *Seita*, 1970
Mixed media on wood
98 x 80 x 20 cm
Museu Colecção Berardo, Lisbon

**Studio DA (Cesare Casati,
Emanuele Ponzio)**, *Pillola*, 1968
Ponteur, Bergamo (BG), Italy
Floor lamps
Plastic, lead
55 x ø 13 cm (each lamp)
Vitra Design Museum

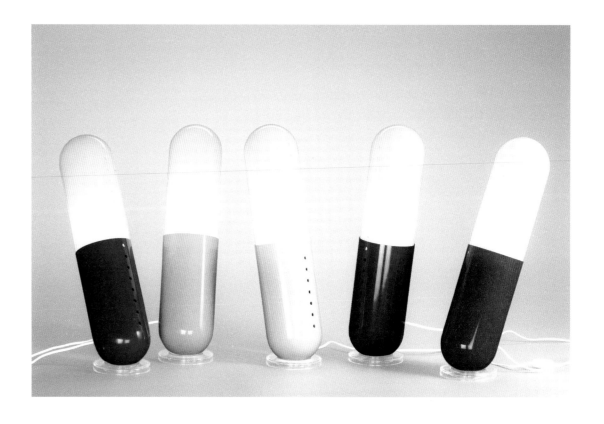

Konrad Klapheck,
Die Logik der Frauen, 1965
Oil on canvas
110 x 90 cm
Louisiana Museum of Modern Art
Gift of The Joseph and
Celia Ascher Collection, New York

Gaetano Pesce, *Moloch*, 1970–71
Bracciodiferro Srl, Genova (GE), Italy
Floor lamp
Photo: Aldo and Marirosa Ballo, Milan

The photograph is of the *Moloch* lamp's serial version and not
of the prototype exhibited in the *Pop Art Design* exhibition.
Aluminium, steel, ABS, glass
230 x 286 x 86 cm
Musée National d'Art Moderne, Centre Pompidou, Paris

Yonel Lébovici, *Fiche mâle*, 1977
Formes et Couleurs, Paris, France
Floor lamp
Polished aluminium
37 x 37 x 83 cm
Vitra Design Museum

George Nelson, Chrysler Pavilion at the
New York World's Fair, 1964–65

The pavilion shown in this photograph from
the George Nelson Archive was replicated
as an architectural model in 1:50 scale for
the exhibition *Pop Art Design*.

Studio 65, *Leonardo*, 1969
Gufram Srl, Balangero (TO), Italy
Seating combination (prototype)
Polyurethane foam, Guflac
60.5 x 266 x 198 cm
Vitra Design Museum

George Nelson, *Sergeant Schultz*, 1947
Koch & Lowy, Avon, MA, USA
Table lamp
Lacquered metal
16 x 17.5 x 14 cm
Mathias Schwartz-Clauss

Andy Warhol, *Mao*, 1972
Acrylic and silkscreen on canvas
209 x 147 cm
Louisiana Museum of Modern Art
Long-term loan
Museumsfonden af 7. december 1966

**Gruppo Strum (G. Ceretti,
P. Derossi, R. Rosso)**, *Pratone*, 1966
Gufram Srl, Balangero (TO), Italy
Sculptural lounge chair
Polyurethane foam, Guflac
95 x 140 x 140 cm
Vitra Design Museum

Martial Raysse, *Souviens-toi de Tahiti en septembre 61*, 1963
Plastic, textile and metal, phosphorescent spray paint, silkscreen on paper, mounted on veneer plinth
171 x 170 x 80 cm
Louisiana Museum of Modern Art

Claes Oldenburg, *Lunch Box*, 1962
Vinyl stuffed with kapok
15.9 x 38.1 x 40 cm
Louisiana Museum of Modern Art

Andy Warhol, *Cow Wallpaper*, 1966/1994
Silkscreen on wallpaper
The Andy Warhol Museum, Pittsburgh

André Cazenave, *Dorra*, 1971
Atelier A, Paris, France
Floor lamps
Fibreglass-reinforced polyester
40 x 60 x 55 cm (left)
13 x 25 x 22 cm (in front)
40 x 60 x 50 cm (right)
22 x 30 x 27 cm (not illustrated)
Alexander von Vegesack, Lessac

Achille and Pier Giacomo Castiglioni,
No. 220 / Mezzadro, 1954/1971
Zanotta spa, Nova Milanese (MI), Italy
Stool
Chromed steel, lacquered sheet steel, beech
52 x 49 x 53.5 cm
Vitra Design Museum

Andy Warhol, *Flowers*, 1970
Silkscreen print on paper
91.5 x 91.5 cm (each sheet)
Louisiana Museum of Modern Art

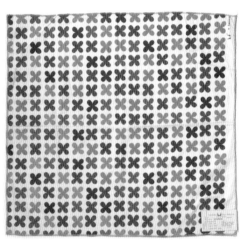

Alexander Girard, *No. 626–629 / Quatrefoil*, 1972
Herman Miller Fabrics, Zeeland, MI, USA
Fabric sample
Cotton
60 x 60 cm (each sample)
Vitra Design Museum

Charles and Ray Eames, *LAR*, 1950
Herman Miller Inc., Zeeland, MI, USA
Armchair
Fibreglass, steel wire, rubber
62 x 63.3 x 62.5 cm
Vitra Design Museum

Gunnar Aagaard Andersen,
Portrait of My Mother's Chesterfield, 1964
Dansk Polyether Industri
Polyurethane foam
83 x 134 x 110 cm
Designmuseum Danmark

Claes Oldenburg, *Soft Saw*, early 1960s
Muslin painted with spray enamel
81 x 17.5 x 4 cm
Moderna Museet
Gift of Pontús Hultén, 2005

Andy Warhol, *Silver Clouds*, 1966
Metallized polyester film, filled with helium
and oxygen
38 x 100 x 150 cm (each cushion)

The photograph is of the original installation
at the Leo Castelli Gallery, New York, 1966.

J. De Pas, D. D'Urbino, P. Lomazzi, C. Scolari, *No. 270 / Blow*, 1967
Zanotta SpA, Nova Milanese (MI), Italy
Inflatable armchair
Transparent PVC film
83 x 110 x 97.5 cm
Vitra Design Museum
Gift of the manufacturer

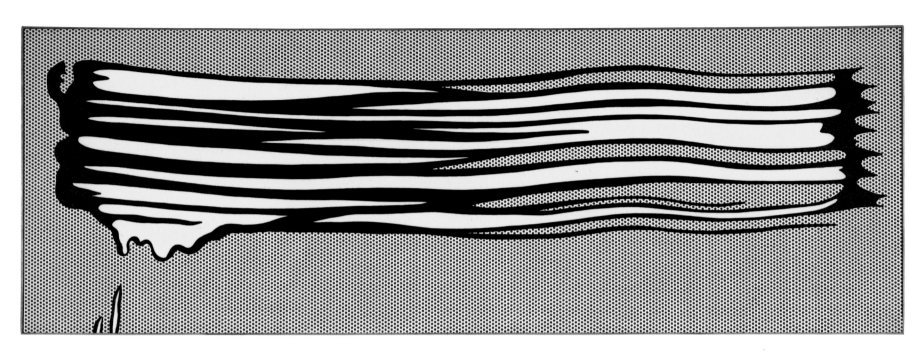

Roy Lichtenstein, *Yellow Brushstroke*, 1965
Oil and acrylic on canvas
93 x 276 cm
Private collection

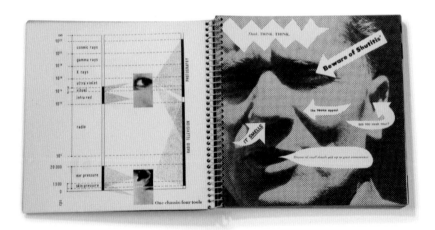

Richard Hamilton, double-page spread
of exhibition catalogue, *This Is Tomorrow*,
Whitechapel Gallery, London, 1956
Offset print
16.5 x 17
Vitra Design Museum

**George Nelson Associates, Inc.
(Irving Harper)**, *Marshmallow*, 1956
Herman Miller Furniture Company,
Zeeland, MI, USA
Sofa
Lacquered steel tubing, vinyl cushions,
aluminium
79 x 131.5 x 80 cm
Vitra Design Museum

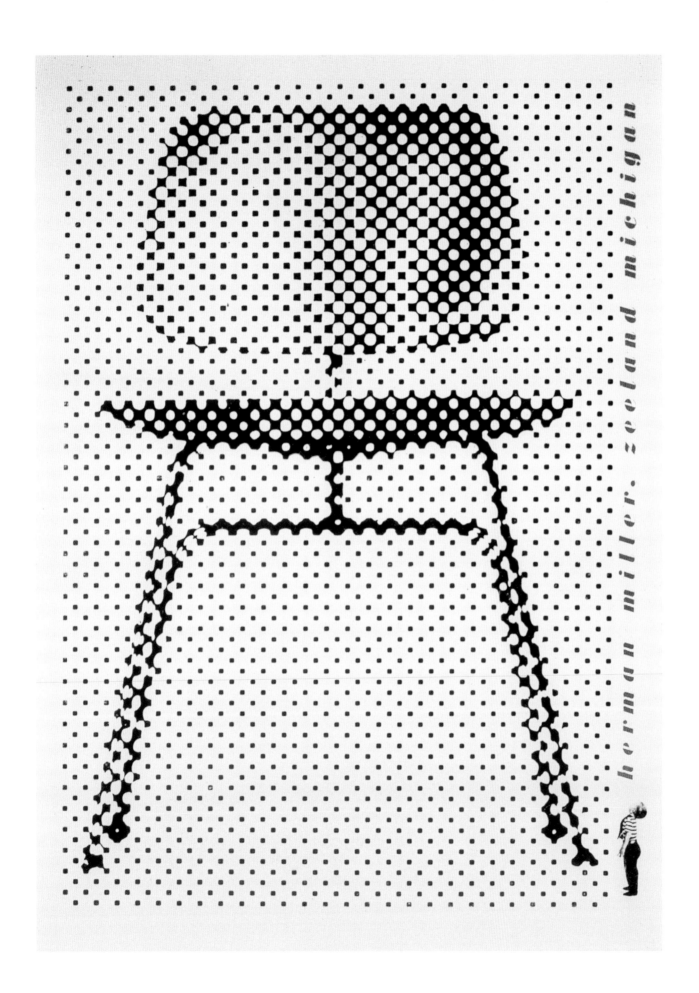

Ettore Sottsass, untitled, 1958
Il Sestante Gallery, Milan (MI), Italy
Plate
Enamel on copper
ø 30.5 cm
Museo Casa Mollino

Eames Office (Charles Kratka),
full-page advertisement, *DCM* chair by
Charles and Ray Eames for Herman Miller,
ca. 1950
Reproduction
Courtesy Eames Office

Peter Stämpfli, *Machine à laver*, 1963
Oil on canvas
130 x 154 cm
Museu Colecção Berardo, Lisbon

Herbert Hirche, *HF 1*, 1958
Braun oHG, Frankfurt am Main, Germany
TV receiver
92.6 x 54.2 x 45.8 cm
Vitra Design Museum

Andy Warhol, *Brillo Box*, 1964
Synthetic polymer paint and silkscreen
ink on wood
43.2 x 43.2 x 35.6 cm
The Andy Warhol Museum, Pittsburgh

Andy Warhol, *Marilyn Monroe*, 1967
Silkscreen print on paper
91 x 91.4 cm
Louisiana Museum of Modern Art

Verner Panton, *Living Tower*, 1969
Vitra/Herman Miller AG, Basel, Switzerland
Living landscape
Wood, foam rubber, fabric
200 x 200 x 67 cm
Vitra Design Museum

Studio 65, *Bocca*, 1970
Gufram Srl, Balangero (TO), Italy
Sofa
Polyurethane foam, Guflex fabric
85 x 209 x 81 cm
Vitra Design Museum

Ettore Sottsass, *Ultrafragola*, 1970
Mirror
Acrylic glass, mirror glass, neon strip lighting
197 x 100.5 x 14.5 cm
Vitra Design Museum

Tom Wesselmann, *Smoker Banner*, 1971
Hand-stitched vinyl
140 x 155 cm
Private collection, Siegen, Germany

Gaetano Pesce, *UP 5 & 6 / La Mamma / Donna*, 1969
Cassina & Busnelli, Novedrate (CO), Italy
Armchair with foot rest
Polyurethane foam, nylon jersey
92 x 117 x 137 cm (*UP 5*); ø 60 cm (*UP 6*)
Vitra Design Museum

Allen Jones, *Chair*, 1969
Polyester, leather, lambskin, artficial hair
79 x 59 x 99 cm
Vitra Design Museum

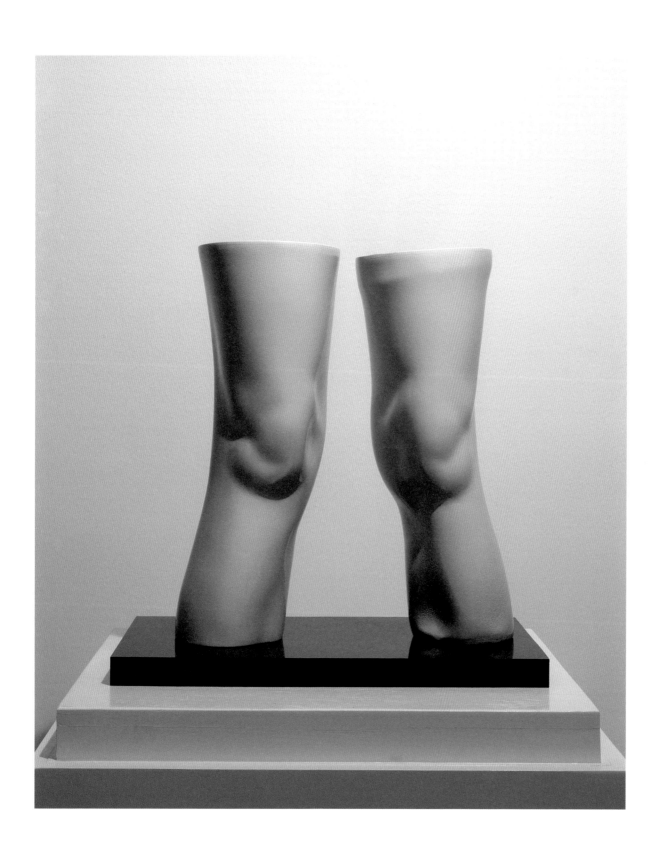

Claes Oldenburg, *London Knees*, 1966
Cast latex painted with coloured
polyurethane
38 x 41 x 27 cm (with black base)
ARoS Aarhus Kunstmuseum

Niki de Saint Phalle, *Lysistrata*, 1966
Model for a stage set
Plaster, paint
13.2 x 26.4 x 9.4 cm
Micky Tiroche Fine Arts, London

Gaetano Pesce, *UP 5 & 6 / La Mamma /*
Donna, 1969
Preliminary model (1:5)
Hard polyurethane foam, painted and lacquered,
brass
29 x 29 x 36 cm (*UP 5*); ø 14 cm (*UP 6*)
Vitra Design Museum

César, *Le grand pouce*, 1968
Bronze
183.5 x 103 x 83 cm
Louisiana Museum of Modern Art
Gift of the Louisiana Foundation

Gaetano Pesce, *UP 7 / Il Piede*, 1969
Sculptural seat
Polyurethane foam
80 x 65 x 165 cm
Volker Albus

Roy Lichtenstein, *The Temple*, 1964
Silkscreen
60.5 x 45 cm
The Israel Museum, Jerusalem
Gift of Daryl Y. Harnisch, New York, to
American Friends of the Israel Museum,
Jerusalem

Studio 65, *Capitello*, 1971
Gufram Srl, Balangero (TO), Italy
Armchair
Polyurethane foam, Guflac
78 x 110 x 120 cm
Vitra Design Museum

André Cazenave, *Tête d'Aphrodite*, 1970
Atelier A, Paris, France
Wall lamp
Synthetic resin
31.8 x 18.4 cm
Alexander von Vegesack, Lessac

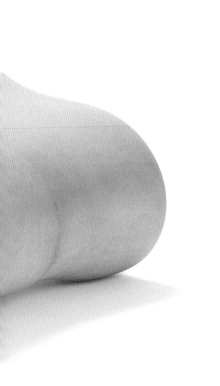

Alexander Girard, *No. 3025 / Brick* (from
the *Environmental Enrichment Panel* series), 1971
Herman Miller Textiles, Zeeland, MI, USA
Fabric panel
Printed cotton
221 x 134.5 x 0.3 cm
Vitra Design Museum

fig. 1
Claes Oldenburg, *Vacuum Cleaner*, 1964–71
Aluminium, vinyl, plastic, rubber, lightbulb, cord
162.6 x 73.7 x 73.7 cm
Private collection

Pop – The Dissolution of Art and Design

Mathias Schwartz-Clauss

fig. 1

fig. 2
Richard Hamilton, *Just what is it that makes today's homes so different, so appealing?*, 1956
Collage
26 x 25 cm
Kunsthalle Tübingen, Zundel Collection

fig. 3
Anonymous, catalogue title page, *Parallel of Life and Art*, Institute of Contemporary Arts (ICA), London, 1953

fig. 3

The Beginnings of Pop Art

The 1956 collage *Just what is it that makes today's homes so different, so appealing?* (fig. 2) by British artist Richard Hamilton has gone down in art history as the 'birth certificate' of Pop Art, its significance even equated with Pablo Picasso's *Les Demoiselles d'Avignon*, which had heralded the start of Cubism half a century earlier.[1] Pop Art may not have developed any differently in the absence of Hamilton's work, as Cubism without the *Demoiselles* would not have become a vastly different Cubism. Yet in its technique and choice of motifs, as well as in the circumstances of its genisis, *Just what is it* can shed light once again on one of the most influential artistic movements of the modernist era and vividly illustrate its relationship to the field of design.

Initially, the collage came about as a commissioned work with a given theme, purpose and deadline: it was to form the basis for a poster that was to accompany the exhibition *This Is Tomorrow* at London's Whitechapel Gallery. A trained artist and designer, Hamilton had joined forces with painter John McHale and architect John Voelcker to form one of twelve interdisciplinary teams of painters, sculptors, musicians, designers and architects contributing to the exhibition, which was organized by architecture critic Theo Crosby. Most participants were members of the Independent Group – a disparate consortium of intellectuals who had come together for previous exhibitions such as *Parallel of Life and Art* (1953) at London's Institute of Contemporary Arts (fig. 3) and *Man, Machine and Motion* (1955) at the Hatton Gallery in Newcastle. For *This Is Tomorrow*, each team was to design an installation, a promotional

fig. 2

poster and six pages of the exhibition's catalogue. As such, the poster was planned as a co-production and Hamilton initially discussed the envisioned character of the work with McHale. However the latter's extended visit to the United States impeded the collaboration and Hamilton eventually completed the work on his own.[2]

Thus, in as much as representatives of the applied arts and their multidisciplinary work practices were involved in the genesis of this Pop incunabulum from the outset, the motifs of the piece expressly confront the design of our daily living environment. *Just what is it* presents a stage-like interior with a couple provocatively displaying their half-naked bodies, as the outside world and the public look in and intrude on their privacy. Through the window, an American movie theatre marquee illuminates the room, a newspaper lies on the sofa and the television shows a woman chatting on the phone. At the top of the staircase leading down to the living room, the happy housewife – a repetition of the main female figure but in a different guise – vacuums the entryway with a spherical-shaped Hoover. Here, an arrow inscribed with a claim regarding the appliance's extra-long reach breaches the spatial illusion of the image and turns it into an advertisement. A lampshade in the background is decorated with the emblem of the car manufacturer Ford and the pattern of the carpet underneath recalls Action Painting of the sort Jackson Pollock had practised on canvases stretched out on the floor. A historical looking portrait hangs on the wall next to the oversized cover of a *Young Romance* comic book, showing an interior with characters talking in speech bubbles. The oversized lollipop with the label 'Pop' that the bodybuilder brandishes in front of his groin ambiguously points towards a tin of boiled ham at the exposed thighs of the posing Eve. In place of the ceiling, the room opens up to the infinite reaches of outer space with the bottom of the earth looming overhead.[3] Finally, a tape recorder prominently positioned in the foreground seems to be capturing the creation of this new environment, which amounts to a cacophony of disconnected self-representations with the slogan 'Pop' at its centre.

Hollywood, comics, superheroes, the car fetish, space travel and household appliances were the American novelties enthusiastically embraced in soot-encrusted Europe, first and foremost in Britain. At the time, Hamilton and his colleagues from the Independent Group systematically investigated the iconography of automotive styling, science fiction and advertising and studied *The Mechanical Bride: Folklore of Industrial Man* of 1951 in which Canadian communication theorist Marshall McLuhan warned about the platitudes and illusions of advertising: 'The public may smile at the suggestion that it need be perturbed at being the target for a barrage of corn flakes or light bulbs. But this industrial ammunition has the character of exploding in the brain cortex and making its impact on the emotional structure of all society.'[4] Yet the Independent Group did not necessarily see American advertising as an assault on reason. Architects Alison and Peter Smithson, for instance, were quite convinced of the potential contained in the popular iconography originating in America: 'Ordinary life is receiving powerful impulses from a new source. […]

We must somehow get the measure of this intervention if we are to match its powerful and exciting impulses with our own.'[5] Like the Smithsons, Hamilton shared this enthusiasm for industrial standards and, aside from the Ford emblem (an exaggerated and out-of-place decoration citing automobile styles that went out of fashion in America after only one year), he outfitted his interior not with useless junk but with objects that are as tuned for naked functionality as the bodies of the two protagonists: 'We resist the kind of activity which is primarily concerned with the creation of style', begins his statement in the catalogue that accompanied *This Is Tomorrow*.[6]

With their installation loudly marking the entrance to the exhibition, Hamilton's group created yet another collage that quoted from commercial and entertainment media (fig. 4): Oversized figures from street advertisements, such as that of Marilyn Monroe from the poster of the movie *The Seven Year Itch* (1955) or Robby the Robot from a billboard for the film *Forbidden Planet* (1956), and a giant Guinness beer bottle were paired with a continuously playing jukebox and a soft plastic carpet that when stepped on emitted a strawberry perfume. A postcard cliché completed this assemblage of quoted images, objects and scent: a reproduction of Vincent van Gogh's *Fifteen Sunflowers* – at the time, the top seller in the museum shop of London's National Gallery.

Yet the symbolism of this presentation and, in particular, of Hamilton's concentrated collage, signifying an artistic paradigm shift in which the quotation itself would eventually become the

fig. 4

fig. 5
Edward Hopper, *New York Movie*, 1939
Oil on canvas
81.9 x 101.9 cm
The Museum of Modern Art, New York
Anonymous gift

fig. 5

subject, was not recognized in professional circles until 1963 when – independent of the developments in England – Pop Art manifested itself as an artistic movement in the Unites States and assumed its name from a symposium held at the Museum of Modern Art in 1962. Soon thereafter, Hamilton's collage was retrospectively identified as a precursor of Pop.[7] Europe's passionate reception of the American way of life had already been refracted by America's own sober reflection of life's everyday dramas: Edward Hopper's paintings of man's alienation from his daily environment had long hung in museums (fig. 5), Robert Frank's photographic snapshots of everyday life were published internationally, and ubiquitous images in the media devalued the average existence of ordinary people, transforming it into mere imitation → p. 109. Already in 1950, even before the widespread breakthrough of television as a mass medium, an analysis of American mentality came to the following conclusion: 'Recreation came to be enjoyed vicariously. From playing games Americans took to watching them and then listening to them on the radio. Even enthusiasm ceased to be spontaneous and was artificially organized by cheer leaders. Men who enjoyed artificial adventures in the pages of mysteries or westerns, and women who acquired artificial complexions, found little difficulty in adopting artificial emotions: they turned to the radio and the movies for excitement and sensation, laughter and tears and learned about love from the magazines. There seemed to be, in short, a progressive atrophy of the creative instinct of the average American.'[8]

After the military victory of the Second World War, the economy of the United States redoubled its efforts to convince Western Europe and the rest of the world of the advantages of consumer society over communism. Commercial advertising had grown into an alluring, ahistorical superpower that – as understood by McLuhan – exerted a massive influence on the ideas and expectations of society. Companies gave themselves and their products a recognizable face and developed uniform corporate identities with memorable colour codes, typographies and logos in order to compete in expanding markets. Consumer goods that were needed less and less by society but were still to be desired, bought and used were presented as iconic objects in order to maximize visibility and recognition amidst the compressed time span of the entertainment media. Practical considerations, such as a product's extended shelf life, were drowned out by promises of carefree pleasure as eye-catching presence and readability became more central to the purpose of design.

Not only capitalism and communism but also advertising and art were ensnared in an arms race that had begun long before the war. Each of the disciplines ingeniously quoted the other's strategies and motifs and sought to outdo them. And in the early 1960s, 'when high-level mass advertising had adopted many of the strategies and inflections of modern art and was operating at an extraordinary level of sophistication, artists had to dig deeper to find motifs and styles that would distance their work both from the romance of art and from the slick visual cleverness of contemporary ads.'[9] Who better to do so than professionals that had worked in both disciplines like Richard Hamilton, Andy Warhol, James Rosenquist, Ed Ruscha and Gaetano Pesce? Finally, while youth and intellectual protests, internationally burgeoning terrorist movements and the first oil crisis questioned the authority and mechanisms of power and markets in the years between 1968 and 1974, advertising and art developed the vocabulary and grammar of their exchange to such an extent that 'it seemed that the alternatives to corporate, industrial and imperialist America had themselves turned into a colorful, nomadic, psychedelic cliché. Artists became popular figures in unprecedented ways, and links were established between their work and fashion, film and advertising, thereby spreading their influence further.'[10]

Quotation, Reality and Illusion

Meanwhile McLuhan's formulation 'The medium is the massage',[11] with its deliberately ambiguous misspelling of the word 'message', had shown practitioners of Pop Art that a quotation is only understood through a formal break with its context; only then can its actual intention become clear and an interpretation be made possible. McLuhan substantiated his reflections on the interpenetration of content and medium with a discussion of the equal readability of figure and ground – a phenomenon he derived from Gestalt psychology. The example of optical illusions, captivating the gaze by allowing alternating motifs to emerge from the image depending on the onlooker's perspective and to develop a dynamism of their own, found its correlation in such objects that appear as flat images. And indeed, the tilting of figure and ground, the reversal of image and means of representation and the morphing of two-dimensional image and three-dimensional object became central methods of both Pop Art and design for interchanging reality and illusion. Along these lines, Warhol's *Brillo Boxes* → p. 167 of 1964 are three-dimensional objects that are nevertheless composed of bold two-dimensional surfaces, which lose nothing of their flatness in object form but, on the contrary, serve to characterize the object as 'superficial' in both senses of the word. Tom Wesselmann's wall installations combining flat Colour Field paintings, photographic perspectives and insertions of real objects provoke a way of looking that continually oscillates between surface and space, while Ruscha's isolated words → p. 139 transform flat letters into three-dimensional blocks as they progress from left to right. Ettore Sottsass's chair *Malatesta* → p. 134 and his mirror *Ultrafragola* → p. 171, on the other hand, are three-dimensional objects constructed to appear from all angles as two-dimensional.

The constitution of an illusion of reality from various media and disparate elements is likewise a central theme in the works of Pop artist James Rosenquist. His 1961 painting *I Love You With My Ford* reads literally as an American response to Hamilton's *Just what is it ...* due to its quotation of the same media → p. 22: design (in the form of a symmetrical car grill in glossy chrome), photography (in the close-up of a woman's lips whispering in a man's ear), painting (with the enlarged spaghetti still life as a satirical comment on Pollock's drippings), music (the work's title being an adaptation of the song lyrics 'I want you, I need you, I love you with all my heart'[12]), film (in the vertical sequence of zoomed-in images in a widened cinematic format) and literature (with the construction of the picture plane from two adjoining canvasses, like the double-page spread of an open book). The strikingly dimensioned sections of the painted collage do not fit together to form a unified scene but rather co-exist in disconnected fashion, which only emphasizes their differences even further.[13]

At the time, Hamilton had already addressed the multimedia theme in yet another collage for *This Is Tomorrow*: a halftone photographic print of a talking face that underwent such enlargement that the dotted grid itself had become the image and on which arrows bearing inscriptions and pointing to the brain and to the five sense organs were affixed, drawing attention to various types and effects of communication → p. 164. Above all, however, this work seems implicitly aimed at the era's most popular medium – the television, which was imported from America and whose picture is a grid of individual points of light. It was the dissemination of this now-ubiquitous mass medium in the 1950s that first gave rise to a uniform popular culture in the United States. Not in a state of social communion but passive and isolated at home, television viewers perceived a reality defined by catchwords, advertising and make-believe whose million-fold multiplication in real time made their own reality pale in comparison – a method of opinion-building still very much in effect today.[14] In particular, commercial advertising was quick to understand how to exploit the tremendous power of persuasion offered by telegenically packaged messages. As a result, the consumer and media society of the 1950s aroused, more

fig. 7

than ever before, questions of how our image of the world takes shape, what is reality and what is imagination, what is genuine and what is artificial and, not least, how to generate an emotional attachment to a product. Precisely these questions preoccupied artists, designers and all others operating at the intersection of these disciplines.

Furniture as Art

Herman Miller, a medium-sized furniture company in Michigan that knew how to take advantage of the postwar construction boom, became a veritable melting pot for new design strategies by bringing together some of America's most creative minds and hands. As head of the company's design department, designer, architect and author George Nelson commissioned projects from independent designers such as Charles and Ray Eames, Alexander Girard and Isamu Noguchi, and these in turn provided the company

fig. 6

and its products with a language that adopted an almost postmodern approach in its heterogeneity while incorporating much of the flat, eye-catching imagery of print media. These designers shared an interest in the connections between art and technology, between tradition and modernity; in a mode of living that does not retreat from but rather opens up to the outside world; and, not least, in treating business as culture and culture as business.

The success of this strategy was personified by Charles and Ray Eames in their union as private and professional partners and

made manifest in their furniture. Now, over a half-century later, their creations still fit in with the times and, in this enduring quality, resemble the works of such Pop artists as Andy Warhol, Roy Lichtenstein and Robert Indiana. In the early 1950s, the Eameses developed the first plastic chairs for serial production as montages of evocative lines and coloured surfaces – an alphabet of signs and symbols that could be interchangeably combined in seemingly endless configurations: rocking chair runners evoking domestic cosiness; an Eiffel Tower chair base referencing the cult of technology; an organic seat shell abstracting the human torso; and 'bikini' padding for woven-wire seats quoting leisurewear. Their almost naked furniture pieces, made of moulded, dyed-through plastic surfaces, were placed in interiors like figures in an abstract painting – an aesthetic that could even be carried on outside since the pieces were also conceived for exterior use (fig. 7). The Eameses' interest in the visual impact of their furniture is further demonstrated by their incessant measuring of a design's effectiveness through photos of the individual development stages that Charles Eames took from various angles – only this sort of objectified image could confirm the success of a particular form.

As early as 1945/46, the Eameses demonstrated the readability of their plywood furniture by presenting it as two-dimensional images. In a solo exhibition at America's leading art museum, New York's Museum of Modern Art, which took place almost immediately after their work first appeared, a number of children's furniture pieces were

fig. 8
Roy Lichtenstein,
Magnifying Glass, 1963
Oil on canvas
16 X 16 inches

fig. 8

mounted on the wall and presented as a relief. In addition, a conceptual collage prepared for an exhibition at the Detroit Institute of Arts in 1949 shows that early on the Eameses had ceased to make formal distinctions between furniture, painting, sculpture and decor (fig. 6). The various elements equally occupy all levels of a stage-like exhibition space, while a colour scale along the right edge marks the transition to the spectators' area.[15] Consecrated in a museum setting, the furniture and its marketing were not only to change our way of living but also our perception of everyday objects, whose design was now recognized as an artistic achievement. Given their great commercial and media success, one can even presume an influence on the Colour Field school of painting that emerged in the United States during the 1950s, for the Eameses' designs anticipated in spirit the monochrome surfaces of Pop Art as did the paintings of Barnett Newman, Kenneth Noland or Hans Hofmann, under whom Ray Eames had actually studied. They also established an identity of thing and image similar to that of the later hermetic works of Jasper Johns, in which popular icons reflected the subject matter and its representation as objective object and subjective idea. Thus, before Pop Art made an icon out of consumer goods, designers like Charles and Ray Eames, manufacturers such as Herman Miller and institutions like the Museum of Modern Art had already popularized design as an autonomous art form.

Over the decades of their collaboration with the Eames Office staff, the couple increasingly concentrated their interdisciplinary interests and talents on communication design – on photography, film, multimedia lectures, books and exhibitions. Even the readability of their furniture as quotation-based allusions and its manufacturing process, which allowed continuous variation in the reproduction phase, had anticipated methods that would later become established in the fine arts – as Pop Art. In George Nelson's office, an ad was created that emphasized the furniture's proximity to art by affixing it with the label 'collector's item'.[16] An image designed by Charles

Kratka[17] in the Eames Office transformed an Eames chair into a graphic artwork by blowing up the raster of a photo of the chair to such an extent that it dissolves into an oversized apparition for the tiny tot standing next to it in the image → p. 165. 'Forms must first be made "illegible," in order to be "seen"', Nelson argued.[18] And in 1956, his employee Irving Harper conveyed this approach in an actual piece of furniture: the *Marshmallow* sofa, which adds a confectionery item magnified to gigantic proportions to the inventory of interior furnishings and is contemporaneous with Hamilton's lollipop in the art world → p. 164. The sofa's design can almost be seen as supplying a three-dimensional model for Roy Lichtenstein's trademark Ben-Day dots that would be developed some years later. Yet the concept that Nelson and Lichtenstein shared is that of the simultaneity of two parallel worlds: the one of real, existing objects and the other of the artificial and medial reproduction that makes them larger than life itself – like an inversion of the Polaroid system in which the camera spits out a miniaturized version of reality while the original still stands before it (fig. 8).[19]

Compared to figures like Nelson or the Eameses and due to their specializations and origins, Isamu Noguchi and Alexander Girard seem exotic outsiders in the circle of designers that worked for Herman Miller. The Japanese-American Noguchi was already a renowned sculptor when he began designing sculptural furniture for Herman Miller in 1944, establishing a link to Japan and its refined culture of daily life. The Italian Girard worked for Herman Miller as an expert on decor and atmosphere. With textiles inspired by Native American, Indian and Mexican motifs, he imported folk art into the modern interior at the same time that Warhol, having grown up in an Eastern European immigrant family, was creating a stir with his naïve drawings as a commercial artist in New York. Girard's achievements are less tangible than those of his colleagues, and his influence on design has long been neglected, as has the inspiration that Pop Art –

fig. 9
Achille and Pier Giacomo Castiglioni,
installation for ANIE, Rai,
15. Mostra Nazionale della Radio
(15th National Radio Exhibition),
Palazzo dell'Arte, Milan, 1948

fig. 10
Achille and Pier Giacomo Castiglioni,
installation for the Rai Pavilion,
36th Milan Trade Fair, 1958

fig. 11
Archille and Pier Giacomo Castiglioni,
installation for the Pesticides for Agriculture
Room of the Montecatini Pavilion,
33rd Milan Trade Fair, 1955

fig. 10

fig. 9

fig. 11

from Robert Rauschenberg or Peter Blake to Warhol and Judy Chicago – took from folk art, an anonymous, traditional and easily accessible mode of creation that actually knows no distinction between fine and applied art. Girard was also the first to use typography to ornament the surfaces of industrial products. He conceived vibrant patterns and colour combinations for home textiles long before the signalling effect of contrasting colours in Pop Art intensified into Op Art. In 1961 he provided the furnishings for one of the first theme restaurants – La Fonda del Sol → p. 88-89 in New York – in which colours, symbols and graphic forms of a nostalgic Mexico came together with industrial Eames furniture;[20] and in San Francisco he transformed a former brothel into a showroom for Herman Miller → p. 84-85 in which simple and straightforward design boldly liaisoned with florid decor.[21] With his steady disregard for the difference between high and low, Girard imbued sterile International Style interiors with a new, primal vitality.

A New Topography of Objects

A Similarly radical renewal could be found in European design of the 1950s and 1960s, especially in Italy, which learned of the developments in the United States via its architecture and interior design magazines – whose writers and editors were often active architects and designers themselves – much in the same way that Americans learned of the work being done in Europe.[22] As the country's trade show, media, design and fashion capital, Milan served as Italy's bridgehead to the international scene. The collaboration of locally anchored industry with traditional crafts and applied arts along with a flair for current trends produced a body of design work perfectly capable of holding its own in America – though not in terms of production numbers but certainly with regard to formal and technical innovations.[23]

Two of Milan's most imaginative and productive designers were Achille and Pier Giacomo Castiglioni. Their work was imbued with a deep distrust towards any and all forms of styling and with a high esteem for objects of daily use that unassumingly fulfil their function.[24] During the 1950s they attracted particular attention with their trade show stands in which they not only stylized and enlarged the articles they were promoting – practices that have always been a part of advertising – but also placed them in such a way that transformed the viewer's surrounding environment, similar to the monuments in the imagery of Giorgio de Chirico's *Pittura metafisica*. Even before, in 1948, they scored a coup when, as part of a national radio exposition, they affixed to the façade of Milan's Palazzo dell'Arte a mock-up of a construction site in which workers appeared to be installing a giant radio receiver, thus causing advertising to ironically comment on itself (fig. 9). In 1958, for yet another radio and television exposition, they built an exhibition stand in the form of an oversized pinball machine, and in publicity campaigns for the Montecatini chemical company (1955) and the Rai public radio service (1958) they contorted antennae and insects into giant creatures that, as they encroached upon viewers, made the whole scene look more like a war of the worlds than a show of civilian technology (fig. 10 and 11).[25] Similarly, at the first World's Fair of the postwar era, held in Brussels in 1958, André Waterkeyn used a method of extreme magnification to create his *Atomium*, a symbol for the peaceful use of nuclear energy, while Robert Brownjohn, Ivan Chermayeff and Thomas Geismar designed the American pavilion as a piece called *Streetscape*, in which advertising referenced itself in a jungle of shop logos and street signs (fig. 12).[26]

Thus, the transfer of widely practised advertising strategies into works of art by figures like Claes Oldenburg, James Rosenquist, Tom Wesselmann, Andy Warhol and Allan D'Arcangelo did not constitute a break with established viewing habits but rather continued the exchange of motifs and methods that had been going on between art and design for some time. Pop Art simply made explicit the already-occurring dissolution of the exclusive autonomy of art and artists and thus questioned art's elitist understanding of itself. In particular,

fig. 12

fig. 13
Allan D'Arcangelo, *US Highway 1*, 1962
Acrylic on canvas
121.9 x 139.7 cm
Smithsonian American Art Museum,
Washington DC
Purchase made possible by the American
Art Forum

fig. 14
Claes Oldenburg preparing the exhibition
Claes Oldenburg, Green Gallery, New York,
1962

fig. 13

fig. 14

figs. 15 and 16

it countered the then-prominent habitus of Abstract Expressionism, which was effusively celebrated as the predominant manifestation of freedom. Unlike this earlier movement, Pop Art has remained internationally successful up to the present day because it has retained its ability to capture the vitality stemming from a certain collective and, in the meantime, global perception – namely, the awareness of the loss of hierarchies and their substitution with the concept of equality, as well as of the necessity of embarking on a quest for one's own identity amidst the tangled thicket of media.

The same effect of an overwhelming immersion in another world, as evoked by the exhibition stands of the Castiglionis, was generated in the United States – albeit without a trace of critical irony – by the commercial strips documented in Las Vegas by Robert Venturi, Denise Scott Brown and Steven Izenour in 1965–66 and contemporaneously discussed by Eugene Smith in nationwide slide presentations under the title 'Why Ugliness – Why Not? It's the American Way' → p. 114. Perceived from the already intrinsically artificial space of the car, these shopping and amusement miles of the ever-sprawling cities of America appear like vast gaming machines in which the aim is to correctly construe the disjointed flashing signals and achieve a higher score than fellow competitors. But the view through the windshield is itself a two-dimensional view, and hence the commercial strip, just like every roadway sign, is oriented to the simultaneity of two- and three-dimensionality.

The *Highway* series that Allan D'Arcangelo began painting in the early 1960s reproduces this double impression of flattening and enlargement in clearly delineated fields of colour that recreate the car driver's field of vision using suddenly appearing, ever-growing, looming signals as points of reference (fig.13). Like the exhibition stands of the Castiglionis, these paintings thus address a state of attention triggered by media and mobility as well as a mode of perception shaped by the sudden and the unexpected: by the continuous shifting of perspectives,

proportions and questions of meanings and priorities that determines our reality far more than the notion of an unbroken illusionistic perpetuation of an unchanging world. Comparing, therefore, the advertising strategies of the Castiglionis with Claes Oldenburg's enlargements of everyday objects, which he exhibited in 1962 at New York's Green Gallery, for instance, or the perspectival distortion of furniture that appeared a year later in his *Bedroom Ensemble*, it becomes clear that Oldenburg's sculptures would have functioned perfectly well as highway advertising for a drugstore or in the shop window of a Fifth Avenue department store in Manhattan – even though they exaggerate the commodity in such a way that robs it of its originally intended attractiveness (fig. 14).

Confronting Oldenburg's soft sculptures and their almost human physicality and interior disposition with Gunnar Aagaard Andersen's *Portrait of My Mother's Chesterfield* of 1964 – a material experiment in which the inherent dynamics of polyurethane foam resulted in a portrait of a chair as well as a chair itself – clearly demonstrates the similar manner with which Pop Art and design engaged with the corporeal individuality of everyday objects. → p. 160-61. Moreover, the twofold readability of Andersen's chair is also instructive in its elucidation of design's key role between art and technology. During the heyday of Pop Art, the acceleration of technological development and mass communication propelled the ongoing contest between commercial design and artistic commentary, with representational strategies coming thick and fast and appearing simultaneously in both disciplines. Distinctions between them could only be made by labelling and framing; but both the label, especially the term 'Pop Art', and the frame, whether a picture frame or podium, were vigorously rejected by designers on a quest for true life and by artists in pursuit of the life of goods.

Already in 1957 the Castiglionis designed furniture that was a sculptural metaphor – manifestos in the form of assemblages of

fig. 17

anonymously designed objects of daily use, relating both to Marcel Duchamp's ready-mades and the images and objects from the beginnings of Pop Art, while simultaneously forging a similar linkage between the private and the public spheres. The *Sella* (Saddle) → p. 24 stool, conceived by the Castiglionis as a seat to lean on when talking on the phone and citing the bicycle as an Italian national fetish,[27] and their *Cacciavite* (Screwdriver) side table, with its screwed-in legs resembling oversized versions of its namesake, are indeed 'examples of "visual thinking"'[28] that lend the object a double meaning as symbol and device (fig. 15 and 16). Like the Eameses' furniture pieces, they address the very identity of object and image, of medium and message, that also marks Jasper Johns's paintings of the American flag collaged with newspaper cuttings or Lucio Fontana's slashes and Piero Manzoni's folds in canvas,

fig. 18

which at the time both artists began creating in Italy. The paintings and what they represent became one.

Cult and Artificiality   The respect for things with an intrinsic sense of purpose and a significance resembling that of magical icons was central also to the work of Ettore Sottsass, who had travelled from Italy to America in 1956 to work for several months in George Nelson's New York office. The commodity fetishism encountered by the designer on every street corner and in the media – which, according to Nelson, go hand in hand, bringing about a perpetual degradation of consumer goods that, in turn, pressures industry to strive towards

continuous improvement and thus promotes the common good by fuelling the economic cycle – ran up against his own conception of design as the formulation of a living relationship between things and their users. Throughout his career, Sottsass gave objects architectural forms in the same way that, in reverse, he stylized his architecture as an object. In both disciplines he thus transformed a functionality aimed at domination into a functionality favouring interaction (figs. 17 and 18).

Influenced by his travels to India in 1961, Sottsass heightened the relationship between object and user into a quasi-ritual relationship in which articles of daily use are stylized as shrines and everyday life is sublimated to cult status. A starker contrast than the one between underdeveloped India and industrial America can scarcely be imagined. In both countries, however, he discovered a fundamental commonality that formed the basis for his idea of a culture in which forms, colours and patterns are not merely superficial trappings but signals of an underlying message that constitutes things as symbolic participants in a cycle of growth and decay – a view reminiscent of Alexander Girard's interpretation of folk customs. As for the latter, the Eameses joined him in 1957 to make the short film *Day of the Dead* about the ephemeral artefacts of Mexico's All Souls' Day festivities – a colourful, frolicsome celebration of transience.[29] Thus, in the eye-catching surfaces and emblematic forms characteristic of the creations of all these designers, themes were formulated that over the course of art history would reappear as Pop Art: in Warhol's reproductions of

fig. 20
Advertising photographs for the beanbag
chair *Sacco* designed by Piero Gatti, Cesare
Paolini and Franco Teodoro, 1968–69

fig. 19

fig. 20

media clichés and Lichtenstein's comic strip art, as well as in Indiana's typographical numbers and words signs.

Such almost esoteric approaches seem diametrically opposed to the characteristic artificiality of Pop Art, which is often perceived as superficial or emotionless and cool; and yet the two phenomena belong to the same time period and are not as divergent as it might seem at first glance. In the 1950s and 1960s, artificiality increasingly became a topic of scientific deliberations, as expressed in the search for artificial materials, artificial intelligence and artificial environments. Able to go from a hard state of matter into a soft one, or vice versa, and fabricated in virtually any desired shape or colour (and even transparent), plastics allowed industry to develop products and applications that inundated the market with a veritable flood of new and affordable commodities: from the Eameses' fibreglass seat shells to the first monobloc chairs produced entirely from a single mould, and from Tupperware that preserves foods with an airtight seal to the Barbie doll, which was modelled after a comic strip character in the German tabloid *Bild* → p. 136, 139, 142. In particular, colours played a major role in shaping the period's typical aesthetic of intensive signs and signals, no longer applied on objects from the outside but now an integral part of the material, which in turn could be fully formed into the desired object.

For the field of design, this represented a challenge that was tackled most directly by Danish designer Verner Panton and later by the Italian Gaetano Pesce: 'The colour must fit the form and the material exactly, otherwise the product will be wrong; but this is seldom the case.'[30] The artificiality of plastic remained evident, but what seemed provocative and fake to a more staid generation was perceived above all by youth, increasingly wooed by the world of commerce, as an equally authentic and exciting expression of a new, progressively synthetic world. After all, it was youngsters and artists who frequently sought the stimulation of hallucinogenic,

synthetic drugs in their quest for freedom and intensive experiences. These substances likewise accompanied the emergence of political and social oppositions, which – like a still-malleable plastic – always seemed to formulate the opposite of what was embodied in the obsolete models of the past (fig. 20).

Thanks to the inventions of the 1950s and 1960s, the creation of artificial intelligence also moved within reach and continues today to be viewed by science and society alike as both a dream and a nightmare. Advances in electronics and automation spawned a plethora of modern devices that facilitated and interlinked work processes as well as public and private life in marvellous new ways. 'We humans are ever more conditioned by the presence of new structures, new horizons and new materials', wrote Sottsass in 1964 of the 'electronic landscape' that had taken shape over the course of just twenty years.[31] In particular, computer technology experienced rapid development and was deployed in ever-broader and more complex applications, even leading to the first academic conference on the creation of artificial intelligence, which took place at Dartmouth College in New Hampshire in 1956.

Already in 1953, the Eames Office took Claude Shannon's communication theory as the basis for a short film using graphics, photos, moving images and sound to simply and vividly explain how the precepts of data transmission could be applied to both direct oral and medial communication as well as to technology, architecture and art → p. 32. In 1957 the office made a film for IBM employing a cartoon format to give audiences at the Brussels World's Fair a better understanding of the processing of data by computers.[32] Commissioned in the late 1950s by the office machine manufacturer Olivetti to design the first Italian computer, the *Elea 9003*,[33] Sottsass departed from the sprawling monstrosities of conventional mainframe computers and packaged the elaborate room-filling electronics in compact cabinet-like housings that concealed all the technology inside and made only

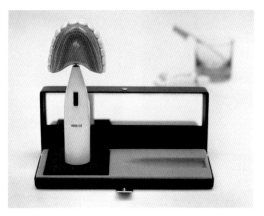

fig. 21

the coloured operational elements and the mechanically run data tapes visible → p. 33. The actual interface, however, was left to Tomás Maldonado of the Ulm School of Design, who was assigned the task of sorting the switches of the central console unit into clearly arranged groups. As information technology progressed, it apparently became harder and harder for individual product designers to convey its complex structures in a clear and orderly design. Thus, the electronic revolution that sparked a discourse on real and virtual worlds was already in full swing and has continued to influence society ever since.

Early on, the electronics manufacturer Braun, cooperating with the Ulm School of Design, had made a trademark of its radical expurgation of all hints of fashionable allure from design as well as its simplification of formal elements into clearly legible, functional symbols – underscored by a total abstention from colour – which became an example for the entire industry. The stringent formal reduction of electric razors, record players, radios and television sets into quasi three-dimensional pictograms, each stylized as an archetype of its category, created models that responded to the rapid consumption of the 1950s and 1960s with the promise of timeless reliability and soon became cult objects themselves. However, the image that Braun adopted for itself was not at odds with pop culture, as proven by the current-day success of Apple, whose product lines have unreservedly embraced and continued to develop Braun's design principles. Even Sottsass's charging of objects with a cult-like aura only theoretically opposes this conception, for like Braun's chief designer Dieter Rams, Sottsass was merely searching for formulations through which an object could convey its purpose in the most direct and convincing manner possible. Pop Art, too, held the functional design of everyday objects in high esteem and frequently rubbed shoulders with the discipline. The work of Richard Hamilton, an unabashed admirer of Rams's designs, is an excellent example of the 'irony of affirmation'[34] with which Pop Art tended to approach

the hype of a thoroughly styled everyday life (fig. 21). As he himself wrote, 'Domestic appliances, audio equipment, chairs, automobiles, planes, computers have been submitted to some of the best and most inventive minds of our time; for me to place the achievements of a few industrial designers above that of most practitioners in the fine arts implies a recognition of the fragile boundaries between specializations in the plastic arts today.'[35]

The advanced technology that had still seemed menacing during the Second World War was greeted with optimism during the economic boom of the 1950s. In light of the opposing power blocs of the Cold War, however, people still toyed with horror scenarios – in the realm of science fiction, for instance. The cinematic icon Robby the Robot thus exemplified a veritable invasion of tin robots, inspiring fantasies of omnipotence in the minds of many a young lad → p. 31. Especially in Japan, thousands of models were produced and sold to America and Europe.[36] Around 1950, the field of cybernetics also came to the fore as a science examining the relationships between human behaviour, message communication and decision and game theories. By the late 1950s, however, Eduardo Paolozzi's sculptures → p. 30 expressed serious forebodings about hybrids of man and machine, and human life itself increasingly came across as a product: in 1961, one year after the birth control pill was released onto the market in the United States, the experimental foundations for deciphering the genetic code were laid – a task which was eventually completed in 1966. At the same time, the achievements of highly specialized sciences and technologies loomed large in the public eye and an artificial world beyond the earth even appeared within reach after the Soviets catapulted the first satellite into space – and into the headlines – in 1957, followed by the first manned spacecraft in 1961. 'We are in pursuit of an idea, a new vernacular, something to stand alongside the space capsules, computers and throw-away packages of an atomic/electronic age,' wrote British architect Warren Chalk of the Archigram group in

1964, describing his architectural vision.[37] With his *Biosphère* → p. 223 created for the United States pavilion at the 1967 World's Fair in Montreal - a giant dome made of acrylic honeycomb cells within a steel frame – Richard Buckminster Fuller raised the idea of human settlement on the moon as an answer to the housing shortage.[38] Thus, the 1950s and 1960s were so saturated with artificiality that they could almost be seen as authentic again.

Collective Expressions

Meanwhile, there arose a creative counter-model to the conception of the modern artist as a lone wolf, particularly in the London-based Independent Group and in the interdisciplinary milieu of American composer John Cage in New York: namely, the collective. Although Pop artists certainly endeavoured to make their mark with personal styles, works like Jasper Johns's flags, targets and beer cans already exhibited a fundamental position of Pop Art in letting the artist disappear in a state of anonymity behind the mere reproduction or materialization of the image. Nevertheless – in keeping with the arguments of McLuhan – compositional and perspectival breaches like abrupt thematic shifts, excessive proportions and carelessly applied paint sought to make the quotation identifiable. Yet at the same time that Pop artists were making themselves invisible, in line with Marcel Duchamp's ready-mades and in antithesis to Abstract Expressionism, industrial products were being promoted with the name of the designer, whose signature on the label vouched for artistic authenticity. However, Pop Art did not view auteur design as representative of everyday life, and very few of its works depict objects that can be linked with the name of any specific designer. Instead, the images and objects almost exclusively present anonymous designs or objects reduced to the point of anonymity. Pop Art primarily availed itself of creative processes that were independent of the originating individual, thus mirroring what was common practice in the field of industrial design. The most famous examples of artistic teamwork from this period are certainly the Factory studios that Andy Warhol orchestrated in New York between 1962 and 1987 → p. 9. Paintings were created there on the basis of silkscreens, music and films were produced, and even a magazine was published. Earlier, Jasper Johns and Robert Rauschenberg had not only made art together but had also jointly produced shop window displays; John Cage had collaborated with Rauschenberg and choreographer Merce Cunningham in bringing fine art to the stage as performance with music and dance; and Allan Kaprow had organized his first happenings, which not only included numerous participating artists but also actively involved the audience.

fig. 22

The design offices of Nelson and the Eameses, however, had long before been working in interdisciplinary teams and had also collaborated with each other on a number of projects. The resulting synergy culminated in the project 'Art X'. Developed in 1953 by Nelson, the Eameses and Girard, this multimedia presentation on art as communication became a groundbreaking demonstration of the suggestive power unleashed by seemingly unrelated impressions

fig. 23
Saul Steinberg, drawing on a *LAR*
armchair by Charles and Ray Eames,
1950–52
Vitra Design Museum
Long-term loan Lucia Eames

fig. 23

from various media presented simultaneously or in rapid succession. The arts faculty at the University of Georgia had asked Nelson for a proposal on how to make instruction more efficient and effective. Nelson subsequently invited his colleagues to jointly demonstrate an enhanced method of instruction to the university. However, due to the geographic distance between them, they all had to prepare their parts separately. Thus, the unrehearsed presentation, consisting of lectures, films, slide shows, music and even olfactory effects coordinated by Girard, must have seemed like a wholly new type of *Gesamtkunstwerk* (fig. 22). But it was also a lesson, demonstrating how the industrial methods of united competences, prefabrication and technological reproducibility can be applied even to arts education.[39] Based on this experience, Nelson logically concluded that educational materials befitting a modern society should be prefabricated as a serial product: 'Find the great teachers in every area, squeeze them to the last drop, pour the precious distillate through a Mitchell camera and put the results in a million cans. It certainly is an application of the industrial method. What, if anything, is wrong with it?'[40] With his multiplication of images showing a soup can with various contents, Andy Warhol essentially did just that in his Factory: art became a product compatible with the masses.

The declared educational goal of the experimental lesson at the University of Georgia was to cross the boundaries between the disciplines in order to foster the intuition and promote an understanding of the surrounding environment. When the Eameses were commissioned by the United States government to provide visitors to the 1959 American National Exhibition in Moscow with insights into everyday American life, they adopted a similar approach since the task at hand involved encouraging communication across borders: lifting the Iron Curtain and suggestively acquainting the Soviets with the advantages of a free market economy. Beneath a geodesic dome designed by Buckminster Fuller, they simultaneously projected over 2,200 photos and a good

many film clips on seven screens, accompanied by voiceovers and specially composed music → p. 110. Viewers were bombarded with this rapid-fire succession of images entitled *Glimpses of the USA*.[41] Yet the climax came in a short clip from Billy Wilder's *Some Like It Hot* in which Marilyn Monroe flirtatiously winks at the camera. While the American star was scarcely known to the local audience, the scene invariably set off storms of applause at each showing. Even if only visible for a few brief seconds, the gesture and Monroe's face spoke a direct and unequivocal language.[42]

With Marilyn's seductive, well-proportioned features, the stereotype of feminine beauty was brought to life. The use of this face – the same visage that Andy Warhol would stylize into a pop icon par excellence after Monroe's death in 1962 – is entirely typical of the exploitation of women in advertising and design. Although the streamlined female form dominated product design already in the 1930s, it was American design of the 1940s and 1950s that really heated up the cult of commodities with its 'sex sells' effect. The curving form also had its technical advantages, being optimally suited for fabrication in sheet metal and plastics – the materials from which the surfaces of many consumer goods were produced – as well as for the minimization of a vehicle's air resistance. Viewed in this light, the fibreglass furniture designs of Charles and Ray Eames – forerunners of the monobloc chairs – are mere shells. Their female contours enticed the cartoonist Saul Steinberg, a friend of the Eameses, to create a telling combination of furniture and caricature in which he drew a naked seated female figure directly onto the surface of a fibreglass chair (fig. 23).

The Conflation of Public and Private

It almost seems an irony of fate that, of all things, the omnipresent visual media are those responsible for our persistent conception of Pop Art as consisting of two-dimensional works. True, it is principally concerned with images that change our perception of reality, but Pop

fig. 24
David Hockney, *Tea Painting
in an Illusionistic Style*, 1961
Oil on canvas
232.5 x 83 cm
Tate, London

fig. 25
Edward Kienholz, *Roxys*, 1960–61
Installation of a brothel (detail)
Mixed media

fig. 24

fig. 25

Art is also an integral part of a culture that explores the full range of disciplines – from painting, sculpture and design through music, film and theatre to literature – as well as the spaces between them and does so with a success unrivalled by any other art movement of the twentieth century. The ambivalence of simultaneously being image and object, for example, is also found in the mixed media combination of numerous Pop Art works in which the flat image support is coupled with three-dimensional elements and thus becomes an object itself: as a shaped canvas like David Hockney's *Tea Painting in an Illusionistic Style* (fig. 24) of 1961 or as an enlargement of a two-dimensional object with a diversity of surfaces as in the case of Warhol's matchbooks of 1962.[43] However, it seems that sculpture was especially suited to represent a few central motifs of Pop Art. First and foremost, it was dedicated to our relationship with everyday objects and commodities as well as to the problem of the private sphere being made public, or the public sphere invading the private one – a problem which Hamilton's collage addressed a full half-century before the advent of blogs, Facebook and Twitter. In sculpture, a medium predestined for the public sphere, Pop Art formulated its most explicit critiques of society's ills.

One of the most prominent and productive representatives of this genre is Claes Oldenburg, who had taken up provocative positions similar to Edward Kienholz, George Segal and Duane Hanson (fig. 25). Oldenburg's sculptures and his written comments oscillate between affirmation and criticism of consumer and media society, similar to the fluctuating positions of his painting comrades.[44] Like the Castiglionis, he was interested in the banal, anonymous object of daily use, untouched by the styling of advertising. At the same time, his monumental works for cities and parks deliberately invert

fig. 26

our notions of mastery over an object. In most cases, he populated the public space with personal consumer items, interpreting it as the private sphere's surrealist realm of action: 'Scale – the relation between minor thing and major formats – was central to almost everything Pop art explored.'[45] Yet while the distortion of this scale as a means of irony served to inflate banal objects into monuments, it could simultaneously do vice versa: mock heroic tributes. In the field of design, only few took these sorts of liberties. George Nelson was certainly a pioneer who pushed the boundaries when, just two years after the war, he designed the bedside table lamp *Sergeant Schultz* with a small steel helmet serving as a lampshade → p. 153.

Oldenburg's characteristic emphasis on the corporeality of objects is thrown into sharp reverse with his design of the monumental sculpture *London Knees* → p. 174, which isolates a section of the human body as an object. A pair of knees underneath an imagined miniskirt (whose demonstrative absence only heightens the provocation of the short hemlines with which the London-based Mary Quant revolutionized fashion at the time) comprises a giant object of voyeuristic desire. While such explicit representations of the human body are the exception in Oldenburg's oeuvre, erotic body parts are an otherwise entirely typical Pop Art motif. On the face of it, it seems to articulate the exploitation of sexuality by advertising and product design and express the concomitant loss of personal integrity. At the same time, however, it reveals the increasing indiscretion with which the postwar media thrust private details into the public spotlight. Even in artistic circles, private predilections were increasingly monitored amidst the widespread surveillance of politics and business, especially during the McCarthy era. Jasper Johns's *Target With Plaster Casts*, arraying plaster casts of mouth and nose, ear, hand,

fig. 27
Saul Bass, cover for the catalogue of the first annual exhibition of the Society of Contemporary Designers, Los Angeles, 1950

fig. 28
Andy Warhol, *Marilyn Monroe's Lips*, 1962
Diptych
Synthetic polymer, silkscreen ink and pencil on canvas
210.7 x 415 cm
Hirshhorn Museum and Sculpture Garden, Smithsonian Institution
Gift of Joseph H. Hirshhorn, 1972
Photo: Lee Stalsworth

fig. 27

foot, heel, nipple, penis and bone over a bull's eye target as if they were shooting gallery figures, can unmistakably be read in this context as a commentary on the persecution to which Johns and other homosexual artists of the period were subjected → p. 205.

On the other hand, the private and intimate domain was also sometimes made public as part of a strategic offensive. The exhibitionism of home stories, with which pop culture celebrities presented themselves in order to seem more approachable to their fans, was already prevalent in the 1940s and 1950s. Designers, too, took advantage of this form of editorial advertising, showing how they lived with their designs in their own homes. But it was also society itself and particularly youth who exposed themselves in order to break away from the mores of the pre-war generation from which they felt alienated (fig. 26). As commercial advertising sought to offer visions for this liberated yet undecided subset of consumers, the conditions for exerting an influence on their personal preferences could not have been better. And while the sadomasochistically packaged female figures in Richard Lindner's paintings or Allen Jones's functional sculptures push sexual role-play to an ironic extreme → p. 173, the exposed genitals in Tom Wesselmann's *Nudes* and *Seascapes* no longer come across so unequivocally as symbols of a lost personality. Similarly, Warhol's reproduction of Marilyn's smile, resembling the multiple printing of a photograph of a pair of eyes that graphic designer Saul Bass had conceived as a cover motif, leaves open the question of whether it is an homage to the sex icon, a caricature that literally ridicules her or a menacing threat in its incessant reproduction (figs. 27 and 28).

Yet the shifts in meaning to which the private sphere was subjected, from advertising through artistic criticism to satire, were not reflected in design until the late 1960s. The symbolism of the clichés, which thanks to plastics technology could now be translated into three-dimensional objects, was already in place and ensured that iconic works like the *Bocca* sofa, overtly quoting art history from the

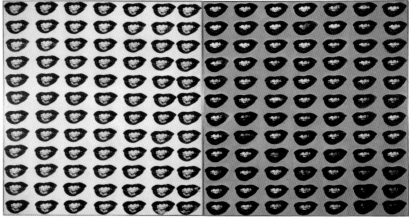

fig. 28

Surrealism of Dalí to the Pop Art of Warhol, essentially marketed themselves → p. 170. Yet there were also designs with a critical underlying tone that nevertheless found willing and courageous producers – Gaetano Pesce's chair *La Mamma (Donna)*, for instance, which stylizes a woman chained to a ball as a 'prisoner of herself' → p. 172.[46]

Endless Pop

In the first two decades after the war, it was art that took on motifs and strategies of design in order to investigate a reality shaped by consumption and media. From the mid-1960s, however, design in general, and Italian design in particular, increasingly sought to demonstrate its proximity to Pop Art, the dominant art movement of the time, and create objects wholly dedicated to the image and its message. The themes remained the same but the relationships and signs had changed: Without Lichtenstein's antique ruins as a medially regurgitated cliché → p. 178 or Oldenburg's enlarged and drooping product sculptures, a soft chair consisting of a capital lying on the floor would have been inconceivable. Likewise, without monumental ice cream cones or huge vacuum cleaners (fig. 1), there would presumably be no gigantic plastic lawn sold as a play and lounge surface for the living room → p. 154. With its artistically sublimated motifs and strategies, design of the 1960s and 1970s borrowed an image of Pop Art that fluctuates opaquely between commodity cult and commercial critique. Meanwhile, those artists who knew how to market themselves became rich stars, whose works are held in public collections or have become the property of a happy few. Particularly in Italy, the traditional role of the designer as a mediator between art and everyday life was transformed into that of a sculptor of multiples for wealthy and educated buyers whose correspondingly spacious apartments were adorned with works of art to match.

Traced in this overview less in chronological terms than through a thematic kaleidoscope, the reciprocal relations between Pop Art and design continue to prevail even in the present. Yet in the period between the mid-1950s, when art developed into Pop Art by adopting design strategies, and the late 1960s, when design re-appropriated the same strategies, the spiral in which this dialogue of disciplines circulates had turned full circle. Even today, its facets still dazzle us, not least because the terms 'Pop Art' and 'design' themselves have become catchwords the world over and impart much less insight than image.

Patrick Caulfield's 1972 painting *Dining Recess* provides a striking example with its depiction of a room containing a tidy yet lonesome ensemble of Eero Saarinen's *Tulip Chairs* of 1956 with the accompanying table → p. 131. The sculptural elegance of this group does not quite fit in with the room's rustic panelling, and yet it all seems quite natural. Outside it is dusk and the room is almost dark. Hanging over the middle of the table, the bright round circle of a pendant lamp cuts through the flatness of the painting like a peephole opening up for the viewer. As in Roy Lichtenstein's early work *I Can See the Whole Room! … and There's Nobody in It!* (fig. 29), which changed hands in late 2011 for more than 43 million dollars, it is up to us to let reality into the image and allow the image itself to become real. At the end of an era in which art and design changed our image of the world, and at the beginning of a new epoch in which the seeming contradictions between the two have been solved, we – the observers of this scenario – are waiting to see what unfolds.

★

fig. 29

1 See John-Paul Stonard, 'Pop in the Age of Boom: Richard Hamilton's *Just what is it that makes today's homes so different, so appealing?*', *The Burlington Magazine* 149, no. 1254 (September 2007), 607–620. Stonard's article provides a comprehensive, highly informative analysis of the work.

2 Assisted by his wife Terry and by Magda Cordell, Hamilton used ads, comics and articles from American magazines presumably supplied by McHale as the basis for the collage. See ibid., 609.

3 As shown by Stonard, the segment of the earth that appears along the top edge of the poster is not an image taken from outer space but a collage of various aerial photographs, the fact being that the first satellite did not go into orbit until 1957. See ibid., 615–16.

4 Marshall McLuhan, *The Mechanical Bride: Folklore of Industrial Man* (New York: Vanguard Press, 1951), 34.

5 Alison and Peter Smithson, 'But Today We Collect Ads', *Ark*, no. 18 (November 1956): 49.

6 Richard Hamilton, statement in Theo Crosby, ed., *This is Tomorrow*, exhibition catalogue (London: Whitechapel Gallery, 1956), unpaginated.

7 Jasia Reichardt, 'Pop Art and After', *Art International* 7, no. 2 (25 February 1963): 42–47.

8 Henry Steele Commager, *The American Mind: An Interpretation of American Thought and Character Since the 1880's* (London: Oxford University Press, 1950), quoted in George Nelson, *Problems of Design* (New York: Whitney Publications, 1957), 67.

9 Kirk Varnedoe, 'Advertising', in Adam Gopnik and Kirk Varnedoe, eds., *High & Low: Modern Art, Popular Culture*, exhibition catalogue, (New York: Museum of Modern Art , 1990), 335.

10 Mark Francis, *Pop*, rev. ed. (London: Phaidon, 2010), 160.

11 McLuhan's observation that every medium imbues its content with a specific attitude is summed up in the title of his 1967 book *The Medium is the Massage: An Inventory of Effects*, written together with the graphic designer Quentin Fiore (New York: Bantam). The title actually goes back to a misprint of the word 'message'. McLuhan adopted it to underscore the physical and psychological effects of media and lend force to his thesis that 'the medium is the message', which soon became a catchphrase itself, threatening to diminish its originality and persuasiveness.

12 In May 1956, Elvis Presley's version of 'I Want You, I Need You, I Love You' became a hit.

13 'Collage is a very contemporary medium, whether it's done with little bits of paper or in the cinema. The essence of collage is to take very disparate imagery and put it together and the result becomes an idea, not so much a picture. It's like listening to the radio and getting your own idea from all these images that are often antidotes – acid – o each other.' (James Rosenquist, quoted in Julia Blaut, 'James Rosenquist: Collage and the Painting of Modern Life', in Sarah Bancroft and Walter Hopps, eds., *James Rosenquist: A Retrospective*, exhibition catalogue, The Menil Collection and The Museum of Fine Arts Houston et al. [New York: Solomon R. Guggenheim Museum, 2003], 17.)

14 Communication science uses the term 'dispersed audience' to describe this phenomenon. This audience 'exhibits no specialization of roles and has no custom or tradition, no codes of behaviour or rites, and no institutions.' (Gerhard Maletzke, *Psychologie der Massenkommunikation: Theorie und Systematik* [Hamburg: Hans-Bredow-Institut, 1963], 30).

15 A similar approach was followed by Friedrich Kiesler, who caused a sensation in Europe with his experimental stage designs in the 1920s and published the book *Contemporary Art Applied To The Store And Its Display* (New York: Brentano) in the United States in 1930. Described as design's 'bad boy' (Elaine De Kooning, 'Design's Bad Boy', *Architectural Forum* 86, no. 2 [February 1947]: 88–89), the multi-talent was also an important link between the European and American avant-garde and in 1954 exhibited his *Galaxy* works, combining paintings and installations, at New York's Sidney Janis Gallery (which was later instrumental in promoting Pop Art).

16 In 1948 George Nelson introduced the term 'collection' to Herman Miller's advertising strategy with the first furniture catalogue he oversaw since joining the company in 1945.

17 Kratka began working at the Eames Office as a graphic designer in 1947. See Marilyn Neuhart with John Neuhart, *The Story of Eames Furniture* (Berlin: Gestalten, 2010), 154–161.

18 Nelson, *Problems of Design*, 70.

19 Polaroid released the first instant camera onto the market in 1948.

20 The uniforms of the La Fonda del Sol staff were designed by Rudi Gernreich whose colourful, boldly patterned fashion designs had already been featured in press photographs taken in the Eames House in the 1950s.

21 Girard 'out-Victorianed his uninhibited predecessors with an application of gold leaf and blue, crimson, and violet paint that would make them swoon with envy'. ('Barbary Coast: Girard Designs a New Herman Miller Showroom', *Interiors* 118, no. 7 [February 1959], 87.)

22 The most successful publication in this regard was the internationally distributed journal *Domus*, which primarily reported on architecture, art and design in Italy but also gave equal coverage to developments around the world. The estate of Charles and Ray Eames, for instance, contains a nearly complete set of all issues from 1946 to 1970.

23 For instance, employees of the Pirelli tire company and furniture makers in the Brianza region joined together to form Arflex, the company that produced the first furniture upholstered with foam rubber based on the designs of architect Marco Zanuso.

24 Their extensive collection of such objects attests to the esteem in which they held them and which they shared with such Pop artists as Jasper Johns, Claes Oldenburg and Jim Dine.

25 The exhibition pavillon for Montecatini promoted chemical insecticides. For further information on these projects, see Sergio Polano, *Achille Castiglioni: Complete Works, 1938–2000* (London: Phaidon, 2002).

26 'Exaggeration has always been part of the American tradition.' (Nelson, *Problems of Design*, 51) This statement no doubt applies to Italy with equal weight.

27 The pink stand supporting the bicycle seat refers to the jersey worn by the rider with the fastest overall time in the Giro d'Italia. The designs of the Castiglionis, which were presented in 1957 at the *Colori e forme nella casa d'oggi* (Colours and forms in the home of today) exhibition in Como, did not go into serial production until many years later, manufactured under the names *Sella* and *Mezzadro* by the Zanotta company.

28 Polano, *Achille Castiglioni*, 9.

29 *Day of the Dead*, directed by Charles and Ray Eames with Alexander Girard (Santa Monica: Eames Office, 1957), film (15 minutes, colour).

30 Verner Panton, interview by Barbara Til, in Wolfgang Schepers, ed., *'68 Design und Alltagskultur zwischen Konsum und Konflikt*, exhibition catalogue, Kunstmuseum Düsseldorf and Galerie Karmeliterkloster Frankfurt am Main (Cologne: DuMont, 1998), 42.

31 Ettore Sottsass, 'Paesaggio elettronico', *Domus*, no. 381 (August 1961), 39.

32 *The Information Machine: Creative Man and the Data Processor*, directed by Charles and Ray Eames (Santa Monica: Eames Office, 1957), film (10:01 minutes, colour).

33 Sottsass worked with Hans von Klier and Andries van Onck on the project, which was completed in 1959.

34 With the term 'irony of affirmation', Hamilton quoted Marcel Duchamp's comments on *The Bride Stripped Bare by Her Bachelors, Even*, a collection of drafts and sketches from 1915 to 1923 for his piece *The Large Glass*, that Hamilton had reconstructed for a Duchamp retrospective held in 1966 at the Tate Gallery in London. See Richard Hamilton, 'concept/technology > artwork', in Bo Nilsson, ed., *teknologi, idé, konstverk—Richard Hamilton*, exhibition catalogue (Stockholm: Moderna Museet, 1989), 22–24.

35 Ibid., 22.

36 See Jacques Goimard, 'Eux les robots', in Dorothée Charles, ed., *Robots: Collection Rolf Fehlbaum*, exhibition catalogue, Fondation Cartier pour l'Art Contemporain Paris (Arles: Actes Sud, 1999), unpaginated.

37 Warren Chalk, 'Living City', Amazing Archigram, 4, 'Zoom' issue, 1964, as quoted in Beatriz Colomina, 'Escape from Today', in Jochen Eisenbrand and Alexander von Vegesack, eds., *Open House: Architecture and Technology for Intelligent Living*, exhibition catalogue, Zollverein Essen et al. (Weil am Rhein: Vitra Design Museum, 2006), 243.

38 Colomina, 'Escape from Today', 243.

39 There are strong paralells between this presentation, which Nelson called 'Art X' and the Eameses named 'A Rough Sketch for a Sample Lesson for a Hypothetical Course', and the lectures and exhibitions of the Independent Group from the same period. It is not clear when Alison and Peter Smithson became acquainted with the Eameses. In 1955, however, *A Communications Primer* was shown at the London Institute of Contemporary Arts, while the poster that the Smithsons and their group made for *This is Tomorrow* shows Peter Smithson and Nigel Henderson demonstratively sitting on Eames chairs in the middle of the street in a petty-bourgeois residential neighborhood. In 1956 an article by art critic and Independent Group member Lawrence Alloway mentioned the 'Art X' project as well as the film *A Communications Primer* (Lawrence Alloway, 'Eames' World', *Architectural Association Journal*, July/August 1956, 55).

40 Nelson, *Problems of Design*, 81.

41 The tremendous success of *Glimpses* can be compared to that of the exhibition *The Family of Man*, curated four years earlier by Edward Steichen together with Robert Frank and presenting over 500 photographs of living conditions in 68 countries around the world. It was 'perhaps the most successful of all MoMA exhibitions', in which each of its nine million visitors could feel like 'a member of a universal humanity' (Mary Anne Staniszewski, *The Power of Display: A History of Exhibition Installations at the Museum of Modern Art* (Cambridge, MA, and London: MIT Press, 1998), 293.

42 See Pat Kirkham, *Charles and Ray Eames: Designers of the Twentieth Century* (Cambridge, MA, and London: MIT Press, 1995), 323; Beatriz Colomina, 'Enclosed by Images: The Eameses' Multimedia Architecture', *Grey Room*, no. 2 (Winter 2001), 6–29.

43 In their double role as a medium for images and advertising as well as a worthless, throwaway functional object, matchboxes and matchbooks were a frequent motif of Pop Art. In his matchbooks, Warhol used sandpaper to imitate the striking surface used for lighting the matches.

44 'I am for Kool-art, 7-UP art, Pepsi-art, Sunshine art, 39 cents art, 15 cents art, Vatranol art, Dro-bomb art, Vam art, Menthol art, L&M art, Ex-lax art, Venida art, Heaven Hill art, Pamryl art, San-o-med art, Rx art, 9.99 art. […] I am for the art of things lost or thrown away, coming home from school. I am for the art of cock-and-ball trees and flying cows and the noise of rectangles and squares. I am for the art of crayons and weak grey pencil-lead, and grainy wash and sticky oil paint, and the art of windshield wipers and the art of the finger on a cold window, on dusty steel or in the bubbles on the sides of a bathtub. […] I am for U.S. Government Inspected Art, Grade A art, Regular Price art, Yellow Ripe art, Extra Fancy art, Ready-to-eat art, Best-for-less art, Ready-to-cook art, Fully cleaned art, […] tomato art, banana art, apple art, turkey art, cake art, cookie art.' (Claes Oldenburg, 'Store Days', quoted in Suzi Gablik and John Russell, *Pop Art Redefined* [New York and Washington: Praeger, 1969], 97–99).

45 Varnedoe, 'Advertising', 351.

46 Gaetano Pesce, quoted in Mario Mastropietro, 'Gaetano Pesce: Progetti n. 34, 44. Serie di imbottiti, UP', in *Un' Industria per il Design* (Milan: Lybra Immagine, 1984), 212.

Mutations of Pop

Marco Livingstone

fig. 1
James Rosenquist, *President Elect*, 1960–61
Oil on masonite
226.1 x 505.5 cm
Musée National d'Art Moderne, Centre
Georges Pompidou, Paris

fig. 1

fig. 2

P op Art has almost as many definitions as the number of artists around the world to whose work the label has been attached. Often claimed a quintessentially American phenomenon, its earliest manifestations occurred simultaneously and independently in Britain and the United States and were quickly echoed around Western Europe. Some purists delimit it to the period between 1961 and 1964; that is, from just before the word 'Pop' became the preferred term for describing this new development, rooted in postwar consumer society, that occurred in representational painting, sculpture and printmaking,[1] to just after the assassination of President John F. Kennedy (the icon of the era, fig. 1) – an event that cast the first of many dark shadows over an initially optimistic decade. A more dispassionate observer, however, would claim that Pop Art continued to develop and mutate in many forms over the next few decades through the work of dozens of artists in an increasing number of countries as far afield and culturally distinct as Australia, Japan, Latin America and even Communist Eastern Europe.[2] Having gone somewhat out of fashion during the 1970s, despite the ever more substantial reputations of some of its main practitioners, it came back with a vengeance during the 1980s, as the first of several new generations of artists looked back to it for inspiration. And even in the very pluralistic climate of early twenty-first century art, when belief in a dominant style or tendency has long given way to a preference for a multiplicity of modes, Pop continues to be a force to be reckoned with.

There are, however, additional factors that complicate any attempt to summarize the ebb and flow of Pop from its first stirrings in the mid-1950s to its most current formulations. While some of the first-generation Pop artists remained faithful to a Pop aesthetic throughout their careers – as in the case of Andy Warhol, Roy Lichtenstein (fig. 3) and James Rosenquist in the United States – others, including such prominent figures as the British painters Peter Blake and Richard

Hamilton, moved in and out of Pop throughout their lives, never rejecting their alliance with the movement but not wishing to be constrained by its precepts either. Such is also the case with Jasper Johns and Robert Rauschenberg. Their groundbreaking work, made in New York during the mid- to late 1950s – Johns's paintings of commonplace objects such as flags, maps and targets (fig. 2), and the collage aesthetic of Rauschenberg's combines of printed materials and found objects – was to prove a fundamental influence on the early history of Pop half a decade later. Yet Johns never embraced the term or attached much importance to his influence on Pop artists, quite rightly given that he was more concerned with the object quality of his paintings and sculptures and with questioning the very function of representation than with the social significance of the objects to which he was referring. As soon as Pop appeared on the scene, he steered his art into more ambiguous territory, partly so as to avoid any identification with consumer imagery. As for Rauschenberg, while powerfully attracted to the flood of images that he saw as symptomatic of the modern world, as is most obviously evinced in the silkscreen paintings he began to produce in 1962, he was perhaps too intent on representing a sense of random energy and multiple visual stimulations to be easily contained within the more classical stasis that characterized much of Pop's formal language.

Perhaps more confusingly still, some of the undisputed masters of Pop, including Tom Wesselmann in the United States and Patrick Caulfield in England, were uncomfortable with the label and sought to distance themselves from it. Wesselmann expressed his dissatisfaction with it already in 1963, telling G. R. Swenson in an interview conducted for *ARTnews* magazine: 'I dislike labels in general and Pop in particular, especially because it overemphasizes the material used. There does seem to be a tendency to use similar materials and images, but the different ways they are used denies any kind of group intention.'[3] Yet

fig. 3
Roy Lichtenstein, *Washing Machine*, 1961
Oil on canvas
141.6 x 172.7 cm
Yale University Art Gallery
Gift of Richard Brown Baker, B.A. 1935

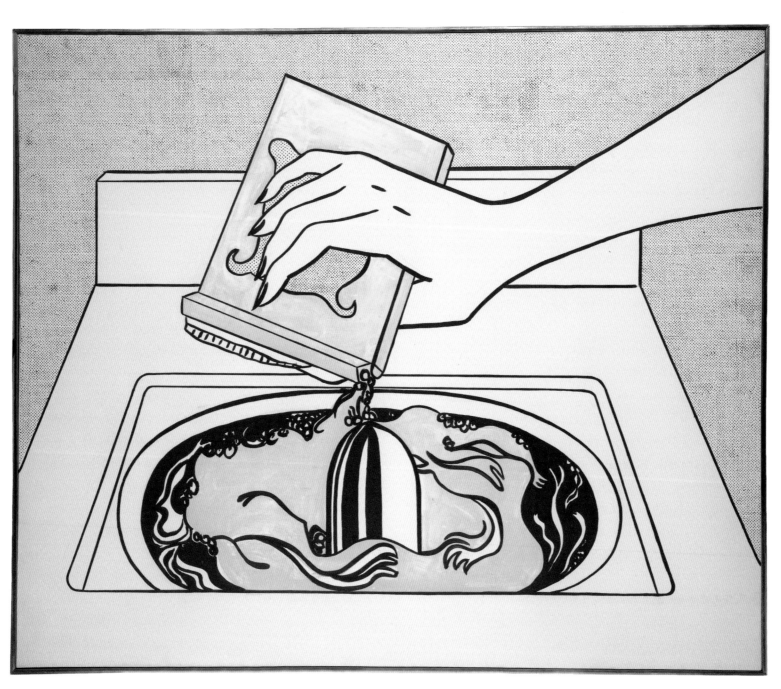

fig. 3

fig. 4
Patrick Caulfield,
Dining/Kitchen/Living, 1980
Acrylic on canvas
179.1 x 179.1 cm
Tochigi Prefectural Museum
of Fine Arts, Japan

fig. 5
Tom Wesselmann, *Still Life No. 18*, 1962
Mixed media and collage on canvas
ø 122 cm
Courtesy The Estate of Tom Wesselmann

fig. 5

what could be more Pop than the celebration of abundance, consumer delirium and fast foods of his still lifes (fig. 5), the orderly and bluntly literal recreations of his suburban bathrooms, or the joyous eroticism of his *Great American Nudes*? Caulfield's inherent contrariness, meanwhile, led him not only to reject the term 'Pop' but also to distance himself from the movement itself, which he saw as a late incarnation of social realism and therefore as something to be avoided. For him, it was not just a semantic issue but one that affected fundamental decisions regarding his choice of subject matter. Judging his colleagues and friends to be preoccupied with representing what was 'up to date', he preferred to pursue imagery that was 'more ambiguous in time': 'I felt there was more scope in not choosing that kind of subject matter. It was coming mainly from American culture, as far as I could see. In fact I don't think that was really the sort of life that one was leading, anyway. One wasn't leading the polished chrome, racy life that these images suggest.'[4] Despite his professed intentions, however, he remained one of the great Pop painters right through to the end of his life in 2005, seamlessly marrying his astute observations of contemporary (and

fig. 4

often slightly out-of-fashion) interiors to a pared-down and hugely sophisticated pictorial language (fig. 4).

Despite the ascendancy of American Pop in the early 1960s and the prophetic use of Pop imagery half a decade earlier by such artists as the New York collagist Ray Johnson (fig. 6), it was rather in 1950s Britain that some of the earliest examples of the genre could be found, particularly within the context of the Independent Group and, separately, in the student work of Peter Blake. Indeed, it was

through the discussions of the Independent Group that the seeds of one branch of British Pop were sown. These were small gatherings of artists (such as Hamilton, Eduardo Paolozzi and Nigel Henderson), architects (among them James Stirling, Colin St John Wilson and Alison and Peter Smithson) and writers (notably the art critic Lawrence Alloway and the architectural historian Reyner Banham) that took place at the Institute of Contemporary Arts in London between 1952 and 1955. They turned their attention to many areas of visual culture that had been under the radar of 'fine' artists or had even been deemed beneath contempt: car styling, advertising, design, technology, engineering, pin-up magazines, Hollywood movies and science fiction, for instance. All of these, often in unexpected proximity, were soon to become intrinsic to the iconography and structure of Hamilton's work in particular, both in its incipient Pop phase of the late 1950s – in such works as *$he* (fig. 7) – and in its more squarely Pop formulations of the following decade.

It was at the Independent Group's inaugural meeting in April 1952 that Paolozzi, in a rapid-fire presentation of images on an epidiascope, first showed the collages of scrapbook images cut from American magazines, advertisements and other printed sources that to this day remain part of the archaeological foundations of Pop Art. Although exhibited only later as artworks in their own right, and reproduced in facsimile as a portfolio entitled *Bunk!* as late as 1972, they demonstrated – in their often humorous and ebullient juxtaposition of images from the mass media – an enormous prescience in setting the terms for much of the collage-based Pop that was to follow in the studios of younger artists. In similar

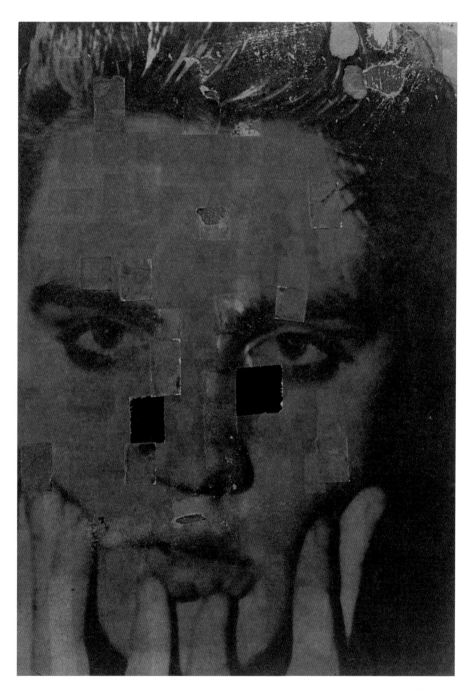

fig. 6

spirit, Hamilton's contribution to the exhibition *This Is Tomorrow* at the Whitechapel Gallery in 1956, in which teams of artists and architects associated with the Independent Group presented environment-evoking installations, was a small collage of his own (produced not as an exhibited work but for reproduction in the catalogue and as a poster) that has come to be recognized as *the* seminal Pop work: *Just what is it that makes today's homes so different, so appealing?* Here, pressed tightly together, are many of the motifs that were soon to be mined by Hamilton himself and others: Hollywood cinema, television, comic books, soft-porn magazines, cars, domestic products born of new technology, furniture, fast food and even explorations into outer space. So genuinely popular and enduring did this collage become, functioning as ground zero for any exhibition of Pop Art, that Hamilton was eventually persuaded of the need to produce a small edition of high-spec printed reproductions of it in order to meet demand → p. 20.

The term 'Pop', first published in an article by Alloway in 1958,[5] emerged from the discussions of the Independent Group and specifically in the wake of *This Is Tomorrow*. It was initially used, however, to describe the ephemeral products of contemporary culture rather than as a stylistic category for the Group's own art. In a letter written on 16 January 1957 to fellow Independent Group members Alison and Peter Smithson, Hamilton first made a case for an art that could carry the name, listing its characteristics as 'Popular (designed for a mass audience); Transient (short term

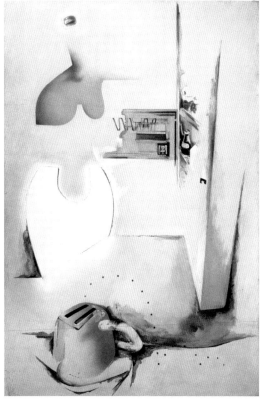

fig. 7

solution); Expendable (easily forgotten); Low Cost; Mass Produced; Young (aimed at youth); Witty; Sexy; Gimmicky; Glamorous; Big business'.[6] Although he was still thinking of what we would now regard as source material for the art that was to follow rather than defining a new artistic direction, most of these terms have proven highly accurate as descriptions of the Pop Art that emerged during the 1960s in New York, London, Los Angeles, various European cities and beyond.

Peter Blake's early forays into Pop imagery during the 1950s came about not through an intellectual engagement with iconography drawn from areas outside the canon of high art, as was the case with the Independent Group artists, but as a much more direct and intimate expression of his experiences and enthusiasms as a child, teenager and young man. Born in 1932 and separated from his parents during most of the Second World War, when he and his sister were evacuated for their safety, he developed a nostalgia for his lost childhood. Paintings of the mid-1950s depicting children with their comic books or wearing badges that declared their allegiance to a Saturday morning cinema club, though executed in a naive figurative style, are among his many works that presage Pop Art. *Children Reading Comics* (fig. 8), for instance, is one of two early paintings by Blake that contain detailed renderings of comic-strip images, half a decade before Warhol and Lichtenstein independently hit upon the idea of making grand paintings from the individual frames of such strips. In other paintings and collages

fig. 9

fig. 8

Blake celebrated the popular entertainments that were part of his life: wrestling matches, circuses, fun fairs and freak shows, as well as jazz and pop music. An avid collector of folk art and printed ephemera, he was a natural Pop artist, treating postcard reproductions of great works of art with the same lack of snobbery that characterized his use of glamour photographs of film stars or pop musicians as material that could be incorporated directly into collage paintings such as *Girlie Door* (fig. 9). The flat, brightly coloured surfaces of enamel paint that feature in his works between 1959 and 1961, and the bold chevron designs and geometric patterns that declared their upbeat mood, were to have an immediate and profound impact on the development of British Pop in the work of artists such as Caulfield and Peter Phillips.

The work that today is most immediately associated with Pop Art was produced in New York in the early 1960s, especially by the 'hard core' – Warhol, Lichtenstein, Wesselmann, Rosenquist and the sculptor Claes Oldenburg – but also by Jim Dine, George Segal,[7] Larry Rivers, Robert Indiana, Richard Artschwager, Allan D'Arcangelo, John Wesley and others. On the West Coast new art was being created with a similar sensibility and attention to popular contemporary imagery: there were painters such as Ed Ruscha, Billy Al Bengston, Joe Goode and Vija Celmins in Southern California and Wayne Thiebaud and Mel Ramos in Northern California, as well as others, most notably Ed Kienholz, Wallace Berman and Bruce Conner, whose messier and more sprawling Funk Art took Pop into darker territories akin to the Junk Art and live happenings being created in New York by Dine, Oldenburg, Allan Kaprow and Red Grooms. How does one explain this sudden profusion of representational art rooted in the everyday, in the urban environment and in the mass media; this spark of creativity that embraced the visual languages of graphic art, comic books, glamour photography, advertising (in its slick Madison Avenue configuration and in its most low-brow forms), billboards, consumer product design and packaging as points of reference for a bold and even wilfully vulgar new form of art?

For one thing, American Pop artists were, on the whole, considerably older than their British counterparts (many of whom were barely in their twenties in 1960), and one might think they were therefore more detached from the teenage enthusiasms of popular culture, comic books, rock 'n' roll music and sexual discovery celebrated in much of Pop Art. Lichtenstein, for example, was in his late thirties when he made his first comic-book paintings, partly to entertain his adolescent sons. Where the Americans had an advantage, however, was in their proximity to and familiarity with the pop culture that served as the backdrop to their art. Compared, moreover, to their British counterparts, whose training was mostly within an art-school context,[8] it is notable that many of the major American Pop artists had first-hand experience in the commercial sector. Warhol was already a celebrated, award-winning graphic artist during the 1950s, noted for the flair of his drawing style, before he reinvented himself as a painter at the turn of the decade. Long before embarking on his billboard-scale paintings, Rosenquist had worked as an actual billboard painter in Minnesota and then on Times Square and other prominent locations in New York City. Ruscha's word paintings of the 1960s and later, which are among his most original contributions to Pop Art, developed from his early training in typography, just as Artschwager's involvement with the commercial production of furniture served as groundwork for his subsequent creation of sculptures in the form of tables, chairs and other domestic items. Wesselmann came to art late, having discovered his taste for drawing humorous cartoons while serving in the army. Thiebaud had a short spell in the animation department of Walt Disney Studios and worked for a full decade as a freelance cartoonist and commercial illustrator before studying painting. From 1953 to 1958, Wesley worked for an aircraft company as an illustrator, just as he was starting to paint. One could even link Oldenburg's eye for the mystery of the everyday object to the two years he spent working as a cub reporter for the Chicago News Bureau from 1950 to 1952.

Yet although there was certainly an abundance of visually appealing material available to American artists a decade or more after the end of the Second World War, particularly as they had not significantly suffered the privations experienced by Europeans, much of it had existed in some form or other earlier in the century without acting as such a powerful stimulus for painters and sculptors. Thus, the new sense of prosperity that prevailed during the 1950s must have had a role in creating the atmosphere for an 'aesthetics of plenty', Pop Art being suffused with the materialism of capitalist culture. Even if at times, or in the work of certain artists, this is greeted with ambivalence, if rarely with open hostility, an acknowledgment of material abundance and the hard-sell tactics of the commercial sector are profoundly embodied both in the imagery and in the bold formal strategies and strong colours employed in much of Pop with the express purpose of knocking the viewer between the eyes. For Warhol, who had a knack for getting straight to the point, the secret was very simple: 'Pop,' as he told Gene Swenson in 1963, is about 'liking things.'[9] And, tellingly enough, two of the first survey exhibitions of the new tendencies that came to be known as Pop stressed the role played in this art by the everyday object: *New Painting of Common Objects*, curated by Walter Hopps at the Pasadena Art Museum in 1962,[10] and *6 Painters and the Object*, curated by Lawrence Alloway at the Solomon R. Guggenheim Museum in New York in 1963.[11]

In addition, American Pop artists appeared in a very specific historical context. In part, theirs was a shared reaction against the lofty ideals and spiritual overtones of the art made by the generation before them and that only then had been granted solemn museum status: namely, that of Abstract Expressionists such as Mark Rothko, Barnett Newman and Willem de Kooning. This is not to say that they disdained the work of their predecessors. On the contrary, many of the Pop artists, along with Johns and Rauschenberg, had great respect for Abstract Expressionist painters and appropriated some of their characteristics, such as large scale and 'all-over' compositional strategies, sometimes even parodying their gestural brushwork.[12] Nevertheless, they recognized the need to cut themselves loose from what was becoming a stultifying influence. In their view, contemporary art, especially abstract painting, was becoming too polite and rarefied and too detached from the lives of ordinary people. The Pop artists, initially with little knowledge of similar work being made by their peers, sought to drag art back into the real world. Not everyone welcomed this development with open arms. One prominent critic, Max Kozloff, who was later to write a monograph on Jasper Johns, published an article in March 1962 in which he spoke sympathetically of the work of Dine, Peter Saul and Robert Watts but expressed reservations about Lichtenstein, Oldenburg and Rosenquist, concluding: 'The truth is, the art galleries are being invaded by the pin-headed and contemptible style of gum chewers, bobby soxers and, worse, delinquents.'[13] His moral outrage may now strike us as stuffy and pompous, but he was by no means alone among art critics in sounding like an embattled parent scolding a teenage child for playing his pop records too loud.

Whereas previous avant-garde movements had sought to *épater les bourgeois*, the Pop generation seemed content, instead, with getting a rise out of the defenders of high culture while remaining on the friendliest of terms with the middle class. Unlike much of the modern art that had preceded it, Pop was designed to be understood at various levels of sophistication rather than directed exclusively to an audience that was highly visually educated. In most of its incarnations it presented itself as user-friendly, accessible, entertaining and fun, even at the risk of being dismissed as low-brow. This is not to say that Pop artists lacked in ambition. By inviting the 'masses' to enjoy art, dismissing the view that it should remain the preserve of the cultured elite, they were declaring war on many long-held assumptions about the role of art, its dissemination and its reception. Interviewed in 1963, Lichtenstein made it clear that part of his purpose was to test the boundaries of taste to the point of his art being judged unacceptable. Describing Pop Art as 'the use of commercial art as a subject matter in painting', he immediately went on to broach the question of his subversive and combative intentions: 'It was hard to get a painting that was despicable enough so that no one would hang it – everybody was hanging everything. It was almost acceptable to hang a dripping paint rag, everybody was accustomed to this. The one thing everyone hated was commercial art; and apparently they didn't hate that enough either.'[14]

The Pop paintings created by Warhol and Lichtenstein in 1961 and 1962, initially with no knowledge of each other's work, represent Pop at its purest and most bluntly extreme. By basing their paintings on found images of the 'basest' kind – frames from comic strips, crudely drawn lurid advertisements from popular newspapers, do-it-yourself paint kits and the like – they challenged the authority of the fine art tradition, particularly by mimicking the cheap printed look of their sources rather than subjecting them to refined artistic interpretation. Warhol immediately abandoned the comic-strip paintings when he learned of Lichtenstein's involvement with the same range of images,

fig. 10

but in the paintings of ads, postage stamps, labels, dollar bills and consumer products such as Coca-Cola bottles and Campbell's Soup cans that followed (fig. 10) he engaged in a similar level of provocation. Lichtenstein, for his part, by making paintings of objects as 'dumb' as a ball of string, a golf ball, an ad for a turkey or a schematic rendering of a great work of art, proposed an equally extreme levelling between art and commerce in its most mundane form. Moreover, both appeared to have relinquished the artist's conventional decision-making about such matters as composition, often favouring a centralized placement of the found motif and, in Warhol's case, a strategy of mechanical repetition evoking assembly-line production. Each also devised processes that replicated or parodied the printing methods of their source material: Warhol through tracing, stencilling and (from mid-1962) photo-silkscreening; Lichtenstein by his adoption of a grid of dots similar in appearance to the Ben-Day dots of half-tone printing used in newspapers and comic books.

Despite throwing in their lot with the anonymous graphic artists and unsung ad-men with whom they engaged in a kind of unofficial collaboration, Pop artists worldwide proved paradoxically to be stubborn individualists. This was in part simply a matter of self-preservation, self-promotion and marketing, since each artist needed to establish his (and they were almost all men) particular stamp, style, method and domain of imagery in order to distinguish himself from

fig. 11

his peers. However, the reality was less cynically motivated than such a reading would suggest, for each artist came to Pop through his own personal history and sensibility, something that not even the common fund of material could erase. Thus, Oldenburg's plaster and then sewn-cloth surrogates of items of food and clothing had a handmade quality that personalized them and accentuated the sense that many of these sculptural objects were stand-ins for the human figure; the soft sculptures, particularly, in the way they drooped and found their 'natural' position, were shown to be as prone to gravity as our own bodies. Rosenquist, for his part, inherited from Surrealism a taste for collage-based random associations of images, dream states and schematized painted surfaces, all of which he married to the large-scale work and disorientation he had experienced as a painter of billboards. In his *Great American Nudes* and in other works of the 1960s, in which he combined broadly painted passages in vibrant colours with collages of printed and photographic images and store-bought objects, Wesselmann undertook to reinterpret categories from the history of art: nudes, portraits, still lifes and landscapes. Challenging himself further to reshape these traditions through overt references to Matisse and other modern masters, he sought to revivify moribund formats and to entwine the most intimately private experiences with a public expression that would have felt familiar to anyone accustomed to the urban landscape of the postwar period.

British Pop of the early 1960s is as varied as its American counterpart. Nevertheless, a fairly cohesive group emerged from the Royal College of Art, after a 27-year-old American student named R. B. Kitaj began in 1959 a highly influential two-year period of study at the school alongside David Hockney, Allen Jones, Peter Phillips and Derek Boshier, who had just embarked on their three-year course. So subversive were these students considered that Jones was expelled at the end of the first year, but by then the seeds of a group ethos

were already sown. Playing with styles and motifs as constituent parts of paintings that could be quoted and mixed at will, they included some popular imagery in pictures that often had a narrative thread or that required decoding. Compared to the instant impact and harsh, hard-edged aesthetic cultivated by many of the New York artists, these English painters preferred to engage the viewer in a slower, more painterly and more playful process. Taking their cue from Kitaj, who advised them to make art that directly reflected their personal enthusiasms, each artist found his own distinct voice: Hockney making paintings that celebrated his homosexuality (then still taboo and even illegal in Britain), his vegetarianism and his love of poetry (fig. 12); Boshier adapting his reading of Marshall McLuhan and Vance Packard to his left-wing politics in narrative paintings that were highly critical of American influence on British society and of encroachments on individual identity; and Phillips making some of the largest paintings in the early history of British Pop, with imagery derived from the heraldic design of pinball machines and fun-fair games (fig. 13). Jones's 1962 series of shaped canvases representing London two-decker buses in motion are still among his most salient contributions to this phase of Pop, but it was after moving to New York in 1964 for two years that he found his true voice as a Pop artist in paintings derived from fetishist illustrations of the female figure (fig. 11). Kitaj's own passions were for literature and history and not for popular culture, and he quite rightly insisted therefore that he was not a Pop artist, notwithstanding his influence.

British Pop encompassed a great variety of artists of different generations. Joe Tilson, who like Blake and the Pop-inflected abstract painter Richard Smith had studied at the Royal College of Art in the mid-1950s, put his carpentry skills to use in the early 1960s making brightly painted wooden constructions suggestive of children's toys (fig. 15). Blake, Hamilton and Caulfield, all mentioned earlier, were

fig. 12
David Hockney, *Cleaning Teeth,*
Early Evening (10pm) WII, 1962
Oil on canvas
182.7 x 122 cm
© David Hockney
Astrup Fearnley Museet, Oslo
Photo: Prudence Cuming Associates

fig. 13
Peter Phillips, *For Men Only – Starring MM*
and BB, 1961
Oil, wood and collage on canvas
274.5 x 142.5 cm
Centro de Arte Moderna –
Fundação Calouste Gulbenkian, Lisbon

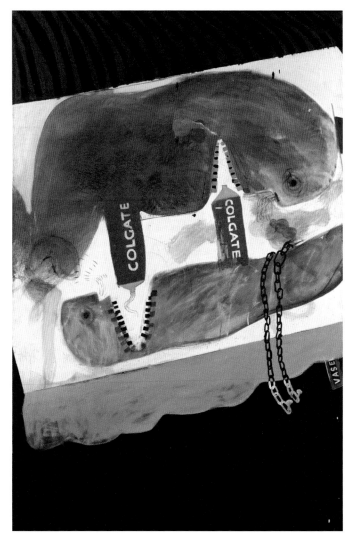

fig. 12

fig. 13

fig. 14
Clive Barker,
Rio – Homage to Marlon Brando, 1968
Chrome-plated bronze
36.8 x ø 30.5 cm
MMK Museum für Moderne Kunst,
Frankfurt am Main
On permanent loan from the
Friends of the Museum für Moderne
Kunst e.V., Frankfurt am Main
Acquired with funding from the
Tischgesellschaft 2005

fig. 15
Joe Tilson, *For Jos, January 1st*, 1963
Oil on wood relief
182.8 x 243 cm

fig. 14

among the most original and articulate voices in British Pop during the 1960s, but there were many others who were also responsible for enriching the movement. Among sculptors alone there was not only Paolozzi but also the American-born Jann Haworth, whose figures and objects sewn from cloth had a high-spirited and self-consciously female quality; Clive Barker, whose polished and chrome-plated casts of commonplace objects such as Coca-Cola bottles, dartboards and artist's palettes drew attention to the glamorous potential of the everyday (fig. 14); and Nicholas Monro, whose brightly coloured figures and objects in fibreglass are among the most humorous and free-spirited works in Pop. The painters Antony Donaldson and Gerald Laing, both of whom came closer in some ways to the clean look and simplified imagery of American Pop, and the virtuoso draughstman Colin Self, who made beautifully detailed and volumetrically rendered pencil

fig. 15

and colour crayon drawings of a whole range of images from stylish glamour models to the lowly American hot dog, took Pop into entirely different territory.

Pop-related developments on mainland Europe during the same decade warrant a separate essay, given that in almost every case the circumstances and intentions were distinct from those of the English-speaking initiators of Pop and that with few exceptions the term 'Pop' is not generally applied to the work of the artists in question.[15] Nevertheless, it is worth mentioning that these important contributions

and expansions of the definition of Pop encompass, most notably, *nouveau réalisme*, a movement not just paralleling but even anticipating the first phase of Pop. Among its artefacts are sculptures using mass-produced objects by artists such as Arman (whose accumulations of identical objects offered a distinct response to industrial mass production, fig. 17), César, Christo, Gérard Deschamps, Yves Klein, Niki de Saint Phalle, Daniel Spoerri and Jean Tinguely; tinted photographic paintings by Martial Raysse; and *décollages* of printed posters by *affichistes* such as François Dufrêne, Raymond Hains, Jacques de la Villeglé and Mimmo Rotella. Also of note are the camouflage paintings and mechanically-rendered photographic parodies of art historical sources by Alain Jacquet (fig. 16); the *figuration narrative* created, with an eye to the pictorial language of European comic strips, by painters such as Bernard Rancillac, Hervé Télémaque and the Icelandic artist Erró; the delightfully vulgar and mocking über-Kitsch of Sigmar Polke's early work; and the sardonic *Kapitalistischer Realismus* of Konrad Lueg and, especially, Gerhard Richter, whose austere deployment of blurred photographic imagery brilliantly and ambiguously translated into paint can be seen as a serious and melancholic questioning of the tenets of Anglo-Saxon and especially American Pop.

Pop Art has never been a narrowly definable style. Already with the original generation of Pop practitioners who emerged in the 1950s and 1960s there was a very wide range of stylistic options being proposed by artists who conformed in one or more ways to the

fig. 16
Alain Jacquet, *Déjeuner sur l'herbe*, 1964
Silkscreen on paper
175 x 195 cm
Musée d'Art Moderne de la Ville de Paris

fig. 17
Arman, *Home, Sweet Home*, 1960
Accumulation of gas masks in wooden
box and plexiglas
160 x 140.5 x 20.3 cm
Musée National d'Art Moderne,
Centre Georges Pompidou, Paris

fig. 16

fig. 17

fig. 18
Gary Hume, *Young Woman*, 1998
From the portfolio *Portraits*
Silkscreen on paper
90.8 x 61 cm
Tate, London

fig. 19
Jeff Koons, *New Hoover Convertibles, Green, Red, Brown,*
New Shelton Wet/Dry 10 Gallon Displaced Doubledecker,
1981–87
Vacuum cleaners, plexiglas and fluorescent lights
251 x 137 x 71.5 cm
Tate, London / National Galleries of Scotland,
Edinburgh

fig. 18

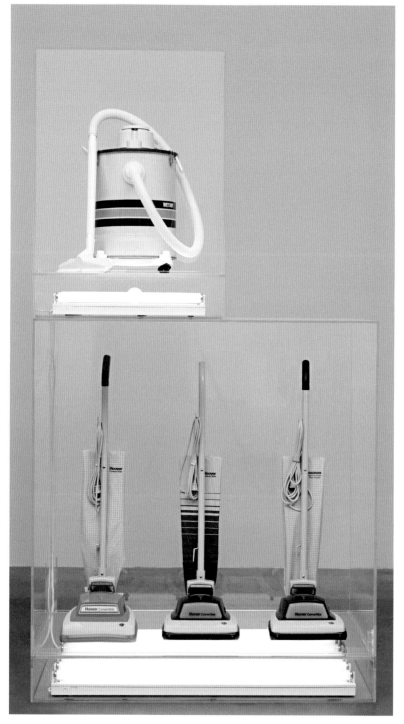

fig. 19

definitions one might propose in terms of attitude, sensibility, subject matter, imagery, materials, methods and involvement with popular culture and the mass media. Just as some of these first-generation Pop artists shunned the label or proved loath to adhere too closely to its unwritten set of precepts, so such ambiguities have become even more marked in the work of much younger artists who have established their reputations in the past four decades. After all, by the 1980s Pop Art was understood as a historical movement that had peaked in the 1960s and could no longer accept new adherents into its ranks. Any new Pop-inflected art had to create its own twist, its own perspective and its own dynamic in order to make its presence felt.

For artists starting out in these more recent decades, much of the vocabulary and syntax of Pop – which at its inception had been greeted with horror or at least suspicion by many within the art establishment – had become so familiar as to be accepted as a language that could be learned, adopted and extended. Some have self-consciously borrowed from its visual and conceptual strategies, just as earlier Pop works had themselves been modelled on

fig. 20

forms and images taken from outside the fine art tradition. Jeff Koons (the quintessential Pop Post-Pop artist, fig. 19) in the United States, Gary Hume (fig. 18) and Julian Opie (fig. 20) in Britain and Takashi Murakami (fig. 21) in Japan all produce work that sits comfortably alongside that of their Pop predecessors. Both Opie (who resists the term 'Pop') and Murakami (who takes it in his stride) are happy to link their art to the popular culture to which they make reference, cheerfully blurring the distinctions between art and commerce and between high and low with a confidence that even first-generation Pop artists would envy.[16] Others, such as Damien Hirst, have gleefully adopted the self-marketing techniques first exploited by Warhol, as well as certain methods from classic Pop, while exploring imagery and subject matter that have very different overtones.

The consumer culture that provided the visual material and the social setting in which Pop Art thrived has continued to expand and to become an intrinsic and inescapable part of the fabric of daily life for most of the populations of the developed world. While the original generation of Pop artists were responding and adapting to new technologies and pictorial forms that had dramatically changed the visual landscape – cinema, television, mass-circulation magazines, comic books, Madison Avenue advertising – younger artists, born since the late 1950s, take these areas of visual expression and marketing for granted, divested of exoticism and novelty. Many of the themes addressed by leading contemporary artists were first conspicuously voiced by Pop artists during the 1960s: celebrity culture, glamour and even the notion of the artist as pop star. Likewise the vogue since the 1980s for appropriation and parody, with both style and imagery there for the taking pret-a-porter, has its roots in Pop's provocative announcement of the death of originality. In short, Pop-derived strategies, themes and images

fig. 21

have become prevalent in the work of younger generations of artists worldwide. Journalists used to ask if Pop Art was just a passing fad, wondering how long it could last. The evidence shows that they need not have worried: it continues to evolve and mutate well into the early twenty-first century, a full fifty years after its first appearance.

★

1 Other terms, such as 'Neo-Dada', 'New Realism', 'Common Object Painting' and 'New American Sign Painting', were proposed by critics before 'Pop Art' finally took precedence in 1962. A symposium on Pop Art held at the Museum of Modern Art, New York, on 13 December 1962 provided the institutional seal of approval for the term. Its participants were Dore Ashton, Henry Geldzahler, Stanley Kunitz, Hilton Kramer, Peter Selz and Leo Steinberg. See 'A Symposium on Pop Art', *Arts* 37, no. 7 (April 1963): 36–45, reprinted in full in Steven Henry Madoff, ed., *Pop Art: A Critical History*, Documents of Twentieth Century Art (Berkeley and Los Angeles: University of California Press, 1997), 65–81.

2 Pop's international dimension was recognized early on in the longwinded subtitle of the first survey exhibition dedicated to it held in New York (Sidney Janis Gallery, 31 October–31 December 1962): *The New Realists: An Exhibition of Factual Paintings & Sculpture from France, England, Italy, Sweden and the United States*. The exhibited artists were Peter Agostini, Jim Dine, Robert Indiana, Roy Lichtenstein, Robert Moskowitz, Claes Oldenburg, James Rosenquist, George Segal, Harold Stevenson, Wayne Thiebaud, Andy Warhol and Tom Wesselmann from the United States; Peter Blake, John Latham and Peter Phillips from England; and Arman, Enrico Baj, Gianfranco Baruchello, Öyvind Fahlström, Tano Festa, Yves Klein, Martial Raysse, Mimmo Rotella, Mario Schifano, Daniel Spoerri, Jean Tinguely and Per Olof Ultvedt from France, Italy and Sweden.

3 G. R. Swenson, 'What is Pop Art? Interviews with Eight Painters', pt. 2, *ARTnews* 62, no. 10 (February 1964): 40–43, 62–67.

4 Patrick Caulfield, in conversation with Marco Livingstone, December 1980. Quoted in Marco Livingstone, *Patrick Caulfield: Paintings* (Aldershot and Burlington, VT: Lund Humphries, 2005), 30.

5 Lawrence Alloway, 'The Arts and the Mass Media', *Architectural Design* 28, no. 2 (1958): 84–85.

6 This private letter was not published at the time, though the definition itself was later widely quoted in publications on Hamilton and on Pop Art. A facsimile of the full two page letter is reproduced in the first pages of the unpaginated catalogue accompanying the exhibition *Pop Art is...*, held at the Gagosian Gallery in London, 27 September–10 November 2007.

7 In his preface to the catalogue accompanying the exhibition *Dine, Oldenburg, Segal: Painting/Sculpture*, held at the Art Gallery of Ontario, Toronto, 14 January–12 February 1967 and the Albright-Knox Art Gallery, Buffalo, 24 February–26 March 1967, Brydon Smith remarked that the three artists featured in the exhibition did not share the 'cool' and uncommitted attitude of Pop artists such as Warhol and Lichtenstein; on the contrary, each of them was a 'hot' artist intent on expressing his feelings and fantasies (*Dine, Oldenburg, Segal: Painting/Sculpture* [Toronto: Art Gallery of Ontario, 1967], 3). The passionate nature of Dine's art and the humanitarian impulses behind Segal's sculpture place these major artists somewhat at a tangent to mainstream Pop, to which they nevertheless made a huge contribution.

8 Blake is an exception to the case, having been trained in commercial art as well as in painting and having continued to undertake commissions as a graphic designer (most famously co-designing the cover of the Beatles' *Sgt. Pepper's Lonely Hearts Club Band* LP with his first wife, American Pop sculptor Jann Haworth, in 1967) in parallel with his career as an artist. Hamilton's intermittent use of precise forms of technical drawing can be accounted for—at least in part—to his youthful experience as a jig and tool draughtsman. From age 14, Phillips was at art school, where he picked up a whole range of technical skills that were to serve him well as a Pop painter.

9 For the full interview with Warhol, see G. R. Swenson, 'What is Pop Art? Interviews with Eight Painters', pt. 1, *ARTnews* 62, no. 7 (November 1963): 24–27, 60–63. On the opening page of his book *POPism: The Warhol '60s*, co-authored with Pat Hackett (New York: Harcourt, Brace, Jovanovich, 1980), 3, Warhol explained, somewhat inscrutably, that after Abstract Expressionism, 'Pop Art took the inside and put it outside, took the outside and put it inside', adding: 'The Pop artists did images that anybody walking down Broadway could recognize in a split second—comics, picnic tables, men's trousers, celebrities, shower curtains, refrigerators, Coke bottles—all the great modern things that the Abstract Expressionists tried so hard not to notice at all.'

10 The exhibition ran from 25 September to 19 October 1962 and featured eight artists: Dine, Robert Dowd, Goode, Phillip Hefferton, Lichtenstein, Ruscha, Thiebaud and Warhol.

11 As mentioned, Alloway had been a prime participant in the Independent Group in London and was the first to publish an article in which the term 'Pop Art' appeared (see note 5). In 1963 he had only recently moved to New York. The artists included in his Guggenheim exhibition were six of the major New York-based Pop artists: Dine, Lichtenstein, Oldenburg, Rauschenberg, Rosenquist and Warhol. That same year it travelled to the Los Angeles County Museum of Art, where it was paired with a companion exhibition entitled *Six More*, in which artists working in California were featured: Bengston, Goode, Hefferton, Ramos, Ruscha and Thiebaud.

12 The respect did not go both ways, at least not when Pop first appeared. After the *New Realists* exhibition at the Sidney Janis Gallery in New York (see note 2), in which the work of leading Pop artists was presented for the first time in a major group exhibition, a protest meeting was called by the Abstract Expressionists under contract with the gallery. Consequently Adolph Gottlieb, Phillip Guston, Robert Motherwell and Rothko all resigned from the gallery, leaving only de Kooning (the Pop artists' favourite) to exhibit there.

13 Max Kozloff, '"Pop" Culture, Metaphysical Disgust, and the New Vulgarians', *Art International* 6, no. 2 (March 1962): 35–36.

14 For the full interview with Lichtenstein, see Swenson, 'What is Pop Art?', pt. 1: 25–27.

15 For a more detailed discussion of European art of the 1950s and 1960s relating to Pop, see Marco Livingstone, *Pop Art: A Continuing History* (London: Thames and Hudson, 1990), 47–61 and 141–159.

16 Opie and Murakami, like Keith Haring before them, have marketed items that sell for small sums but that they present as of a piece with their more substantial works. Opie has also delighted in creating exhibition catalogues for his solo shows that look like mail-order catalogues, further blurring the distinction between fine art and low-brow merchandising.

MIT / Monsanto, House of the Future,
Disneyland, Anaheim, 1957–67

Alison and Peter Smithson, front door
of the House of the Future, 1955–56
Experimental house for the *Daily Mail Ideal
Home Exhibition*, London

Bernard Judge, *Judge House*, Los Angeles, 1962
Julius Shulman Photography Archive

Richard Buckminster Fuller, *Biosphère*, 1967
United States pavilion, *Expo 67*, Montreal

223

Jean Maneval, *Bulle six coques*, 1964–68
Shown at the Internationale Kunststoffhaus-
Ausstellung (International Plastic House
Exhibition) in Lüdenscheid, 1971, under
the name *Orion*

Matti Suuronen, *Futuro House*, 1968
Photographed location: Philadelphia, 1970

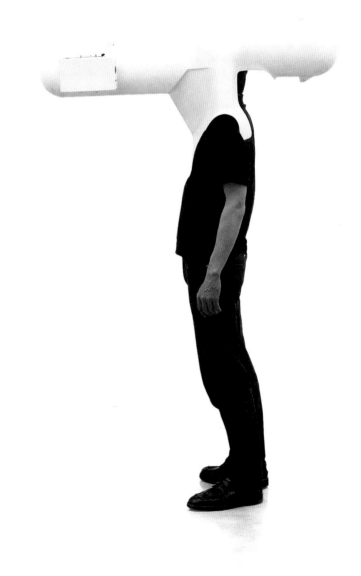

Matti Suuronen, *Venturo House / CF-45*
(*Casa Finlandia* series), 1971
Interior
Photo: Lehtikuva

Walter Pichler,
TV-Helm (Tragbares Wohnzimmer), 1967
White lacquered polyester, integrated
monitor with TV connection
59 x 120 x 43 cm
Walter Pichler, WP/S 6702

Cesare Casati and Emanuele Ponzio,
nightclub of Hotel Grifone, Bolzano, 1968
Interior

Quasar, *Structure Gonflable*, 1968
Installation at the Musée des Arts Décoratifs, Paris

Hans Hollein, *Mobiles Büro*, 1969
Transparent PVC film
Courtesy Generali Foundation, Vienna

fig. 1
Verner Panton, *Phantasy Landscape*, 1970
Detail from the exhibition *Visiona 2* at the
Cologne Furniture Fair
Installation using bi-elastic Mira-X fabrics
by Bayer

The Plastic of Inner Space

Brigitte Felderer

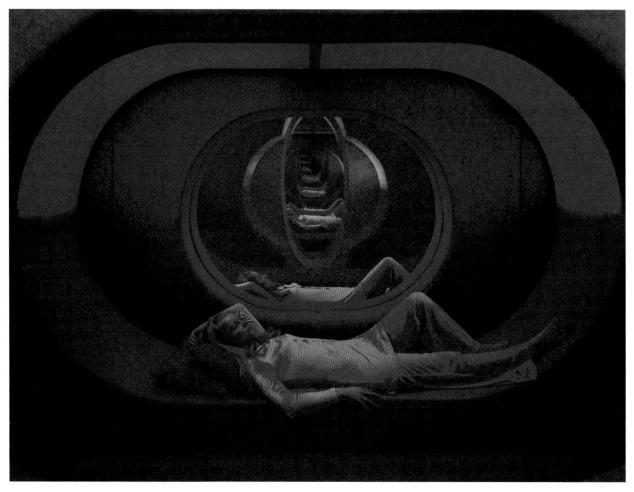

Verner Panton, *Phantasy Landscape*   fig. 1

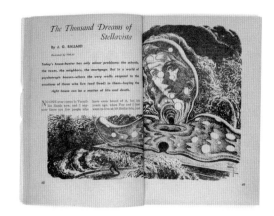

fig. 2

'Dammit, I can't arrest a house for attempted homicide, can I?'[1] The police officer's reaction displayed belligerence but, above all, a sense of helplessness. The perpetrator was not a person but a house that had gone haywire and could scarcely be controlled, no longer functioning as intended. Howard Talbot, the lawyer who had bought the villa with his wife a few months earlier at a bargain price, barely managed to escape with his life. In the middle of the night, he awoke to discover a palpable surge in the air pressure inside his bedroom. Shock waves pulsated through the air and made it almost impossible to breathe. The walls of the room along with its floor melted into an oppressively narrow sphere. The house, constructed from 'plastex', lost its stability and hence its form, which initially resembled an enormous orchid with a heart-shaped swimming pool at its core and the living areas contained in its petals. Against such an attacker, there was little the police could do. The aggressive plastic house could only be deactivated and not a moment too soon. Yet the deformed rooms and corridors still bore evidence of the structure's hidden personality.

English writer James Graham 'J. G.' Ballard described this surreal villa in his short story 'The Thousand Dreams of Stellavista', first published in 1962, as one of the curious estates of Vermilion Sands, a run-down millionaires' colony. The place is, of course, a product of fiction, yet it does suggest certain aspects of Palm Springs. With no one building like any other, the glamour of bygone days still lingers, while many houses either stand empty or offer a final refuge behind their bizarre facades for one-time celebrities. The houses are made out of 'plastex' and are, 'it goes without saying, [. . .] psychotropic'[2] – meaning they respond to the needs of their inhabitants: doors open by themselves, seats appear out of nowhere when needed and then disappear again. As a result, the idiosyncrasies of the occupants, their psyches, leave living traces in the unstable structure of the plastic, even after their physical death.

Each of the homes in Vermilion Sands remains a mutable encapsulation of all the emotions felt within its walls. The mental states that were experienced inside them settle into the structure and become stored as the building coagulates into a walk-in, inhabitable realm of the subconscious that continues to react to new impressions and new occupants. The dwellings might respond with unanticipated reflexes at any time – for who can be expected to keep their feelings in check while in the seclusion of their very own home? Every annoyance, every dispute, every tension can quickly lead to overreactions in the underlying structure of the villa. Thus, the real estate agents of Vermilion Sands have to summon all their powers of persuasion when it comes to finding buyers for psychotropic houses with a difficult biography. Previous occurrences of eccentric suicide parties or scandalous murders have an adverse effect on a house's market position, even if 'the vinyl chains in [its] plastex were hand-crafted literally molecule by molecule':[3] too many aggressions and traumatic memories may have been deposited in the 'memory drum' of the domicile.

This Ballardian dystopia does not explore outer space as a potential imagined realm of technical possibilities. It conceives of an inner space[4] and documents the deep psychological impact of applied technology, which promises utmost comfort while continually generating new needs.

In the plastex houses of Vermilion Sands, living concepts that resist the cliché of a clear-cut, ready-made existence, of a psychologically and erotically hygienic life, take shape. In contrast, a very different conception of private life was presented in the House of the Future, a Disneyland attraction that was developed by the chemical company Monsanto in cooperation with the Massachusetts Institute of Technology and Walt Disney Imagineering and was viewed by over 20 million visitors between 1957 and 1967. In this streamlined

fig. 3

fig. 3
Woman in rubber suit, photograph published in John Sutcliffe's fetish magazine *AtomAge*, no. 18, 1978

fig. 4
Advertising photograph for black vinyl swimsuits by Rudi Gernreich, 1963

single-family home of the future, the plastic surfaces do not harbour dark passions but are simply easy to clean. The furnishings do not materialize according to the unspoken individual wishes of their users. Housewives are assisted in their day-to-day work routines, the environment is child-friendly, and at first glance the plastic walls are indistinguishable from the solid quality of conventional houses. While the Disneyland model facilitates the smoothly functioning order of nuclear families, in Vermilion Sands such conventions are thwarted: the plastex houses form an environment that remains mercilessly authentic and the psychotropic residences are never anonymous. Inner spaces turn outward; things inhabitants have suppressed or concealed become psychosculptures that defy standards through constant change.

'Dynamic. Shortliving. Ever changing' – these were the criteria for a man-made plastic space that Austrian designer and architect Hans Hollein put forth in his 1960 master's thesis at the University of California in Berkeley.[5] The ambiguous term 'plastic' describes the expansive flexibility and adaptability of architecture, of living environments 'made by man' – a demand that seems realizable, not only on a metaphoric level, in the very materiality of plastic and even extends beyond the material → p. 227.

In Ballard's visions of strange fiction, the inexhaustible malleability of plastex seems to erase the boundaries between virtual and concrete space. There is no longer any safety zone in which individuals can

fig. 4

entrench themselves against their own fantasies. The tingle of fear that comes with temporarily renouncing a self-imposed sense of reality in order to deliberately engage in the reality of induced dreams can no longer be switched on and off at will. A technology influenced – not to say, impaired – by the unconscious cannot simply be overridden or deactivated. Even the desires that might reside beyond individual perception materialize in the protean plastex. The inhabitants of psychotropic houses can literally suffocate and perish as a result of their own wishful thinking. The reality of the virtual realm reacts to each input and expresses each change in concrete form: software becomes manifest.

Inner space became accessible in real terms in Verner Panton's *Phantasy Landscape* (fig. 1), which he presented in the *Visiona 2* exhibition at the 1970 Cologne Furniture Fair.[6] The Danish designer projected ideas of a then-still-relevant concept of freedom into the seemingly infinite vastness of his constructed 'inner space' and visualized the qualities of a private refuge. In his view, only in the context of speculative fantasy and an ongoing, careful examination of oneself can visions be found that transcend personal constraints and everyday functional parameters. Yet for Panton privacy never meant an uncritical escapism but rather an intrinsically social place – the universe in which people can finally rediscover themselves as authentic, well-maintained individuals contrary to the constraints of reality.

fig. 5

fig. 6

fig. 6
Haus-Rucker-Co, *Gelbes Herz*, 1968
Pneumatic space capsule at the inaugural
presentation in Vienna

In 1973 the cosmetics company Max Factor commisioned the Vienna-born fashion designer Rudi Gernreich, who had fled the National Socialists in 1938 and immigrated to Los Angeles, to design a visionary fashion concept for the launch of its new cosmetics line Futura (fig. 5). The designer was not only known for his scandalous monokini but also for having used vinyl in his collections going back to the mid-1950s: as a see-through insert for evening dresses – if such were not constructed entirely out of seamless vinyl – or as waterproof swimwear. The choice of material was scandalous in and of itself, since until then it was only used in the discreet fetish scene or as an industrial product. For Max Factor, the idea was to create a form of urban armour that made sense in a world whose social spaces were defined by anonymity – in which the difference between proximity and distance had become unclear and old, familiar social signs, such as clothing, played a new role instead of primarily marking class differences. As Gernreich himself said: 'I see the conditions today like this: anonymity, universality, unisex, nudity as fact and not as kick, and above all reality. By reality, I mean the use of real things: blue jeans, polo shirts, T-shirts, overalls. Status fashion is gone. What remains? Something I am obliged to call authenticity.'[7] The fashionable attire of the future, as envisioned by Gernreich, was to guarantee this very authenticity. The designer conceived of plastic uniforms that were meant to create 'public privacy' in the social exterior space of the future, in contrast to the 'private privacy' of one's own home. Social armaments were to be exchanged for soft, flowing garments whose transparency permitted immediate corporeality. Contemporary clothing was to be characterized by the naked body preserving its communicative significance despite being covered. The body was no longer to be a bearer of status symbols but a medium of pleasure and attraction in a place that forms a counter world to conventional constraints. Along these lines, a free

and conscious exploration of highly personal desires and needs was to yield a socially critical power.

As depicted in these scenarios and experimental schemes, plastic functions as an infinitely adaptable medium of living schemes, moving towards a society in which leisure time reigns supreme and people have long been freed from the burden and toil of day-to-day work and duty. The plastex of Ballard, the Pantonian cave and Gernreich's uniforms for the outside world were visionary in their synthetic, plasticized materiality. The malleability of plastic corresponded to a critical view of fixed identities as well as to the sociopolitical project of authentic models of life that aimed to break away from the stereotyped roles and social norms of the postwar era. Yet, the fascination with plastic had already begun to wane by the early 1960s. In the grand scheme of things, there is no happy ending to the story of this fascination but, in the spirit of Verner Panton, 'even a failed experiment can be more significant than a triviality'.[8]

fig. 7
Fictive inhabitant of Alison and Peter
Smithson's House of the Future, shown
operating the self-cleaning bathtub, 1956

fig. 8
Alison and Peter Smithson, volumetric
drawing of a housing scheme featuring
two versions of the House of the Future,
1957

fig. 7

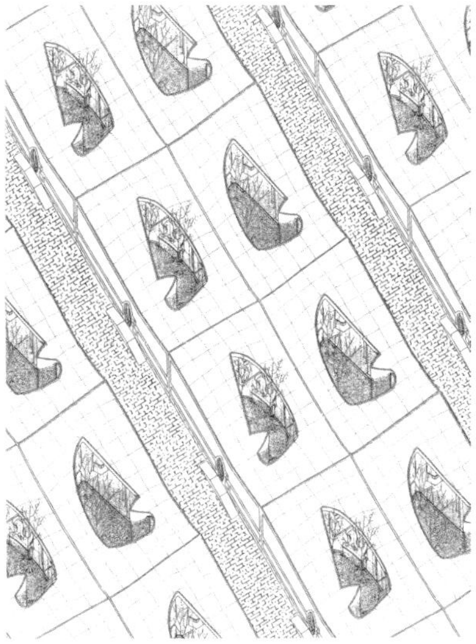

fig. 8

1   J. G. Ballard, 'The Thousand Dreams
of Stellavista', in *Vermillion Sands* (London:
Vintage, 2001), 206; originally published
in *Amazing Stories* 36, no. 3 (March 1962).
2   Ibid., 186.
3   Ibid., 188.
4   Ballard repeatedly returned to this
concept in both his literary and non-fiction
writings. See J. G. Ballard, 'Time, Memory
and Inner Space', in *A User's Guide to the
Millenium: Essays and Reviews* (London:
HarperCollins, 1996), 199–201; originally
published in *The Woman Journalist* (1963).
5   Hans Hollein, 'Plastic Space' (master's
thesis, University of California, 1960), 32.
6   The exhibition was organised in
cooperation with Bayer. See Sabine Epple,
'Verner Panton as Interior Designer', in
Alexander von Vegesack and Mathias
Remmele, eds., *Verner Panton: The Collected
Works* (Weil am Rhein: Vitra Design
Museum, 2000), 156–201, especially 184.
7   Rudi Gernreich, in intervew, 1971,
quoted in Marylou Luther, 'Looking Back
at a Futurist', in Peggy Moffitt and Willliam
Claxton, eds., *The Rudi Gernreich Book*
(New York: Rizzoli, 1991), 30.
8   Verner Panton, quoted in Epple,
'Verner Panton as Interior Designer', 184.

Tu vuo' fa' l'americano: The Assimilation of the American Way of Life in Italy, 1950–1980

Dario Scodeller

fig. 1

When Italian Prime Minister Alcide De Gasperi landed in Washington shortly before noon on 5 January 1947, Italy was still a republic without a constitution. He had been invited to the United States by Henry Luce, the publisher of *Life* and *Time* magazines, the latter of which was a sponsor of the Cleveland Council on World Affairs. It was the first time an Italian prime minister had been received in the United States.

Held at the Cleveland Arena, where only five years later, in March 1952, Alan Freed was to organize the Moondog Coronation Ball – the first rock and roll concert in history, two topics were up for discussion at the conference in which De Gasperi addressed the Council: 'What does the rest of the world expect of the U.S.? and What is the U.S. going to do about it?'[1]

Three days later, when he spoke before the New York Chamber of Commerce on 13 January, his words were almost prophetic:

> 'I think that because we are a poor nation with nothing to lose in the face of world upheaval, [. . .] we are the most fervent advocates of the freedom of communication between one nation and another, financial communication, economic communication, spiritual communication, [. . .] the most fervent followers of an international order in which, alongside the United States of America, [. . .] we may see the emergence of the United States of Europe.'[2]

The Constitution of the Italian Republic was promulgated on 27 December 1947, two weeks after the United States Army left Italy. Eighteen months had passed since *Life* magazine had written: 'Italians Send Their King Packing'.[3]

A year later, in the autumn of 1948, a young intellectual called Fernanda Pivano – who had translated Edgar Lee Masters' *The Spoon River Anthology* into Italian in 1943 – met Ernest Hemingway in Cortina d'Ampezzo, a small town in the Dolomites. During the war, the writer Cesare Pavese, who had fallen in love with American literature in the 1930s, had asked the young Pivano to translate Hemingway's *A Farewell to Arms*, 'a book absolutely banned in Italy by Mussolini'.[4] The SS found the translation contract during a raid on the Einaudi publishing house in Turin and Pivano was arrested. Hemingway, who visited Italy in 1948, heard the story and wanted to meet her.

Wonderful photographs of those days in the Dolomites survive and in one of them Hemingway, his fourth wife Mary and Pivano are standing in front of a huge, streamlined Buick, which the writer had brought over from the United States. The photograph was taken by Pivano's partner, a young, semi-unemployed architect from Turin. His name was Ettore Sottsass.[5]

1950s: Fashions, Modes of Consumption, Attitudes

Although the president of Westinghouse International, William E. Knox, declared that 'you can't do business with a poorhouse',[6] the European aid program proposed by United States Secretary of State George Marshall had a major effect on Italy, which in the decade between 1948 and 1958 underwent an 'economic miracle'. Literature, radio, cinema, newsreels, magazines, cartoons, television, music, fashion, games and sports were the media through which Italian society was introduced to, and later assimilated, the American way of life – a process that also coincided with its transformation into a consumer society.

In the early 1950s, Adriano Olivetti commissioned artist Renato Guttuso to paint a large fresco in the Olivetti shop in Rome. Entitled *Boogie Woogie* (fig. 1), it portrayed a crowd going wild for the dance brought over by American soldiers. In Via Margutta, the *Roman New Orleans Jazz Band* played in noisy street parades and the 'long-haired' young artists that America had banished to the margins of society took refuge in the city.[7] In short, the initial enthusiasm of

fig. 2

fig. 2
Franco Mosca, drawing for a page
of the Vespa Piaggio calendar, 1951

fig. 3
Covers of *Epoca* magazine, June 1953,
March 1954, August 1954, August 1962

young Italians for America and its myths was triggered after the war by jazz music; for, as Renzo Arbore has recently put it, 'jazz was improvisation and improvisation meant freedom'.[8]

Among the Italian-Americans returning to Italy, there was one who was to play a key role in the Americanization of the recently formed Italian television and later, during the 1980s, in Silvio Berlusconi's commercial television project. His name was Mike Bongiorno. After the war, Bongiorno had worked for an Italian radio station in New York and as a Voice of America broadcaster. Moving to Italy in the early 1950s, he began making documentaries on the reconstruction for American television. Magazines of the time wrote: 'Mike tours the peninsula in a black Oldsmobile convertible with red leather seats. He wears jeans with a studded belt, carries a hand-operated recorder and uses a tape that allows him to edit reports by himself'.[9]

In 1954, while Hemingway – back in Venice and rather the worse for wear after two successive plane crashes in Africa – moved back and forth between the Gritti

fig. 3

hotel and the tables of Harry's Bar, the acclaimed Marlon Brando arrived on the Lido, along with Elia Kazan, for the screening of *On the Waterfront* at the Venice Film Festival. Yet Hollywood stars weren't the only ones arriving from across the ocean: according to a March 1947 newsreel, the Americans had deported the mobster Lucky Luciano to Italy after pardoning him for his crimes in return for his collaboration with the United States Army during the war.[10]

The glittering world of Hollywood and pin-up girls, which also inspired a Vespa Piaggio calendar (fig. 2), was mirrored in the picture stories of *Grand Hôtel* and *Epoca*, a magazine founded in 1950, based on the model of *Life* magazine, and designed by Bruno Munari.[11] Of 1950s *Epoca*, Stephen Gundle has written: 'The United States fills up the whole magazine', including 'countless advertisements for products such as Shell lubricating oil, Colgate toothpaste, Palmolive hair cream, Lux soaps, Pal razor blades and Squibb products.'[12]

In June 1953, the front cover of *Epoca* featured a provocative Marilyn Monroe, who already looked like the one that was to later appear in Andy Warhol's screen prints. A few issues later, a diagram – which could have been a Pop Art masterpiece – compared the weights and measurements of Monroe, Gina Lollobrigida and Sophia Loren, the three leading figures of the international star system (fig. 4). And while Italy exported to America the Neorealist cinematography of Vittorio De Sica's *Shoeshine* and *Bicycle Thieves* (which were awarded Oscars in 1947 and 1949, respectively), Federico Fellini's *La Strada* and *Nights of Cabiria* (which also won Oscars in 1956 and 1957) imported to Italy the mythology of Hollywood.

The newsreels screened before films were another strong catalyst for the penetration of the American way of life into Italy. Reports preserved in the Istituto Luce archives describe an America that was already, as Guy Debord was to say, 'a society of the spectacle'. Miss America beauty pageants, American fashion shows, sports triumphs

fig. 4
Presentation of the 'ideal' dimensions of
Marilyn Monroe, Gina Lollobrigida and
Sophia Loren, *Epoca* magazine, 1954

fig. 4

and scientific and technological achievements were all turned into spectacle. An event was always a 'media event', and Italians consumed America primarily from the spectator's seat.[13]

Italy's fashion followed its films to America. In August 1951, *Life* published an article entitled 'Italy gets Dressed Up' with the following lead: 'A big, hectic, fashion show attracts U.S. style leaders, poses a challenge to Paris'.[14] The event was organized by Giovanni Battista Giorgini, who today is considered the inventor of Italian pret-a-porter. An expert on the American market from as early as the 1920s, Giorgini opened the Allied Forces Gift Shop in Florence in 1944, immediately after the city was liberated from the Wehrmacht, and sold Italian craft products to the allied soldiers. In 1951 he realized that the American middle classes were more interested in everyday fashion than haute couture and invited American buyers and journalists to visit Florence on their way back from Paris, which in those days was the centre of European high fashion. Complemented by parties and theatre shows, and held from 1952 at the Palazzo Pitti, the Florence fashion show presented the work of young fashion designers as well as that of Italian fashion and sportswear labels. The *Life* article reporting on the success of the initiative wrote: 'When the trunks were packed and the orders totaled up, all agreed that Italy had made a good beginning in its upstart attempt to enter fashion's big leagues.'[15]

When American buyers began arriving in the city for Giorgini's fashion show, Florence had just finished celebrating another American, one who had made a major impact on Italy's architecture: Frank Lloyd Wright. He received honorary citizenship in a solemn ceremony in Palazzo Vecchio in June 1951, while the Palazzo Strozzi held an exhibition devoted to his works.

During the 1960s, television gradually replaced the newsreels and became the main rival of the popular weeklies. Yet even before, between November 1955 and 1959, Mike Bongiorno hosted the now legendary *Lascia o Raddoppia?*, a highly popular television program inspired by the American quiz show *The $64,000 Question*.[16] In September 1956, *The Adventures of Rin Tin Tin* began to be broadcast on television and its success triggered a massive importation of American television series.

1950s Italy was characterized by the coexistence of both an acceptance of the American way of life and an anti-Americanism that was manifested not only on the ideological level. The stereotype of the Americanized youngster in jeans, big belt and baseball cap, ironically played by Alberto Sordi in the 1954 film *An American in Rome*, and in the young Italian who 'wants to be trendy [. . . and] drink whisky and soda', 'dance rock and roll and play baseball', ridiculed in 1956 by Renato Carosone in the famous boogie-woogie song 'Tu vuo' fa' l'americano' (You wanna be Americano), were veritable albeit negative pop models.[17]

In 1953, Hank Kaufman – who thirty years later would reconstruct, together with Gene Lerner, the story of American films in Italy in the *Hollywood sul Tevere* memoirs – wrote: 'Everyone senses that Rome is on the brink of a real film boom'.[18] That year William Wyler filmed *Roman Holiday* with Audrey Hepburn and Gregory Peck in the Cinecittà studios, and later, in 1959, *Ben Hur* with Charlton Heston. A *Ben Hur* scene at the Circus Maximus was filmed by a young assistant director named Sergio Leone, who was to play a key role in the cinematographic rewriting of American imagery. The media circus generated by this overdose of 'Hollywood on the Tiber' is described in *La Dolce Vita*, with which Federico Fellini lightheartedly and cynically brought to a close the golden era of Neorealist films in 1959. A scene in the film shows a young boy singing as he twists and turns. That is Adriano Celentano, described in the popular press as 'one of the most picturesque figures on the Milan music scene, which Adriano joined during a rock and roll festival, [...] where he staged an imitation of Elvis Presley'.[19]

fig. 5
Cover of *Domus* magazine, no. 318,
May 1956

fig. 6
Italian advertisement for the American home
appliance manufacturer Westinghouse, 1950s

fig. 5   fig. 6

1958 was the year the hula hoop craze exploded in Italy and the Sanremo Music Festival was won by 'Nel blu dipinto di blu', popularly known as 'Volare'. The song, sung by Domenico Modugno and Johnny Dorelli, became a symbol of the Italian boom, while Dorelli, who had attended the High School of Performing Arts in Manhattan, was described as 'another Italian from America'.[20]

Since rock and roll concerts were associated with acts of violence and hooliganism, the more refined magazines such as *L'Espresso* and *L'Europeo* addressed the phenomenon from a sociological standpoint: '[T]he men all wear blue cloth trousers and checked sports shirts, tennis shoes and baseball jackets with writing on the back,' wrote Camilla Cederna in *L'Espresso*. 'Nearly all of them have a motorcycle and they started grouping together in gangs about a year ago [. . .]. The Milanese people saw them all together this winter for the first rock and roll competition at the Palazzo del Ghiaccio [. . .]. They were keen to get in without paying [. . .]. In order to disperse them [. . .], they were sprayed with jets of water.'[21] As a result, the 1955 film *Blackboard Jungle*, featuring the song 'Rock Around the Clock' that incited American teenagers, was not distributed in Italy after being expressly denounced by Clare Boothe Luce, the United States ambassador to Rome (and wife of Henry Luce), who in this way played the dual role of anti-Communist outpost for the Eisenhower government and filter against the spreading of an American culture not approved by the USIS (United States Information Service) protocols.

However, in 1959, in an article entitled 'Per chi urla il juke-box' (Who is the jukebox shouting for?), Roberto Leydi put the phenomenon back into perspective, writing that the new musical genre 'has found its main audience in working-class neighborhoods on the outskirts of big cities [. . . and] in dance halls popular with shop assistants and mechanics'. Thus, what in America was pop arrived in Italy as folk.[22] 'The tensions that run through rock and roll in America,' observed Alessandro Portelli, 'dissolve when they touch Italian soil', where this new form of music was principally a most welcome liberation from tradition.[23] And it was none other than the jukebox, promoting the recently introduced 45 revolutions-per-minute music format, that was the principal means of diffusion of this new taste in music.

However, the controversy over pinball machines, called 'flipper' in Italy, better clarifies the issue. 'Pinball machines are being indicted', wrote the newspaper *Il Giorno* in August 1958. 'Fathers, professors, teachers and the heads of philanthropic youth organizations have sent petitions and protests against these American electric billiard games to police chiefs in many cities.'[24]

Thus, in the transition from the contamination phase to the assimilation phase, there emerged an awareness that the American model of existence entails a new way of enjoying time, leisure time in particular: by consuming.

From the 1950s to the 1970s: Consumer Society, Beat Culture and America's Radical Imagery

In 1951 the Museum of Modern Art exhibited Pininfarina's Cisitalia 202 two-seater, thus introducing America to the legend of Italian car design. In 1952 the museum held the exhibition *Olivetti: Design in Industry* and a year later Olivetti opened its first New York shore, designed by the Italian architectural firm BBPR. 'After I took over the company,' said, many years later, Thomas Watson, Jr., president of IBM, 'I considered design one of the principal factors behind IBM's success [. . .], but one evening in the early 1950s, as I was strolling down Fifth Avenue, I was drawn to some typewriters displayed in a shop window with a roll of paper in them and available for passersby to use. [. . .] I entered the shop and found it decorated in modern and striking colours [. . .]. The name on the door was Olivetti.'[25] From then on, Italian design gradually won over America.

fig. 8

Although the touring exhibition *American Design for Home and Decorative Use* had, since 1955, passed through Milan and other cities, Italian notions of the modern interior design of American offices and homes were primarily forged by television series such as *Alfred Hitchcock Presents* and *Perry Mason*, which were broadcast in dozens of episodes by Rai during the 1960s.

In 1952, *Domus* magazine, which had already discovered Charles and Ray Eames and Eero Saarinen, published work by Italian-American designer Harry (Arieto) Bertoia and, in 1956, after the first Knoll shop opened in Milan, put his *Diamond Chair* on its cover. In 1958, Maddalena De Padova began producing Herman Miller's office furniture on license.[26]

Most of all, however, with the industrialization of the 1950s, Italians imported 'the ideology of "comfort", the mechanization of the home, from America: [. . .] the myth of the refrigerator, the electric household appliance [. . .], the competitive desire to attain well-being and security [. . .], social positions that could be assessed concretely in terms of objects possessed so as to permit the prospect of the ultimate luxury: waste.'[27] And thanks to industrial entrepreneurs such as Lino Zanussi (Rex) and Vittorio Merloni (Ariston), who responded to these growing needs, Italy became the world's second largest manufacturer of household appliances (after the United States) and the largest in Europe.

During the 1960s, Italian emigrants returning from America brought with them a new model of kitchen design, in which electrical appliances were built into standard-size furniture. Thus, a new furnishing system began to gain prominence, becoming a popular must-have: the American kitchen featuring fitted furniture and wall cupboards.

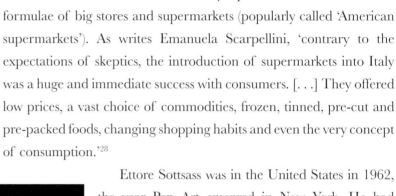

fig. 7

Consumer models were successfully reproduced in the commercial formulae of big stores and supermarkets (popularly called 'American supermarkets'). As writes Emanuela Scarpellini, 'contrary to the expectations of skeptics, the introduction of supermarkets into Italy was a huge and immediate success with consumers. [. . .] They offered low prices, a vast choice of commodities, frozen, tinned, pre-cut and pre-packed foods, changing shopping habits and even the very concept of consumption.'[28]

Ettore Sottsass was in the United States in 1962, the year Pop Art emerged in New York. He had already been there in 1955–56, working in the office of George Nelson, but this time the circumstances were different: he was seriously ill and hospitalized at the Stanford University Medical Center in Palo Alto. During his convalescence, he used a copy machine to produce a magazine that he sent to friends in Italy. It was called 'Room East 128 Chronicle' and its picture montages show a remarkable familiarity with the visual codes of Pop (fig. 10). Following his recovery, Fernanda Pivano accompanied him to San Francisco and New York, where he met the poets of the Beat Generation – Allen Ginsberg, Neal Cassady and Michael McClure.[29]

Until the 1950s, Poe, Melville, Whitman, Hawthorne, Hemingway and Faulkner, translated by some of Italy's most prominent literary figures during the 1930s, were – as Leslie Fiedler writes – 'real presences to the Italian imagination. […] What Italy itself had been to England in the Renaissance, what Germany to Europe when Romanticism was beginning – America is (or has been until only yesterday) to contemporary Italy.'[30] But as early as 1947, Cesare Pavese declared that 'the days when we discovered America have gone.'[31] America was

fig. 10
Ettore Sottsass, illustration on page 4 of the
magazine *Room East 128 Chronicle*, no. 3, July 1962,
published by Sottsass and Fernanda Pivano

fig. 9

fig. 10

fig. 11
Anita Klinz, advertisement for the Italian
cigarette brand *Cowboy* in *Epoca* magazine,
23 June 1951

fig. 12
Album cover of Ennio Morricone's
soundtrack for *A Fistful of Dollars*
(Sergio Leone, dir.), 1964

fig. 11   fig. 12

the dream of an imagined freedom. The reality corresponded little to the literary image that Italians had built up. So what was it that nevertheless moved so many young people even closer to American culture during the 1960s?

Jack Kerouac's *On the Road* was published in Italy in 1959; Ginsberg's *Howl and Other Poems*, published in the United States in 1956, was translated in 1965 and published under the title *Jukebox all'idrogeno*. Pivano wrote a foreword to both of them and these icons of the beat and hippy generations painted a different picture of America.

In the 1960s, Italian society embraced consumerism, on the one hand, but, on the other, warmed to the America that was fighting for civil rights, the America conveyed in protest songs. Tellingly enough, the Marilyn depicted by Mimmo Rotella in 1963 (fig. 9), the year before Pop Art arrived at the Venice Biennale, was a torn film poster. In other words, the 1950s' acceptance of American role models was followed by a reworking of these models. In 1968, the sociologist Francesco Alberoni wrote that the American way of life was a means of creating demand: 'The consumption models do not conserve [. . .] the ethical meaning they had in the system that generated them but take on different meanings. [. . .] Their exportation caused a qualitative transformation in the meaning of goods, the consequences of which eventually became catastrophic also for the American system.'[32]

This hypothesis is confirmed by the creative reworking of the Western genre – a phenomenon that on the face of it seems marginal but actually exemplifies the process of assimilation and transformation that American cultural models underwent in Italy. Before being adopted by the local film industry, American Westerns had already given rise in Italy to original and creative comic books that were a huge popular success. *Tex*, for example, first appeared in 1948 and the comic strip *Ringo* in December 1950, four years before *The Ringo Kid* was published in the United States. *Il Grande Blek* dates from

1954 and *Zagor* from 1961. However, the phenomenon reached its peak in the 1960s with the Italian (or Spaghetti) Westerns of Sergio Leone, which totally revamped the narrative and visual codes of their American predecessors, blurring the contrast between good and bad, subduing the rhetorical component and offering a more cynical and disenchanted view of the heroic Wild West.

During the 1970s, an intellectual attitude that sought to emancipate design from the industrial logic it was entrenched in began to take hold, triggered by Sottsass's Californian experience and the influence of the Beat poets. Collective experimental practices, which mixed educational workshops and craftsmanship, art and self-production, searched for a space of free thought in which folk art could influence the modern aesthetic.

Maddalena De Padova found this self-same freedom among the designers who were working for Herman Miller in California: 'When we started working with Miller, my husband and I became great friends with George Nelson, Alexander Girard, Charles Eames and, in their company, I absorbed a totally different culture. [. . .] What I learnt [. . .] from the American system of production was the joy of mixing objects together. [. . .] My friendship with Alexander Girard was decisive. [. . .] He taught me to mix modern furniture with anonymous pieces of folk art. In Italy, in those years, [. . .] Pier Paolo Pasolini was doing the same in his films; you need only watch *Medea* to understand this. Pasolini had a taste for folk art.'[33]

This freedom, understood as the possibility to be inventive, is what Pasolini himself recognized in Allen Ginsberg, as he wrote in his famous letter to the poet in October 1967:

Dear, angelic Ginsberg, last night I heard you say everything that came into your mind about New York and San Francisco, with their flowers. I have told you something about Italy, (flowers only to be found in flower shops.) [. . .] [Y]ou are

fig. 13

fig. 13
Pier Paolo Pasolini in New York,
L'Europeo magazine, 13 October 1966

[. . .] compelled to invent your revolutionary language anew and completely – day by day and word by word. All the men of your America are forced to invent words to express themselves! We here, instead, [. . .] already have our revolutionary language, pre-fabricated, and with its own ethics behind it. [34]

Attacked even in America, the American way of life lost its seductive force, but that did not lessen the fascination Italian culture had for its American counterpart. Models of protest and counterculture were now being imported. Folk rock music, mega-gatherings such as Woodstock, hippy Neo-Nomadism, the new spirituality, trips to India and the sexual liberation proclaimed in the Hite Report were the cultural references that reverberated in the minds of the younger Italian generations from the late 1960s through the second half of the 1970s. [35]

This was the dreamy and tragic America of Dennis Hopper's *Easy Rider* (1969) and the libertarian one of *Zabriskie Point*, which Michelangelo Antonioni filmed in California in 1969–70. In 1972 Francis Ford Coppola painted a harsh picture of Italy as mirrored in America in his Mafia family saga *The Godfather* (and the following year, Martin Scorsese reiterated the lesson of Italian Neorealism in *Mean Streets*,), while the Museum of Modern Art presented the exhibition *Italy: The New Domestic Landscape*, curated by Emilio Ambasz and dedicated to contemporary Italian design.

Shortly before it ceased regular publication in late 1972, *Life* magazine criticized Italy sharply for adopting the model that it itself had helped propagate. In a review of *Italy: The New Domestic Landscape* and a parallel exhibition, held at the Metropolitan Museum of Art, entitled *Art & Landscape of Italy – Too Late to Be Saved?*, Walter McQuade, a member of the New York City Planning Commission, wrote: 'The Italians have virtually taken over design leadership in the domestic landscape. [. . .] Exports thrived [in the 60s] and the Italians themselves plunged into a consumer goods era.' [36] But, as the sceptical title of the Metropolitan Museum exhibition suggests, in the early 1970s Italy was paying the price of this development, with 'an aching economy unable to stem pollution, with unemployment, political paralysis, labor unrest and student rage. [. . .] At the Modern Museum exhibition, 12 of the best Italian designers were invited to step up their efforts from designing exquisite isolated objects to creating "environments" [. . .]. But the big environment, trembling dangerously in the balance, is Italy itself.' [37]

During the 1970s, radical groups such as Archizoom and Superstudio, whose projects were shown in the *Italy: The New Domestic Landscape* exhibition, and Global Tools, which was founded a year later by members of these two groups, Sottsass and others surrounding Alessandro Mendini's *Casabella* magazine, attacked design's production base and tried to orphan it from industry by inserting it into a different cultural context. These attempts were doomed to fail because by then the phenomenon of Pop Art had made it clear that there was no longer any difference between popular culture (folk) and mass culture (pop) in a society pervaded by consumerism and spectacle.

In 1980, shortly before Canale 5, Italy's first commercial television channel, owned by a certain Silvio Berlusconi, began airing the new American television series *Dallas*, the Memphis Group, which was to dominate the world of design for nearly a decade, was formed in Milan. They were all sitting at Sottsass's home, architect and designer Michele De Lucchi later recalled, and as they talked the record player kept playing a Bob Dylan song. The song was 'Stuck Inside of Mobile with the Memphis Blues Again'. [38]

★

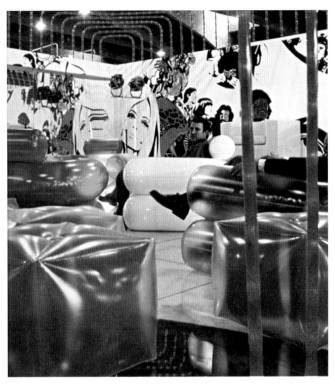

fig. 14

fig. 15

1 'Marshall Flies Home to His New Job', *Life* 22, no. 3 (20 January 1947): 30. Through the Italian ambassador to Washington, De Gasperi requested the United States government to view the trip as an official visit. On 7 January he met President Truman and later discussed the Italian reconstruction and the restoration of economic trade links with the Under Secretaries of State for Political and Economic Affairs. Before leaving, and after complicated negotiations, he obtained a 100-million-dollar loan from the Export Import Bank. De Gasperi addressed the Cleveland Council on 10 January 1947.

2 Alcide De Gasperi, speech to the New York Chamber of Commerce, New York, 13 January 1947 (transcript), La Democrazia Cristiana in Italia, storiadc.it/doc/1947_usa_degasperi3.html. See also Alcide De Gasperi, *Alcide De Gasperi e la politica internazionale: Un'antologia di scritti su 'L'Illustrazione Vaticana' (1933-1938) e di discorsi all'estero (1945-1954)*, eds. Giovanni Allara and Angelo Gatti (Rome: Cinque lune, 1990).

3 'Italians Send Their King Packing', *Life* 20, no. 25 (24 June 1946): 25–29.

4 Fernanda Pivano, *Hemingway* (Milan: Rusconi, 1985), 22.

5 Ibid.

6 'U.S. Foreign Policy, III: Its Most Hopeful Project Depends for Success on the American Businessman', *Life*, 20 January 1947, 34.

7 Alfredo Todisco, 'I "long haired" si rifugiano a Roma', *L'Europeo*, no. 26 (25 June 1950), 7, quoted in Elena Gelsomini, *L'Italia allo specchi: L'Europeo di Arrigo Benedetti (1945- ·1954)* (Milan: Franco Angeli, 2011), 55.

8 Renzo Arbore, interview in 'Renzo Arbore: La vita è tutta un jazz', *Sfide*, Rai 3, 30 April 2012.

9 M. Emanuelli, *Storia della televisione attraverso la stampa settimanale* (Milan: Greco & Greco, 2004), 37.

10 La Settimana INCOM, *Dall'America il bandito Luciano*, Archivio Storico Istituto Luce, 1947-00049. The suggestion that the Sicilian Mafia had backed American and British landing operations in Sicily was confirmed in the papers of the Commissione parlamentare d'inchiesta italiana sulla mafia, 'Relazione su Mafia e politica', May 1993.

11 Already in 1939, Munari had based the cover of *Tempo* on the layout of *Life*, which was designed in 1936. A few years later, in 1954, Munari's graphic design for the title of *Epoca*, which consisted of a white logo on a red stripe that stretched right across the cover of the magazine, was also changed to copy that of *Life*: it was reduced in size and allocated to the top left corner of the cover.

12 Stephen Gundle, *I comunisti italiani tra Hollywood e Mosca: la sfida della cultura di massa, 1943–1991* (Florence: Giunti, 1995), 115–6. 'This extraordinary focus was no exception. In most cases, the illustrated weeklies had foreign correspondents only in the United States and other periodicals, especially those dedicated to cinema (*Cine illustrato*, *Hollywood*, *Novelle film*, and *Film*) and women's magazines (*Storie vere*, *Confessioni*, *Selezione femminile*, etc.) lived almost exclusively off American material.' (Ibid, 116)

13 La Settimana INCOM, the weekly newsreel of the Industria Cortometraggi Milano, was founded in 1946 to replace the Istituto Luce newsreels. It was a news bulletin that was screened in cinemas before the main feature film and reported on Italian and worldwide news and current affairs. Titles of reports include: *Concorsi per Miss America* [The Miss America Pageants] (September 1947); *Moda d'autunno in America* [Autumn fashion in America] (October 1948); *America: La casa di plastica* [America: The home of plastic] (October 1949); *Notizie sulla moda maschile da New York* [News on men's fashion in New York] (January 1951); *Miss America: Atlantic City* (September 1952); *Moda americana del 2000* [American fashion for the year 2000] (October 1954); *U.S.A.: le dieci donne più eleganti del mondo* [U.S.A.: The ten most elegant women in the world] (April 1958); *Milano: un mese d'America in Italia, alla Rinascente* [Milan: America Month in Italy, at the Rinascente department store] (May 1958); *La presentazione di una collezione di costumi da spiaggia a Palm Beach* [The presentation of a swimwear collection in Palm Beach] (May 1959); *L'angolo della moda: USA—Una eleganza davvero economica* [The fashion angle: USA— Truly affordable elegance] (November 1959); *L'angolo della moda: Modelli stravaganti e avveniristici* [The fashion angle: Extravagant

and futuristic models] (February 1960); *California: miss Universo* [California: Miss Universe] (July 1960).

14 'Italy gets Dressed Up', *Life* 31, no. 8 (20 August 1951): 104–112.

15 Ibid., 104.

16 Television broadcasts started in Italy on 3 January 1954, with Mike Bongiorno appearing that same day on *Arrivi e partenze*. *The $64,000 Question* was first aired in America by CBS on 7 June 1955. In Italy, although few homes had televisions, *Lascia o raddoppia?* was watched by an audience of millions gathered in bars.

17 *An American in Rome* was directed by Steno (Stefano Vanzina) and written by Ettore Scola, among others. At the time, baseball was gaining popularity in Roman suburbs; see the short documentary film *L'America a Roma* (Opus Film, Archivio Storico Istituto Luce, 1954-D015605). Alongside baseball, there were also newsreel reports on the Harlem Globetrotters basketball team and the opening of Rome's first bowling alley in 1960.

18 Hank Kaufman and Gene Lerner, *Hollywood sul Tevere* (Milan: Sperling & Kupfer, 1982), 7, quoted in Aurelio Magistà, *Dolce vita gossip: Star, amori, mondanità e kolossal negli anni d'oro di Cinecittà* (Milan: Bruno Mondadori, 2007), 84. Montgomery Clift, Jennifer Jones, Joseph Cotton, Kirk Douglas, Mel Ferrer, Errol Flynn, Henry Fonda, Buster Keaton, Joan Fontaine, Ava Gardner, Audrey Hepburn, Abbe Lane, Victor Mature, Paul Muni, Anthony Perkins, Anthony Quinn, George Raft, Orson Welles, Vera Miles and Shelley Winters all arrived to this 'American' Cinecittà, the so-called Hollywood on the Tiber.

19 Emanuelli, *Storia della television*, 96. A few months after Billy Haley & His Comets arrived in England, Adriano Celentano and His Rock Boys performed in the first Italian rock and roll festival at the Palazzo del Ghiaccio in Milan on 18 May 1957.

20 Emanuelli, *Storia della television*, 76.

21 Camilla Cederna, 'I fusti di Milano, la gioventù dalle ali scottate', *L'Espresso*, 1 June 1958, quoted in Guido Crainz, *Storia del miracolo italiano* (Rome: Donzelli , 1996), 70.

22 Roberto Leydi, 'Per chi urla il juke-box',

L'Europeo, 1 March 1959, quoted in Crainz, *Storia del miracolo italiano*, 77.

23 Alessandro Portelli, 'L'orsacchiotto e la tigre di carta: Il rock and roll arriva in Italia', *Quaderni storici*, no. 58 (1985): 143, quoted in Crainz, *Storia del miracolo italiano*, 77–78. According to Portelli, the teenagers of the 1950s 'triggered the student movements of the following decade' (ibid., 146).

24 Luigi Locatelli, *Tre potenti catene controllano i flippers*, in *Il Giorno*, 30 August 1958, quoted in Crainz, *Storia del miracolo italiano*, 70. In 1959 a decree issued by the Ministry of the Interior abolished pinball machines throughout Italy. By contrast, the number of jukeboxes increased from a few thousand in 1958 to 40,000 in 1965 and album sales surged from five million in 1953 to 30 million in 1964.

25 Thomas Watson, Jr., quoted in *Design Process Olivetti, 1908–1983*, published on occasion of the 75th anniversary of Olivetti (Milan: Olivetti, 1983), 46. Inside the shop, an entire wall was covered with a 23-metre-long bas relief created by Italian artist Costantino Nivola, using the sand casting technique he invented while playing with his children on the beach near his home in Springs, East Hampton, to which he had moved during the war. The Olivetti Corporation of America was founded in 1950 and in the early 1960s it merged with the Underwood Typewriter Company.

26 For a summary of the connections between Italian and American design, see Alberto Bassi, 'L'america in Italia: l'aspetto del design durante il boom economico', in Gilberto Ganzer, ed., *Harry Bertoia, 1915–1978: Atti del convegno, 23 November 2007* (Pordenone: Comune di Pordenone, 2008).

27 Vittorio Gregotti, *Il disegno del prodotto industriale, Italia, 1960–1980* (Milan: Electa, 1982), 238.

28 Emanuela Scarpellini, 'Le reazioni alla diffusione dell'american way of life nell'Italia del miracolo economico', in Piero Craveri and Gaetano Quagliariello, eds., *L'antiamericanismo in Italia e in Europa nel secondo dopoguerra* (Soveria Mannelli: Rubettino, 2004), 353. On the introduction of supermarkets to Italy, see Emanuela Scarpellini, *Comprare all'americana: Origini* *della rivoluzione commerciale in Itali, 1945–1971* (Bologna: Mulino, 2001).

29 On Sottsass's stay in America, see Barbara Radice, *Ettore Sottsass* (Milan: Electa, 1993), 62–65.

30 Leslie Fiedler, 'Italian Pilgrimage: The Discovery of America', *The Kenyon Review* 14, no. 3 (1952): 369–70. *America amara* by Emilio Cecchi was published in 1938 and, as Fiedler writes, 'transformed America from a geographical and social entity to a fact of the Italian imagination' (ibid., 368). The 1930s witnessed a discovery of American literature that culminated with *Americana*, an anthology edited by Elio Vittorini and published with a preface by Cecchi.

31 Cesare Pavese, 'Un negro ci parla', radio review of *Ragazzo Negro [Black Boy]* by Richard Wright, trans. Bruno Fonzi, May 1947, in *La letteratura americana e altri saggi* (Torino: Einaudi, 1951), 189.

32 Francesco Alberoni, 'Pubblicità e società dei consumi', in *Pubblicità televisione e società nell'Italia del miracolo economico* (Rome: Armando, 2011), 102–103. Originally published as *Pubblicità e televisione* (Turin: Rai Eri, 1968).

33 Maddalena De Padova, interview by Giulio Castelli, in Giulio Castelli, Paola Antonelli and Francesca Picchi, *La fabbrica del design: Conversazione con I protagonisti del design italiano* (Milan: Skira, 2007), 226–229.

34 Pier Paolo Pasolini, Letter to Allen Ginsberg, 18 October 1967, translated in Simona Bondavalli, 'Giving Flowers to Policeman: Pasolini, "Flower Children" and *figli di papà*', in Ben Lawton and Maura Bergonzoni, eds., *Pier Paolo Pasolini: In Living Memory* (Washington, DC: New Academia Publishing, 2009), 37–39. Interviewed by Oriana Fallaci in New York in October 1966, Pasolini, who was there to present a film, said: 'Come to America and you will find the finest Left there is today. They are not Communists or Anti-Communists but mystics of democracy. Their revolution consists in taking democracy to extreme and almost crazy consequences' (Oriana Fallaci, 'Un marxista a New York', *L'Europeo* 22, no. 42 [13 October 1966], 65).

35 New magazines such as *Ciao 2001*, which first appeared in 1969, reflected the teenage music phenomena. Singers such as Francesco Guccini and Francesco De Gregori translated American folk rock, especially that of the early Bob Dylan, into Italian. In his 1967 album *Folk Beat No. 1*, Guccini first started using American folk music techniques such as finger-picking, collaborating with New York guitarist Deborah Kooperman. In 1971 Fabrizio De André set a poetic reworking of Edgar Lee Masters's *Spoon River Anthology* to music on the album *Non al denaro, non all'amore né al cielo*. Fashion translated the new trend in its own way: the Fiorucci pin-up girls were ironic Pop transcriptions of the American myth, as were the advertments for Jesus jeans by Emanuele Pirella and Oliviero Toscani.

36 Walter McQuade, 'Italy: Micro-Environments vs. Macro-Mess', *Life* 73, no. 3(21 July 1972), 18.

37 Ibid. Describing the exhibition at the Metropolitan Museum, McQuade wrote: 'Uptown at the Met is a scarifying photographic show of what rampant industrialism can do to brutalize a landscape and demean an ancient culture.' (Ibid.)

38 Michele De Lucchi, interview by Giulio Castelli, in Castelli, Antonelli and Picchi, *La fabbrica del design*, 370.

Richard Brown Baker in his apartment, 1964
Photo: Ken Heyman

Leon Manuchin in his living room, 1964
Photo: Ken Heyman

Bathroom of the Leon Kraushar home, 1964
Photo: Ken Heyman

Kitchen of the Leon Kraushar home, 1964
Photo: Ken Heyman

Dining room of the Robert C. Scull home, 1964
Photo: Ken Heyman

Views of the Gunter Sachs apartment, St. Moritz, 1970
Photos: Ulrich Mack

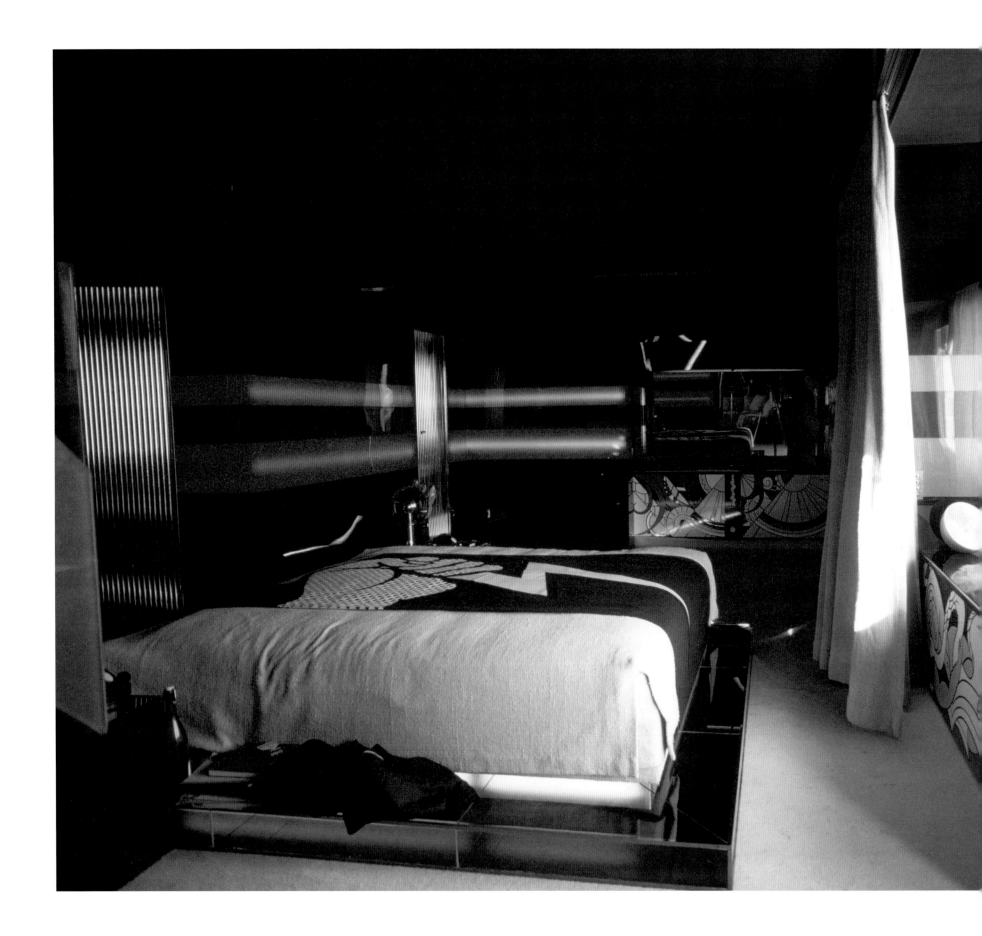

Index
Picture Credits
Selected Bibliography

* Bold numbers refer to pages on
which illustrations or photos appear

Picture Credits

t → top
r → right
l → left
c → center
b → bottom

Literature

Francesco Alberoni. *Pubblicità televisione e società nell'Italia del miracolo economico.* Edited by Gianpiero Gamaleri. Rome: Armando, 2011.

Reyner Banham. *Design by Choice: Ideas in Architecture.* Edited by Penny Sparke. London: Academy, 1981.

Reyner Banham, ed. *The Aspen Papers. Twenty Years of Design Theory from the International Design Conference in Aspen.* London: Pall Mall, 1974.

Elena und Nicolas Calas. *Icons and Images of the Sixties.* New York: E. P. Dutton, 1971.

Giulio Castelli et al. *La fabbrica del design. Conversazioni con i protagonisti del design italiano.* Milan: Skira, 2007.

Michael Crichton. *Jasper Johns,* New York : H. N. Abrams in association with the Whitney Museum of American Art, 1977.

Eames Demetrios. *An Eames Primer.* New York: Universe, 2001.

Peter Dunas. *Luigi Colani und die organisch-dynamische Form seit dem Jugendstil.* Munich: Prestel, 1993.

Mark Francis, ed. *Pop.* Abr., rev. and updated ed. London: Phaidon, 2010.

Suzi Gablik and John Russell. *Pop Art Redefined.* New York and Washington: Frederick A. Praeger, 1969.

Vittorio Gregotti and Manolo DeGiorgi, eds. *Il disegno del prodotto industrial. Italia 1860–1980.* Milan: Electa, 1982.

Hans Höger. *Ettore Sottsass, Jun.: Designer, Artist, Architect.* Tübingen and Berlin: Ernst Wasmuth, 1993.

Lesley Jackson. *The Sixties. Decade of Design Revolution.* London: Phaidon, 1998.

Frederick Kiesler. *Contemporary Art Applied to the Store and Its Display.* New York: Brentano's, 1930.

Pat Kirkham. *Charles and Ray Eames: Designers of the Twentieth Century.* Cambridge, MA, and London: MIT Press, 1995.

Jesse Kornbluth. *Pre-Pop Warhol.* Munich: Schirmer/Mosel, 1989.

Lucy R. Lippard et al. *Pop Art.* Reprint of 3rd ed. (1970). London: Thames & Hudson, 2001.

Marco Livingstone. *Pop Art: A Continuing History.* London: Thames & Hudson, 1990.

Raymond Loewy. *Häßlichkeit verkauft sich schlecht: Die Erlebnisse des erfolgreichsten Formgestalters unserer Zeit.* Düsseldorf: Econ, 1953.

Steven Henry Madoff, ed. *Pop Art: A Critical History.* Documents of Twentieth-Century Art. Berkeley, Los Angeles and London: University of California Press, 1997.

Jack Masey and Conway Lloyd Morgan. *Cold War Confrontations: US Exhibitions and Their Role in the Cultural Cold War.* Baden: Lars Müller, 2008.

Marshall McLuhan. *The Mechanical Bride: Folklore of Industrial Man.* New York: Vangaurd Press, 1951.

George Nelson. *How to See: A Guide to Reading Our Man-Made Environment.* Boston and Toronto: Little, Brown & Company, 1977.

George Nelson. *Problems of Design.* New York: Whitney Publications, 1957.

John Neuhart. *Eames Design: The Work of the Office of Charles and Ray Eames.* New York: H. N. Abrams, 1989.

Leslie Piña. *Alexander Girard Designs for Herman Miller.* Rev. and exp. ed. Atglen, PA: Schiffer, 2002.

Sergio Polano. *Achille Castiglioni: Complete Works, 1938–2000.* London: Phaidon, 2002.

Mary Portas. *Windows. The Art of Retail Display.* London and New York: Thames & Hudson, 1999.

Barbara Radice. *Ettore Sottsass: Leben und Werk.* New York : Rizzoli, 1993.

Barbara Rose. *Claes Oldenburg.* New York: The Museum of Modern Art, 1970.

Nina Schleif. *SchaufensterKunst: Berlin und New York.* Cologne, Weimar and Vienna: Böhlau, 2004.

Arturo Schwarz. *The Complete Works of Marcel Duchamp.* Rev. and exp. ed. New York: Delano Greenidge, 2000.

Mary Anne Staniszewski. *The Power of Display: A History of Exhibition Installations at the Museum of Modern Art.* Cambridge, MA, and London: MIT Press, 1998.

France Vanlaethem. *Gaetano Pesce. Architecture, Design, Art.* London: Thames & Hudson, 1989.

Andy Warhol und Pat Hackett. *POPism. The Warhol '60s.* New York: Harcourt Brace Jovanovich, 1980.

Nigel Whiteley. *Pop Design: From Modernism to Mod.* London: Design Council, 1987.

Tom Wolfe. *The Painted Word.* New York: Farrar, Straus and Giroux, 1975.

Exhibition Catalogues

'68 – Design und Alltagskultur zwischen Konsum und Konflikt. Edited by Wolfgang Schepers. Kunstmuseum Düsseldorf and Galerie Karmeliterkloster Frankfurt am Main. Cologne: DuMont, 1998.

Andy Warhol. The Early Sixties. Paintings and Drawings 1961–1964. Kunstmuseum Basel. Ostfildern: Hatje Cantz, 2011.

Andy Warhol: Rétrospective. Musée National d'Art Moderne/Centre Georges Pompidou Paris. Paris: Centre Georges Pompidou, 1990.

Andy Warhol: Das zeichnerische Werk, 1942–1975. Edited by Rainer Crone. Württembergischer Kunstverein Stuttgart and other locations. Stuttgart: Württembergischer Kunstverein, 1976.

Les années pop, 1956–1968. Edited by Mark Francis. Centre Georges Pompidou/ Galerie 1 Paris. Paris: Centre Georges Pompidou, 2001.

Art and Film since 1945: Hall of Mirrors. Edited by Russell Ferguson. The Museum of Contemporary Art Chicago and The Museum of Contemporary Art Los Angeles. New York: Monacelli, 1996.

Birth of the Cool: California Art, Design, and Culture at Midcentury. Edited by Karen Jacobson. Orange County Museum of Art Newport Beach and other locations. Newport Beach: Orange County Museum of Art ; Munich and New York: Prestel, 2007.

Claes Oldenburg: The Sixties. Edited by Achim Hochdörfer with Barbara Schröder. Museum moderner Kunst Stiftung Ludwig Wien and other locations. Vienna: Museum moderner Kunst Stiftung Ludwig Wien; Munich: Schirmer/Mosel, 2012.

Cold War Modern Design, 1945–1970. Edited by David Crowley and Jane Pavill. Victoria and Albert Museum London. London: V&A Publishing, 2008.

Dada, Surrealism, and Their Heritage. Edited by William S. Rubin. The Museum of Modern Art New York and other locations. New York: The Museum of Modern Art, 1968.

Europop. Edited by Tobia Bezzola and Franziska Lentzsch. Kunsthaus Zürich. Cologne: DuMont, 2008.

Hot Spots: Rio de Janeiro / Milano – Torino / Los Angeles 1956 bis 1968. Edited by Tobia Bezzola. Kunsthaus Zürich. Göttingen: Steidl, 2008.

The Inflatable Moment: Pneumatics and Protest in 1968. Edited by Marc Dessauce. Architectural League of New York. New York: Princeton Architectural Press, 1999.

The Italian Metamorphosis, 1943–1968. Solomon R. Guggenheim Museum New York and Kunstmuseum Wolfsburg. New York: Solomon R. Guggenheim Museum, 1995.

Italy – The New Domestic Landscape: Achievements and Problems of Italian Design. Edited by Emilio Ambasz. The Museum of Modern Art New York. Florence: Centro Di; New York: The Museum of Modern Art, 1972.

James Rosenquist: A Retrospective. Edited by Sarah Bancroft and Walter Hopps. The Menil Collection and The Museum of Fine Arts Houston and other locations. New York: Solomon R. Guggenheim Museum, 2003.

Pop Life: Art in a Material World. Edited by Jack Bankowsky et al. Tate Modern London and other locations. London: Tate Publishing, 2009.

Power Up: Female Pop Art. Edited by Gerald Matt and Angela Stief. Kunsthalle Wien and other locations. Cologne: DuMont, 2010.

Robert Indiana: Der amerikanische Maler der Zeichen / The American Painter of Signs. Schriftenreihe Museum Kurhaus Kleve – Ewald Mataré-Sammlung, no. 41. Museum Kurhaus Kleve and Museum Wiesbaden. Kleve: Museum Kurhaus, 2007.

Robert Rauschenberg: A Retrospective. Edited by Walter Hopps and Susan Davidson. Museum Ludwig Köln and other locations. Ostfildern-Ruit: Gerd Hatje; New York: Solomon R. Guggenheim Museum, 1998.

Roy Lichtenstein. Edited by Diane Waldman. Solomon R. Guggenheim Museum New York and other locations. New York: Solomon R. Guggenheim Museum, 1994.

Sechziger Jahre: Die neuen Abenteuer der Objekte. Edited by Marc Scheps, Ausst.-Kat. Museum Ludwig Köln. Cologne: Museum Ludwig and Oktagon, 1997.

Shopping: A Century of Art and Consumer Culture. Edited by Christoph Grunenberg and Max Hollein. Schirn-Kunsthalle Frankfurt and Tate Liverpool. Ostfildern-Ruit: Hatje Cantz, 2002.

Summer of Love: Art of the Psychedelic Era. Edited by Christoph Grunenberg. Tate Liverpool and other locations. Ostfildern-Ruit: Hatje Cantz; London: Tate Publishing, 2005.

teknologi, idé, konstverk – Richard Hamilton. Edited by Bo Nilsson. Moderna Museet Stockholm. Stockholm: Moderna Museet, 1989.

Jasper Johns: A Retrospective. Edited by Kirk Varnedoe. The Museum of Modern Art New York. New York: The Museum of Modern Art, 1996.

Nelson Eames Girard Propst: The Design Process at Herman Miller. Special issue of Design Quarterly, nos. 98/99. Edited by Mildred S. Friedman. Walker Art Center Minneapolis. Minneapolis: Walker Art Center, 1975.

Olivetti: una bella società. Edited by Manolo De Giorgi and Enrico Morteo. Società Promotrice delle Belli Arti Turin. Turin: Umberto Allemandi & C., 2008.

Out of Actions: Between Performance and the Object, 1949–1979. Edited by Paul Schimmel. The Museum of Contemporary Art Los Angeles and other locations. New York and London: Thames & Hudson, 1998.

Pacific Standard Time: Los Angeles Art, 1945–1980. Edited by Rebecca Peabody et al. Getty Research Institute and J. Paul Getty Museum Los Angeles in association with the Martin-Gropius-Bau Berlin. Los Angeles: Getty Publications, 2012.

Pierre Paulin, Designer. Edited by Catherine Geel. Published on occasion of the exhibitions Pierre Paulin Superdesigner, Design Parade 02 Hyères, and Pierre Paulin Supermodern, Grand-Hornu. Paris: Archibooks; Hornu: Grand-Hornu Images, 2008.

Pop Art, 1955–70. Edited by Henry Geldzahler. Art Gallery of New South Wales Sydney and other locations. Sydney: International Cultural Corporation of Australia, 1985.

Pop Design: Fuori Scala, Fuori Luogo, Fuori Schema. Edited by Luisa Bocchietto. Il Filatoio di Caraglio. Cinisello Balsamo (MI): Silvana, 2008.

Time & Place: Milano – Torino, 1958–1968. Edited by Luca Massimo Barbero and Cecilia Widenheim. Moderna Museet Stockholm. Stockholm: Moderna Museet; Göttingen: Steidl, 2008.

L'Utopie du tout plastique. Edited by Philippe Decelle et al. Fondation pour l'Architecture Brüssel. Brussels: Fondation pour l'Architecture, 1994.

Verner Panton: The Collected Works. Edited by Alexander von Vegesack and Mathias Remmele. Vitra Design Museum Weil am Rhein. Weil am Rhein: Vitra Design Museum, 2000.

The Warhol Look: Glamour Style Fashion. Edited by Mark Francis and Margery King. The Andy Warhol Museum Pittsburgh and other locations. Munich: Schirmer/Mosel, 1997.

Your Private Sky: R. Buckminster Fuller, the Art of Design Science. Edited by Joachim Krausse and Claude Lichtenstein. Museum für Gestaltung Zürich and other locations. Baden: Lars Müller, 1999.

Erwin Wurm, *Melting House II*, 2009
Installation view: Kunstmuseum Bonn, 2010
Wood, styrofoam, synthetic resin, color
135 x 325 x 350 cm
Courtesy Galerie Thaddaeus Ropac, Salzburg (A), Paris (F)

Parallel to *Pop Art Design*, an exhibition on Austrian sculptor and installation artist Erwin Wurm will be shown at the Vitra Design Museum Gallery. Wurm's oeuvre typifies the continuing impact of Pop Art and popular culture on the work of many contemporary artists and designers. In a unique presentation for the Vitra Design Museum Gallery, Wurm – one of the most successful and popular artists of our time – will display several familiar works as well as new pieces, created especially for this temporary exhibition, in which houses seem to mirror human personalities. Full of allusions to our everyday culture, as well as to the neighbouring architecture of Frank Gehry and Herzog & de Meuron, Wurm also makes a topical statement on the relationship of Pop Art and design.